T0330773

BARRIERS AND ACCIDENT PREVENTION

Barriers and Accident Prevention

ERIK HOLLNAGEL
University of Linköping, Sweden

Routledge
Taylor & Francis Group

LONDON AND NEW YORK

First published 2004 by Ashgate Publishing

Published 2016 Taylor & Francis
2 Park Square, Milton Park, Abingdon, Oxon OX14 4RN
711 Third Avenue, New York, NY 10017, USA

Routledge is an imprint of the Taylor & Francis Group, an informa business

British Library Cataloguing in Publication Data
Hollnagel, Erik
  Barriers and accident prevention
  1.Industrial safety - Equipment and supplies 2.Accidents -
  Prevention
  I.Title
  620.8'6

Library of Congress Cataloging-in-Publication Data
Hollnagel, Erik, 1941-
  Barriers and accident prevention / by Erik Hollnagel.
      p. cm.
  Includes bibliographical references and index.

  1. Industrial safety. 2. Accidents--Prevention. I. Title
  ISBN 9780754643012
  T55.H65 2004
  620.8'6--dc22

                                                    2004012248

ISBN 9780754643012 (hbk)

Contents

CHAPTER 2: THINKING ABOUT ACCIDENTS

CHAPTER 3: BARRIER FUNCTIONS AND BARRIER SYSTEMS

CHAPTER 4: UNDERSTANDING THE ROLE OF BARRIERS IN ACCIDENTS

CHAPTER 6: ACCIDENT PREVENTION

Preface

Accidents have probably happened since the first caveman lit the first fire, but for many centuries the consequences of accidents were mostly limited to the people directly doing the work – what we now call the people at the sharp end. The introduction of technology to the work process changed all that. This development may with some justification be linked to the industrial revolution and, even more precisely, to the year 1769 when James Watt patented the steam engine. The industrial revolution introduced the large-scale use of machines as part of human work beginning with mining and manufacturing, and thereby inevitably changed the very nature of work. Machines did not only make production faster and more efficient but also increased the severity of consequences when something went wrong. The replacement of human muscular power by machines created a need for control, which quickly led to increasingly complex technological systems. Since any piece of technology can fail, it was inevitable that more complex technology meant more failures – and also greater consequences of those failures.

This development is excellently illustrated by the story of the high-pressure steam engine, which came into widespread use in steamboats and industrial production in the beginning of the 19th Century (Leveson, 1994). From the very start the use of high-pressure steam engines was marred by a number of cases where the machine exploded, injuring or killing crew, passengers, and workers. According to Leveson, the U.S. Commissioner of patents estimated that, between 1816-1848, there had been 233 steamboat explosions, resulting in 2,562 persons killed and 2,097 injured (a rather remarkable ratio from a contemporary point of view). The steamboat was a new technology, which brought significant advantages, but also – inevitably – significant risks.

As the use of technology became more widespread, the consequences of accidents were no longer confined to the people at the sharp end but could affect both bystanders and people who were completely unrelated to the work process. Beginning slowly, the number of accidents soon started to grow although it was not until the first decades of the 20th Century that accident statistics became commonplace. We are today inundated with statistics about accidents for practically every field of endeavour, but better knowledge of occurrences does not by itself seem to have any dampening effect.

In the second half of the 20th Century, writing about accidents has increased in part to meet the need of improved safety. Many books have been written about accidents, and it is a safe bet that many more are still to be written. There are two main reasons for that. The first is that accidents always have happened and always will happen, barring some cataclysmic – or providential – event. The second is that the understanding of accidents is still approximate and incomplete, and is likely to remain so for a long time, perhaps indefinitely. Taken together this means that there is an unfulfilled need for a better understanding of the nature of accidents. One way of trying to meet this need is to propose a comprehensive explanation of accidents, which is what this book sets out to do.

What is this Book About?

Books about accidents can be written in many different ways and in many different styles. Without claiming anything like a comprehensive classification, the accident literature seems to include the following main types.

- Books that look at classes of accidents rather than single events and which try to go beyond the specifics of the accidents and understand the general principles or lessons from them – specifically in relation to the system characteristics that led to them. Many of these propose an overall view or approach to analysing and understanding accidents. The classical work in this group is without a doubt Herbert. W. Heinrich's book on *Industrial Accident Prevention* from 1931, which has been extended and reprinted several times with a fifth edition published in 1980 (Heinrich, Petersen & Roos, 1980). Another important volume is Charles Perrow's book on *Normal Accidents* (Perrow, 1984, with a second edition in 1999), which put forward the argument that our technological systems now have become so complex that accidents must be seen as the norm rather than exception – commonly referred to as Natural Accident Theory. Other important works are Amalberti (1996), Leveson (1994), Petroski (1994), Tenner (1997), and Woods et al. (1994).

- Books and papers that provide in-depth accounts of major accidents, often combined with analyses that introduce new ways of thinking or provide new points of view. Two recent examples of that are Dianne Vaughan's treatment of the accident with the space shuttle Challenger in 1986 (Vaughan, 1996) and Scott Snook's account of the 'friendly fire' shoot down of two Black Hawk helicopters over Northern Iraq in 1994 (Snook, 2000). Supplementing these are the detailed technical reports from accidents, which nowadays often are available as documents on the World Wide Web.

- Writings that provide systematic accounts of collections of accidents, often with exemplary analyses of each, but without the intention of proposing a grand theory (e.g., Bignell & Fortune (1984). These are usually focusing on specific domains such as trains, aviation, accidents at sea, etc.

- Books that develop proposals for possible 'mechanisms' of accidents and which describe how specific types of causes can be used to explain how accidents happen. This literature has until recently primarily focused on the legendary 'human error', e.g., Rasmussen, Duncan & Leplat (1978), Reason (1990), Senders & Moray (1991), Bogner (1994) and many others.

- Books that examine the role of organisations in accidents. These fall into two major subcategories. One puts the focus on accidents on the organisational level, such as Reason (1997) and Vaughan (1996). The other looks more to the way in which organisations can play a role in safety, either in the form of studies of safety culture (Wilpert & Qvale, 1993) or high-reliability organisations (Weick & Sutcliffe, 2001).

- Finally, there are a growing number of books about accident analysis in relation to engineering and construction, such as Harms-Ringdahl, (2001), Kjellen (2000) and Taylor (1993).

Given these many styles of writing about accidents – and probably a few that have been missed – where does this book fit in? Hopefully in the first category, i.e., books that try to go beyond the specifics and formulate some general principle. It can confidently be stated that this is *not* a book about 'human error', or about any specific type of cause or failure. Neither is it a book about accident analysis as such (see, e.g.,

Hollnagel, 1998, for an example of that). The aim is to offer a framework for understanding accidents so that we are better able to prevent them. This should at the same time provide both a consistent basis for analysing accidents and a method for responding to them in an effective manner – which means something that leads to a reduction in their number and a diminution of their consequences. The framework represents a systemic point of view, according to which accidents are due to complex coincidences rather than distinct, individual causes. The method that goes with the framework is based on the concept of barriers or defences as the effective means against accidents and their consequences. The concept of barriers is obviously not new, as the following chapters will show, but the combination of a systemic view of accidents with barrier functionality is believed to offer an effective solution to accident prevention.

Readership and Outline

This book is intended for practitioners rather than researchers – although both groups hopefully can use it. The reason for this partiality is simple – it is the practitioner who can make changes to practice, not the academic. The intention is that the practically minded reader should be able to read the book without constantly consulting the references and even without caring much about them. On the other hand, the more academically oriented reader should be able to find enough to expand the study of the issues treated in the book. Changes to practice are rather desperately needed if any real reduction in the number of accidents is ever to be achieved. The emphasis is therefore, as the title indicates, on accident prevention and on the role of barriers. The topics treated in the book are organised as follows:

Chapter 1: Accidents and Causes. This chapter provides a broad introduction to accidents, defined as unexpected events that result in unwanted outcomes. It goes on to discuss the range in events and outcomes, i.e., the degree to which events can be predicted and the varying severity of outcomes. Other topics treated are the relation between accidents, incidents and near misses, and the difference between explaining accidents and finding their causes. The chapter ends by discussing the evolving concept of causes and the concomitant change from an absolute to a relative understanding of what a cause is.

Chapter 2: Thinking about Accidents. In order to understand accidents it is necessary to describe them, and the description inevitably involves the use of an accident model. Most approaches to accident analysis and prevention focus on the methods without addressing the issue of the underlying models. Or rather, they imply a certain type of model and assume that it is universally accepted. It is, however, not only useful but also necessary to be aware of which accident model lies behind a description, since this determines both the search principles and the goals of the analysis. This chapter presents three characteristic types of accident models: the sequential, the epidemiological, and the systemic. The three types correspond to the gradual realisation that accidents are due to complex coincidences rather than root causes. The systemic type of accident models represents the current understanding, specifically the role of blunt end – sharp end factors, and also provides the basis for the functional resonance accident model developed in Chapter 5.

Chapter 3: Barriers Functions and Barrier Systems. Although the concept of a barrier is used rather freely in the accident literature, there have been relatively few attempts thoroughly to analyse what a barrier is. The chapter presents each of these and goes on to make a distinction between barrier functions and barrier systems. The former describes what barriers do (to prevent, protect, etc.) whereas the latter describes how it is done, for instance whether entry is prevented by a door or a sign. The chapter introduces four different types of barrier systems called physical, functional, symbolic, and incorporeal; each of these may support one or more barrier functions, but in practice a barrier usually combines two or more barrier systems. As each type of barrier system has its strengths and weaknesses the choice of a barrier to solve a concrete problem is always a trade-off, for instance between cost and efficiency. The relative qualities of the four barrier systems are discussed as a starting point for barrier design. Finally, the chapter considers how other types of barriers, e.g., organisational barriers and actions, can be seen as specific instances of the four systems.

Chapter 4: Understanding the Role of Barriers in Accidents. In the commonly used methods for risk analyses, such as fault trees and event trees, barriers can be represented in a straightforward manner as nodes in the trees. Indeed, if a possible scenario is described as a sequence or tree of possible events, the semantics of a barrier is to block or break the path between two nodes. Where the fault tree achieves this through logical conditions, other approaches represent barriers directly as interruptions of a path. Yet the notion that a barrier is a simple way of hindering something from happening is unfortunately misleading. Barriers often have unwanted side-effects and may even under certain conditions have the opposite of the desired effect. For example, while a cell door may prevent inmates from escaping it may also prevent fire fighters from entering during an emergency. Barriers are furthermore just one of several ways of responding to an accident, and should be seen as a possible tool rather than as a panacea.

Chapter 5: A Systemic Accident Model. In the contemporary view, accidents are seen as emerging phenomena in complex systems, and as the result of an aggregation of conditions rather than the inevitable effect of a chain of courses. In a nominal work situation, people can in principle manage just by following rules and procedures. In practice, however, they must always balance resources against requirements and constantly make adjustments to what they do in order to achieve their goals. Since this efficiency-thoroughness trade-off is necessary for complex systems to work in the first place, it is generally useful rather than harmful. Yet, in addition to its usefulness, it is also a source of variability and may as such help us understand why accidents happen. The occurrence of unwanted effects from performance variability can be explained using the concept of resonance, and the chapter ends by describing a systemic accident model based on the principle of functional resonance.

Chapter 6: Accident Prevention. The last chapter proposes how the functional resonance accident model can be used in accident prevention. This is achieved through four steps that are described in detail and illustrated by a practical example. The steps comprise identifying the essential system functions, determining the potential for variability, defining the functional resonance – which is the main source of risks, and finally deciding on appropriate countermeasures. The method underlines the need of creative – or requisite – imagination and of using an accident model that matches the complexity of the systems being considered. Consonant with the systemic accident model, an important countermeasure is to manage the performance variability in the system, as a functional barrier system that complements the more conventional use of barriers.

Acknowledgements

In February 1676, Sir Isaac Newton famously wrote in a letter to Robert Hooke that 'if I have seen farther than others, it is because I was standing on the shoulders of giants.' Today few people can rightfully claim the same, both because the views are more bewildered and because there are fewer giants around. Yet it is as true today as it was in 1676 that any work is a product of what has gone before and that it may offer a specific, albeit limited, view of what may happen in the future. The perspective put forward by this book reflects the experience from many years of working in projects related to risk and system safety as well as from numerous discussions with friends and foes alike. To the latter I owe a debt of gratitude because they have forced me to improve arguments and revise lines of reasoning. From the former I rely on varied schedule reinforcement to prevent me from wandering completely off the track. Finally, I would like to thank Sue Bogner, Paulo Victor de Carvalho and Richard Cook for detailed comments to a draft version of this book.

Erik Hollnagel, July 2004.

Chapter 1

Accidents and Causes

Accident, n. An inevitable occurrence due to the action of immutable natural laws.
Ambrose Bierce, *The Devil's Dictionary*, ca. 1906.

Introduction

Let me start by describing an accident that happened as I was working on the introduction to this book. There is no special reason for taking this accident as an example, except for the fact that it did take place. In that sense it is typical of the multitude of accidents that happen all the time. Whenever I open a newspaper, listen to the radio, or log on to the Internet, I can most likely find another accident that will serve just as well. Certainly, not a single week goes by without a major accident grabbing the headlines across the media, nationally and internationally.

In this case it was a bus accident that happened in the port of Gedser, Denmark, on May 28, 2002. A double-decked bus that had arrived to Gedser on the ferry from Travemünde, Germany, drove into a roof over a customs booth with the result that the upper deck of the bus was severely damaged; four people were killed and 18 were taken to nearby hospitals. The bus was firmly wedged under the roof, which covered the lanes for private cars and small trucks. Buses and large trucks were supposed to use a different lane, and the driver had missed three signposted warnings about the limited height ahead.

When something like this happens the inevitable question is what went wrong, and what the cause was. In many accidents of this type there is no simple or single cause, for instance in the sense that something failed. There are rather a number of things that go wrong and which together lead to the accident. In this case the driver clearly did not notice the signs, either because they were not clear enough or because he did not pay sufficient attention. (The alternative, that the driver noticed the signs, but then wilfully ignored them, is rejected as

1

being too improbable. Such deliberate malicious actions are usually excluded from accident analysis.) One may then wonder why that happened. One reason for the lack of attention could be that the driver followed the cars in front instead of trying to find his way independently. (That then leads to some thoughts about why the driver was inattentive, where possible factors may have been the time of day, insufficient rest after a long period of driving, eating a heavy meal during the short ferry trip, etc.) These speculations illustrate the step-by-step backwards reasoning that is typical of reactions to accidents.

This accident also shows the importance of barriers. Very briefly, a barrier is something that can either prevent an event from taking place or protect against its consequences. Since this was a potentially dangerous situation – a hazard – a set of barriers had been installed (not least because a number of similar accidents had happened previously). The barriers included signs and indications (for instance, showing lanes for different types of vehicle), the standard warning signs such as limited height ahead, active warnings in the form of blinking signals triggered by a photocell, etc. Despite these barriers the accident happened. Sometimes the barriers fail themselves, for instance, because a lamp does not light, a sensor does not register, or a sign is so dirty that it cannot be read or is covered by, e.g., branches and leaves. None of this was the case in this accident. How can we then understand what happened?

After the accident the roof over the customs booth was immediately removed. (Since the customs booth was no longer used, it could easily have been removed earlier, thereby rendering the accident impossible.) That does not eliminate the possible causes, but it removes the hazard, hence making another accident of this type impossible. The example illustrates that accidents often are due to the combination of an existing hazard (the low height of the roof) and an unexpected event (the driver's presumed inattention). This will be taken up later in the book in the discussion of accident models and the relation between barriers and accidents.

Accidents today rarely happen just because one thing goes wrong, i.e., there are very few cases of single cause failures. Engineers and designers have learned to guard effectively against such conditions and single failure prevention is often part of formal system requirements. This, however, does not rule out accidents that happen when two or more failures occur together, as when a simple performance failure combines with a weakened or dysfunctional barrier. Such combinations are much harder to predict than single failures, and therefore also harder to prevent. Since the number of combinations of single failures can be exceedingly large, it is usually futile to prevent multiple failure accidents by a strict elimination of individual causes. A much more efficient solution is to make use of barriers, since the effectiveness of a barrier does not depend on knowing the precise cause of the event. A fire extinguisher or a sprinkler system, for instance, is an effective barrier against fires regardless of their origin.

What is an Accident?

This book is about the role of barriers in accident prevention, although it also ventures some thoughts on the nature of accidents as such. Despite Ambrose Bierce's bitter definition – which in some sense anticipates both Murphy's Law and Charles Perrow's (1984) notion of natural accidents – accidents are not inevitable. Although it is impossible in practice to prevent every accident, it is fully possible to prevent many and perhaps even most of them. To do so requires that we understand why accidents really happen, so that we can find the most effective ways of guarding against them. This means that we must refrain from taking existing ways of explaining accidents for granted, and instead reflect a little on what takes place during accident analysis and investigation. The argument made in this book is that we need to change our understanding of what accidents are, in order effectively to prevent them.

The book is, in particular, about understanding the role of barriers in accidents. This can be interpreted in two different ways, which both are described further in the following. First, that the failure or absence of a barrier or of several barriers, may be part of why accidents occur. Second, that the existence and proper functioning of a barrier may reduce accidents and their consequences either by preventing unexpected events from taking place or by protecting people from the consequences if the former effort fails. Even when protection cannot be complete, it may be possible to alleviate the effects, hence ensure that the outcome of the accident is not as serious as it could have been. Both aspects will be considered in this book, the first in connection with analysing and explaining accidents, the second in connection with preventing accidents.

A Little Etymology

Etymology is the branch of linguistics that deals with the origin and historical development of language terms (words) by tracing their transmission from one language to another, beginning with the earliest known occurrence. Although it may sound trivial, it is usually well worth the effort to look into the meaning of words, and in particular into how that meaning has developed.

Everybody knows what an accident is. That, at least, is what we assume. But experience shows us that it can sometimes be dangerous blissfully to make such assumptions since it misleads us into talking about things without properly defining what we mean. Even if everybody knows what the word 'accident' means, in the sense that they recognise it and can associate something to it, it does not follow that everyone shares the same understanding of what an accident is. It is therefore prudent to spend some time to discuss the meaning of the words and to begin by exploring their origin.

From the linguistic point of view, the word accident is the present participle of the Latin verb *accidere* which means 'to happen', which in turn is derived from *ad-* + *cadere*, meaning to fall. The literal meaning of accident is therefore that of a fall or stumble. The derivation from 'to fall' is significant, since falling is not something one does on purpose. If someone falls while walking or while climbing, it is decidedly an unexpected and unwanted event. It is, in other words, what we call an accident: an unforeseen and unplanned event, which leads to some sort of loss or injury.

Other definitions of 'accident', such as they can be found in various dictionaries, concur that an accident is an unforeseen and unplanned event or circumstance that (1) happens unpredictably without discernible human intention or observable cause and (2) leads to loss or injury. Used as an adverb, to say that something happens accidentally or happens by accident means that it happens by chance, i.e., without will or intention – and usually also without any expectation that it will happen (at least at that particular moment in time). We may therefore also talk about an accidental occurrence with unwanted outcomes. Similarly, we often say that someone suffered an accident or was the victim of an accident. An 'accident' can thus refer to either an event, the outcome of an event, or the possible cause. This unattractive quality is characteristic of other important terms as well, for instance 'human error' (cf. Hollnagel, 1998). To reduce the possibility of confusion, the term 'accident' shall in this book be used to refer to the event, rather than the cause or the outcome.

According to this definition an act of terror is not an accident, since the outcome is brought about on purpose. The prevention against acts of terror is therefore different from accident prevention since security must consider not only the occurrence of unwanted outcomes but also that these are deliberately brought about. There are nevertheless significant areas of overlap between safety and security, particularly when it comes to protecting third-party recipients against unwanted outcomes.

It is interesting to note that in the Germanic languages the word for accident comes from the Low German *ungelucke* meaning lack of luck [*(ge)lucke*]. In modern German the corresponding word is *unglück*, in Swedish *olycka*, and in Danish and Norwegian *ulykke*. If you fall or stumble you are, of course, out of luck. The word luck itself is possibly related to the word *loop*, signifying something that is closed or locked, or something that has come to a completion – presumably a successful one. So while accident in its etymology refers to the event itself, lack of luck (*ungeluck*) refers to the condition or state where accidents happen, the background or cause, so to speak. Indeed, one has an accident because one is out of luck.

Since we are looking at the meaning of words, and since this book is about barriers as well as accidents, it is appropriate to consider also the origins of the term barrier. Here the situation is a little easier, since the word is the same in the Latin and Germanic languages.

A barrier is derived from the middle age Latin word *barra*, which we also find in the English word bar (as in a bar, but not the place where you drink). A barrier is something that stops, or is intended to stop, the passage of something or someone, usually in a physical sense. So if an accident refers to an event, a barrier refers to that which can prevent the event from taking place.

Definition of Accident. For the purpose of this book, an accident can be defined as a short, sudden, and unexpected event or occurrence that results in an unwanted and undesirable outcome. The short, sudden, and unexpected event must directly or indirectly be the result of human activity rather than, e.g., a natural event such as an earthquake. It must be short rather than slowly developing. The loss of revenue due to an incorrect business decision can therefore not be called an accident, regardless of how unwanted it is. It must be sudden in the sense that it happens without warning. The slow accumulation of toxic waste in the environment is not considered as an accident since in this case the conditions leading to the final unwanted outcome – the disruption of the ecology – were noticeable all along. The final outcome is therefore neither sudden nor unexpected and should more properly be called misfortune, decline or deterioration. In contrast, a collision between two cars in an intersection is short, sudden, and unexpected – and also has an unwanted outcome. Some accident definitions also add that the event must be unintended. This is not done here, for the simple reason that if an event is unexpected then it must also be unintended. Intention is nevertheless related to the understanding of accidents, as it will be discussed below.

If we consider the above definition as a basis for thinking about prevention, it is clear that this either can be directed at the event or at the outcomes. Since an accident is the event plus the outcome, it follows that if we can prevent the event from taking place, we will also have ensured that the outcome does not occur. However, as illustrated by Figure 1.1, even if we cannot prevent the event from taking place, we may still be able to prevent the outcome from occurring. Preventing the accident from happening thus altogether means ensuring that the recipient comes to no harm. In Figure 1.1 the recipient is shown as a person, but it may of course equally well be a social system, a technological artefact or a combination thereof.

Before going any further it is also necessary to define what is meant by a system. The term is ubiquitous in technical (and popular) writing today and is generally used on the assumption that it is so well understood by everyone that there is no need to define its meaning. While this may possibly be so, it never hurts to be on the safe side. In this book the term system is therefore used to mean the deliberate arrangement of parts (e.g., components, people, functions, subsystems) that is instrumental in achieving specified and required goals.

> It is legitimate to call a pair of scissors a system. But the expanded system of a woman cutting with a pair of scissors is also itself a genuine system. In turn, however, the woman-with-scissors system is part of a larger manufacturing system – and so on. The universe seems to be made up of sets of systems,

each contained within a somewhat bigger, like a set of hollow building blocks. (Beer, 1964, p. 9)

As this delightful quote makes clear, the scope of a system depends on the purpose of how it is described. Any system can be seen as including subsystems and components, just as any system can be described as a component or part of a larger system.

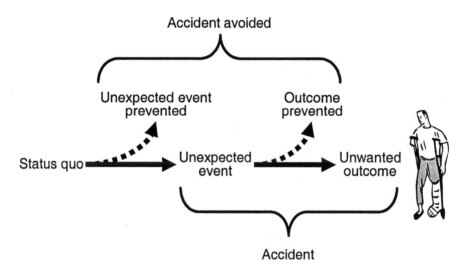

Figure 1.1: The constituents of an accident

Accident versus Good Luck. It is clear that an accident involves more than just an unexpected event. To see that we only need to look at unexpected events where the outcome is desired rather than undesired. The simplest example is winning in the lottery – or suddenly being given a sum of money in the case of those who do not play the lottery. More generally, think of a situation where something happens that is positive but unexpected. In these cases we talk about good fortune, good luck, or about getting a break. Similarly, if the unwanted outcome occurred in situations where it was expected and where it could not be prevented, such as death after a long illness, we talk about bad luck or misfortune but not about accidents. Finally, if the outcome is both positive and expected, we usually think of it as an achievement or as the fulfilment of a goal, i.e., a deliberate bringing about of something attractive and desired.

The four different situations can be illustrated as in Table 1.1, which shows a matrix with four cells corresponding to each of the four outcomes. The use of this kind of representation is common in both risk analysis and decision theory, and provides an effective shorthand characterisation of different conditions or situations. In this case it is useful to clarify what are the defining characteristics of an accident, so that confusion is minimised. The table makes clear that although there are two types of situations where the outcome is unwanted, only one of them should be called an accident according to the definition used here. In the other case the event was expected but the outcome was unexpected. This could, for instance, happen if the user had misunderstood the situation or the functioning of the device s/he was manipulating, or because the user lacked the requisite knowledge, in which case an intended action might fail to achieve its purpose.

Table 1.1: Events and their possible outcomes

	The outcome is unwanted	The outcome is wanted (desired)
The event is unexpected or unpredictable	Accident	Stroke of good luck
The event is expected or predictable	Bad luck, misfortune	Achievement, goal fulfilment

The definition of an accident can also be illustrated as in Figure 1.2, which relies on a graphical representation that often is used in accident investigations and system safety analysis, namely the logical tree. In this case the top node ('accident') represents the occurrence of an accident. The tree shows that an accident occurs if there is an unexpected event *and* an unwanted outcome, i.e., that both conditions must exist at the same time (or rather, for the same event). (Note that the tree, in this case a very small one, is turned sideways so that the leaves are to the left and the root is to the right.)

Accident as Noun and as Verb. While we may say that something *is* an accident, we often also say that something happens *by* accident. The latter is seen in contrast to something that happens deliberately, hence something that is not an accident. The following examples illustrate this difference.

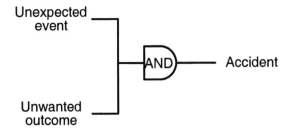

Figure 1.2: Accident defined by a logical tree

On July 17, 1996, TWA Flight 800 crashed in the Atlantic Ocean near East Moriches, New York. The investigation that followed sought to establish whether it was an accident or the result of an intended action, such as an act of sabotage. The latter was something that could not be ruled out at the time, particularly since there were no obvious causes for the crash. On October 31, 1999, EgyptAir Flight 990 crashed into the Atlantic Ocean about 60 miles south of Nantucket, Massachusetts. Again the investigation tried to determine whether it was an accident or not.

In the case of TWA 800, the National Transportation Safety Board (NTSB) determined that the crash was an accident and that the probable cause was an explosion of the centre wing fuel tank, resulting from ignition by a short circuit of the flammable fuel/air mixture in the tank (NTSB, 2000). In the case of EgyptAir 990 the NTSB determined that the probable cause was a result of some inexplicable flight control inputs from the relief first officer, although the reasons for these could not be determined (NTSB, 2002). (Needless to say, this conclusion has not gone undisputed.) In the TWA 800 case, the crash was due to an unusual but nevertheless understandable technical condition, hence was an accident. In the case of EgyptAir 990, the cause was determined to be an unexplainable action rather than a technical malfunction. It is therefore debatable whether this was an accident.

Not everything that happens by accident is, however, an accident. In 1928, the Scottish bacteriologist Alexander Fleming observed that colonies of the bacterium *Staphylococcus aureus* failed to grow in those areas of a culture that had been accidentally contaminated by the green mould *Penicillium notatum*. He isolated the mould, grew it in a fluid medium, and found that it produced a substance capable of killing many of the common bacteria that infect humans.

Thus Fleming's discovery of penicillin happened by accident, in the sense that he had not left the Petri disc in the drawer deliberately or by intention. Yet the discovery of penicillin can hardly be called an accident. So something must not only happen 'by accident' (i.e., be non-deliberate or non-intentional) but must also have a negative outcome before it can be called an accident.

Other things may happen by accident but have negative consequences that are negligible, so that the event as a whole is not considered as an accident. For instance, I may accidentally knock down a cup from the breakfast table so that it breaks, but the outcome is so insignificant that it is discounted (unless, of course, it was a very valuable cup or one of a matching pair).

Accidents, Causes and Consequences

So far the term 'accident' has been used mainly as a common denominator for the set of phenomena that is of interest, which includes accidents proper, incidents, minor events, near-misses, etc., or in other words the whole gamut of performance variations. Common to these are two things already mentioned. First that they carry with them unwanted and undesirable outcomes. Second that they are unexpected.

Unwanted Outcomes

All artefacts and systems are designed to enable the achievement of specific functions and objectives. A videocassette recorder (VCR – or these days perhaps rather a DVD RAM recorder) is designed to let the user record a TV programme from a given channel at a given time. An aeroplane is designed to transport people (or materials) from one point to another, with emphasis on comfort, speed, and safety. A computer network is designed to enable people to communicate effectively with each other and to work in a distributed fashion, again with safety and speed (and capacity) as the main criteria. The list of examples could go on and on.

Every now and then, and occasionally with surprising and deplorable regularity, something may happen that either hinders the system from carrying out its intended function or in some other way brings about an outcome that was not wanted. This has been aptly captured by Murphy's Law, which in its common form states that everything that can go wrong sooner or later will go wrong. (According to Tenner (1997, p. 22), what Captain Murphy actually said was that 'if there's more than one way to do a job and one of those ways will end in disaster, then somebody will do it that way.') If the consequences of something going wrong are severe, we call it an accident. If the consequences are smaller or minor, we may call it an incident, a delay, a mishaps, etc. (A near miss is an event when something could have gone wrong but did not. Near misses will be discussed in more detail below.) Common to all cases is the fact that we do not get what we expected. The VCR may be set to record at the wrong time or set to record the wrong channel. The airplane may be delayed or routed to another airport or cancelled. The network may be attacked by hackers, be too slow, or inaccessible.

The unwanted outcomes can range from minor nuisances and irritations to serious accidents and disasters. In this book they are referred to by the common term accidents, as a short form of saying outcomes with negative consequences or just unwanted outcomes. The reader should beware that the term can cover anything from the minor delays or slightly off-target events to the real accidents. On the low end of the scale are such things as a person falling off a ladder, someone unintentionally deleting a file, or toasting a slice of bread too much. On the high end of the scale are events ranging from collapsing bridges (Tacoma Narrows Bridge, described in Chapter 5), airplanes flying into mountains, or train accidents (derailing, collisions). As these examples show, accidents can occur on all levels and have consequences that range from the trivial and insignificant to the major. Indeed, there may be considerable disagreement on whether all of these should be called accidents. While the low end of the scale represents things that are so trivial that they almost are insignificant, an old nursery rhyme may help to put things into perspective:

> For want of a shoe, a horse was lost.
> For want of a horse, a soldier was lost.
> For want of a soldier, a battle was lost.
> For want of a battle, a war was lost.

Being short of a nail can hardly be described as an accident in itself, but is rather on the scale of a nuisance. Yet while the lack of a nail may seem a trivial and insignificant event, the loss of a battle is not an insignificant event. Thus, when the consequences are fully realised, missing a nail does become part of the accident. (This is, of course, only true as long as we accept the strict causality implied by the nursery rhyme. The wisdom of doing that will be discussed in Chapter 2.)

A trivial, but real, example is the following. In the fall of 2001, I travelled to a meeting in Manchester, UK. After arriving at the airport I went to the ticket machine to get a ticket for the train to the city centre. Following the instructions on the machine, I selected the type of ticket that I wanted, and inserted a ten-pound note. After a little delay, the machine started to make some noises and eventually produced in the out tray a ticket cleanly cut in two pieces and without anything printed on either piece, i.e., neither date, price, type, destination, or anything else. After another delay the machine produced one more ticket of the same type. This happened two more times. I was now beginning to get worried since the machine obviously did not work as I expected or, I assume, as intended. (In the case of such machines there must of course be a high degree of congruence between what the user expects and what the machine has been designed for, i.e., what the designer intended.) Finally, the machine, very kindly, returned the tenner. I then went to the ticket office and bought my ticket there. This is a case where there was an unwanted outcome, which furthermore was unexpected (cf. below). The consequences were not serious, since I got my ten pounds back and had time to buy a ticket and catch the train. The consequences would have been worse if I had not got my money back, and if I had missed the train and if it furthermore had been the last train or that the trains had run very infrequently (as they do in some airports in some countries). Events of this type, though they can be written off as minor nuisances, are subsumed under the label of accident as well as events with serious outcomes such as car collisions, house fires, chemical spills, plane crashes, and the like.

Examples of events with serious unwanted outcomes are unfortunately all too easy to come by. We have already mentioned two flight crashes and the news media provide a constant flow of accidents on an almost daily base from every field of application. Throughout the book a limited set of examples will be introduced to illustrate the arguments and findings, some of them of a serious nature but none of them major accidents. We will not consider natural disasters such as volcano eruptions, tsunamis and tornados, since these cannot be considered accidents. They may well be unexpected and lead to seriously unwanted outcomes, but they are not the result of human activity – except, perhaps, in extremely rare cases.

Lack of Unwanted Outcomes. According to the definition, the absence of an unwanted outcome means the absence of an accident. This might be taken as an indication that all is well. Unfortunately that is not necessarily the case. The reason is that the lack of an unwanted outcome can be due to several conditions or factors, as illustrated by Figure 1.3. The formalism is that of an or-node, which means that the output ('no indication if failure') is true if just one of the inputs is true. One reason could be that everything is working as it should, i.e., that the situation is normal and within the boundaries of safe performance. Another reason could be that the criterion for a failure is too high, in which case there may be a latent condition instead of an unwanted outcome. An example could be the 'safe' level of pesticides in farmed salmon or other cases of pollution, where the criteria sometimes change or are revised based on new findings. Finally, the reason could be that the measurements are too imprecise or taken too infrequently, in which case the unwanted outcome may be missed – unless it manifests itself in another way. This may also lead to a latent condition.

Figure 1.3 makes it clear that there is an important difference between a situation where there *is* no unwanted outcome, and one where the unwanted outcome is not noticed or detected. In many cases the lack of a failure indication should more properly be seen as meaning the lack of an *overt* failure or overt condition. There may, however, easily be a covert condition, something that in the literature is referred to as a latent condition. Latent conditions will be discussed in more detail in Chapter 2 (the epidemiological accident model).

Unexpected Events

While unexpected events often seem to have unwanted or negative outcomes, this is by no means always the case. Imagine, for instance, winning in the lottery. Despite many sanguine hopes, this is usually unexpected – especially if you adopt the philosophical stance of a statistician. But when it happens, it is rarely unwelcome. The opposite is the case of accidents that we have insured against, i.e., expected or possible events but unwelcome ones. The two cases also illustrate the classical paradox that in both cases we pay a small sum, but in the one case hope that an unlikely event does not occur and in the other that it does.

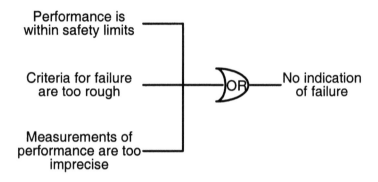

Figure 1.3: Possible reasons for 'normal' outcomes

In trying to understand accidents it is important to look closer into the distinction between an event with an unwanted outcome and an unexpected event. Accidents always have unwanted outcomes and are always unexpected when they happen in the sense that they come without warning. Yet the fact that accidents are unexpected does not necessarily mean that they also are unimaginable. They may therefore, both in principle and in practice, have been expected or anticipated. Whenever a relatively complex artefact or a system is designed, a range of possible malfunctions is usually considered. This is why there are barriers or safety systems built into most complex systems, such as emergency cooling loops in nuclear power plants, back-up computers and power supplies in safety critical processes, spare tires in cars, parachutes in airplanes (the smaller ones at least), fire extinguisher in buildings, life-boats on ships, etc. All these features indicate that one or more possible malfunctions have been taken into account, and that precautions have been included in the system design. The possibility of accidents has therefore in practice been anticipated. A characteristic example is the risk analysis that sometimes is part of a system design, using methods such as a Probabilistic Safety Assessment, PSA, or a Failure Mode, Effects and Criticality Analysis, FMECA. Technically speaking such accidents are said to be part of the design-base and they are consequently called Design-Base Accidents (DBA), a delightful but somewhat incongruous phrase.

Acknowledging that accidents *may* occur does nevertheless not mean that the accidents really are expected, in the sense that it is considered likely that they will occur. On the contrary, they are often considered highly unlikely, with or without justification. Consider, for instance, the British liner Titanic that sank on the night of April 14–15, 1912, after striking an iceberg in the North Atlantic. The ship was equipped with life-boats (although not in sufficient number) and other innovative safety features, such as the watertight panels between sections of the ship. An accident of some kind was therefore anticipated in principle, but it was considered very unlikely that it would ever occur, i.e., it was not expected to happen. In other cases, such as the space shuttle (after the Challenger disaster in 1986), calculations were made to find out how likely specific types of accidents were, and in some sense one can therefore say that they were expected but with a very low probability. In the mid-1990s NASA commissioned a Probabilistic Risk Assessment, PRA, of space shuttle missions. The result was that the probability for a loss of vehicle, or in other words another shuttle disaster, was $7.66*10^{-03}$ per mission. This means that roughly one mission out of 130 could be expected to go wrong, something that hardly can be considered reassuring (Fragola, 1995).

Beyond Design-Base Accidents. Some accidents may be not only unexpected but also unanticipated. In technical terms these are called beyond-design-base accidents (BDBA), meaning that they were not taken into account when the system was designed. A prominent example was the maiden flight of the Ariane-5 launcher on June 4, 1996, which ended in a crash about 40 seconds after takeoff. Sending off a launcher is an endeavour that is both costly and risky, and every practical precaution is therefore taken to prevent anything from going wrong. In this case something went wrong that had not been anticipated or taken into account in the design – although with hindsight it should have been. (The accident happened because a 10-year old software module from the Ariane-4 launcher, the Inertial Reference System horizontal bias module, was reused in Ariane-5. In what must have been the understatement of the year, if not the decade, the first press release from the European Space Agency, ESA, following the accident merely stated that the 'first Ariane-5 flight did not result in validation of Europe's new launcher'.)

A possible relation among different categories of outcomes is shown in Figure 1.4, which characterises outcomes on two dimensions. The X-axis describes the predictability of the event and runs from 'low' at one end and 'expected' at the other. The Y-axis describes the desirability of the outcome, going from 'unwanted' to 'wanted'. This defines a space where the upper right quadrant corresponds to predictable events with wanted outcomes (normal operations), the lower right to predictable events with unwanted outcomes (design-base accidents, DBA), the lower left to unpredictable events with unwanted outcomes (beyond design-base accidents, BDBA), and finally the upper left to unpredictable events with wanted outcomes (serendipity or good luck).

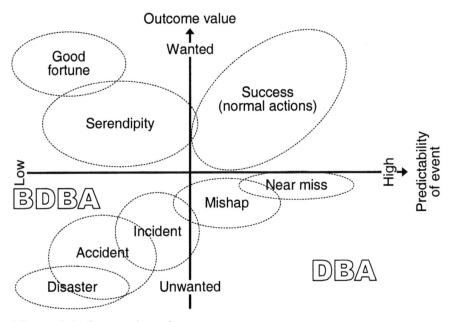

Figure 1.4: Categories of outcomes

Intended Acts and Unintended Outcomes

If someone intends something to happen that is both unexpected and unwanted by others, the event is considered an act of ill will rather than an accident. Intentional acts can range from chicanery (which hardly are accidents), to interference, sabotage, and terror. The unwanted outcome may also be a side effect of something else. Thus when someone breaks into your car, it is usually damaged. The damage was not the intention of the perpetrator (presumably – he or she just wanted to steal something), but it happened nevertheless. Compare that with having the car damaged during normal use. In this case it is a pure accident, since no one intended it to happen either as a main effect or a side effect.

The fact that actions sometimes lead to outcomes that were not considered from the start has been recognised by thinkers and philosophers at least since the days of Niccolò Machiavelli (1469-1527). In modern times, it has been treated extensively under the name of The Law of Unintended Consequences (Merton, 1979). Although unintended consequences often are unwanted as well, Merton astutely pointed out that undesired effects are not always undesirable effects. Yet from a practical point of view we are more concerned about the latter, since we are keen to ensure that they are not repeated.

An important contribution of The Law of Unintended Consequences is the identification of five main sources of such outcomes. These are: ignorance, error, imperious immediacy of interest (i.e., that an individual wants the intended consequence of an action so badly that possible side-effects are purposefully ignored), basic values, and self-defeating predictions. Of these, the prevailing literature on accidents and human behaviour has focused on the first two, ignorance and error, and paid little attention to the last three.

Although the Law of Unintended Consequences is not in itself a theory of accidents, it is useful in trying to understand why people sometimes do things that with hindsight seem groundless or not thoroughly thought out. It is perhaps even more useful as a contribution to the use of barriers, since these sometimes may have consequences that are not only unintended but which are in outright conflict with the objectives.

The Grounding of s/s Stockholm

As an illustration of the definitions proposed so far, consider the following case of the grounding of s/s Stockholm. This must clearly be classified as an accident according to the definition used here since the event was unexpected (as well as unintended) and the consequences were negative (damage to the ship, but fortunately no injury of people).

Accidents involving the grounding of ships can differ in seriousness, as the following three examples will show. The first is the case of the cruise liner The Royal Majesty that ran aground on the Rose and Crown Shoal outside Boston harbour on June 19, 1995 (NTSB 1997). In this case there was only material damage to the ship, although to the amount of about 7 million US$. The second example is the Greek oil tanker Prestige, which suffered a 50-metre gash in the right side of the hull during stormy weather on Wednesday November 13, 2002, off the Spanish coast. Salvage ships attempted to tow the Prestige away from the Spanish coast across the Galician bank and into deeper waters, but on Tuesday November 19, the vessel split in two and sank about 170 miles west of Vigo. The single skinned vessel carried some 77,000 tonnes of fuel oil, of which in excess of 5,000 tonnes were lost before the ship sank. This led to considerable environmental damage in the form of oil spills, the effects of which are still felt.

The s/s Stockholm was built in 1931 to be used in the traffic between the cities of Kalmar on the Swedish mainland and Färjestaden on the island of Öland in the Baltic Sea, a distance of some 10 kilometres. (Today the connection is provided by the 6070 metres long bridge, Ölandsbron, opened in 1972.) It served in this capacity under the name of s/s Öland until 1957. From 1957 she sailed between Finland and Sweden, rebuilt to be able to take cars onboard, and was renamed s/s Korsholm. After 1966 the ship was bought by the Finnish state, and used for various purposes. Between 1985 and 1998 the ship had various owners and uses, and slowly fell into disrepair and was almost a wreck. In 1998 a Swedish company bought it, with plans to restore it to its original condition. The costly renovation was completed in 2000, and the ship began to be used for coastal traffic under the name of s/s Stockholm.

On Thursday July 20, 2000, the ship was travelling from Nyköping to Mem on its normal schedule. The waters are part of the Swedish archipelago, which means that there are narrow passages and many rocks both above and below the surface. On its way out from Nyköping, the ship suddenly experienced a total loss of electrical power (black-out). At the time, two able-bodied seamen were trying to pump out water from the engine room using a portable pump. During this work one of them accidentally hit the regulator for the fuel pump and cut off the fuel to the main generator (cf. Sjöfartsverket, 2000). The captain and the first mate were on the bridge at the time, but the ship sailed under the control of the autopilot. The loss of power meant that the bridge lost control of the steering as well as the propeller pitch. At the time of the power loss the rudder was at starboard, and the ship was heading towards a rock. The captain took over and connected the shaft generator to replace the lost electrical power. At the same time he moved the rudder to port and set the pitch to zero. This was a sensible response, except for the fact that neither rudder position nor propeller pitch could be controlled from the bridge when electrical power was lost. The captain, however, was unaware of that at the moment. After about 10 seconds the shaft generator disconnected due to overload, which meant that the corrective actions were only incompletely carried out.

The ship continued towards port in the direction of an area with shallow water. The captain tried repeated times to reconnect the shaft generator, but without success. The first mate ran to the galley to switch off ovens, cookers and other power-hungry appliances. The captain continued the attempts to regain control of the ship, but finally had no alternative but to stop the main engines and helplessly wait as the ship slowly ran aground at 11:30 on a rocky island named Munken. The stopping of the main engines also caused an emergency clutch-out of the propeller shaft (i.e., disconnecting it from the gear box). After the ship had run aground, the first mate managed to start the emergency diesels manually.

The ship was crewed by a captain, a first mate with the help of two able-bodied seamen and a service staff of eight people. It was licensed to carry 76 passengers. No one was injured or hurt by the accident, and there were no releases to the environment. The bottom of the vessel was bent, and the propeller was severely damaged. The vessel was later towed back to the town of Oxelösund.

The grounding of s/s Stockholm was clearly an accident since it was unexpected and had a negative or unwanted outcome. The initiating action, the loss of electrical power, was presumably also unintended although it is not known with certainty why it happened. On a scale of severity it was a minor one, although probably rather costly.

Accidents, Incidents, and Near Misses

Both of the specific conditions that are part of the definition of an accident can be considered in various degrees. The occurrence of an event may be associated with some uncertainty. Yet when we say that an event is unpredictable it does not mean that we cannot imagine it or think of it. Indeed, when we drive our car in the traffic we know that there is a very small chance of being involved in a collision and of sustaining damage (to the car or to oneself). Still, when it happens we call it an accident. We can think of the possibility that it may happen, and we can imagine that it happens, though unwillingly so, but we cannot predict precisely when or where it will happen. (If that were the case, the logical consequence would be to refrain from driving, at least on that occasion, or to avoid the specific location of the future accident.) So when we speak about a possible accident, the possibility refers to the occurrence of the event. When we deal with accidents in a professional manner – rather than just worrying about them as private persons – we try to describe and calculate the probability that the accident may occur. Indeed, this is what insurance companies do in order to decide how much to charge for an insurance policy.

In the case of the consequences, they can be more or less serious. To take the situation with the car again, the worst outcome of an accident is that the driver or a passenger is killed. A much less serious outcome is that the car is slightly damaged, but that otherwise no one is hurt. And there are clearly many degrees of outcome in between. Technically, the outcomes are usually categorised as accidents (the most serious), incidents (the less serious), and near misses. An accident can be defined, for instance, as an unforeseen event or occurrence, which results in serious property damage or injury, possibly even loss of life. An incident can in a similar fashion be defined as an unforeseen event or occurrence, which results in only minor injury or property damage. Finally, a near-miss can be defined as an occurrence with potentially important safety-related effects which was prevented from developing into actual consequences.

The definition of what is an accident or an incident is specific for each application and domain, and there are no common rules that apply across cases. The difference between accidents and incidents is a question of the severity or seriousness of the outcome. In traffic, for instance, an accident is normally something that is reported to the police or entered into the official databases, whereas an incident is something that is not. What determines the difference is thus to some degree subjective, hence arbitrary, although it is commonly associated with the level of personal injury. In cases where the rescue services or ambulances are called the event is always classified as an accident. In cases where the participants (drivers) can reach an agreement among themselves, the term incident is used – if the event is reported at all.

To illustrate the differences in definition, consider the example of Japan Railways, which for the purpose of statistics on track maintenance uses a classification based on the following three categories: big, small and no-loss accidents/incidents (Itoh et al., 2003). In this system a 'big accident' is defined as something that either involves a loss of more than 500,000 Japanese Yen or causes a delay of more than 10 minutes to the first bullet train (Shinkansen) in the morning. A 'small incident' is something that involves a shorter delay or a smaller loss, while a 'no-loss incident' is a very minor event that causes no appreciable loss or delay to the bullet train (and which therefore is excluded from the statistical analysis). In most other countries, a 10 minutes delay of a train is not seen as an accident, but rather as something that must be expected every now and then. The same goes for civil aviation.

Despite the differences in criteria for what are considered accidents and incidents, it is commonly agreed that failures come in many shapes, which can be characterised according to the severity of their outcomes. The importance of making the distinction is that an incident generally is understood as an event that might have progressed to become an accident, but which for one reason or another did not do so. The difference is in many cases due to the presence of a barrier. Common to both incidents and accidents is that they are conspicuous and that it therefore normally is futile to hide or suppress them – with some notable exceptions, of course.

In addition to incidents and accidents there are also events that, although by themselves they are innocent, under the right – or rather, wrong – conditions may become incidents and accidents. These events are usually called near misses (or near miss events), and are defined as something that could have resulted in some kind of injury or property damage, but which did not. Table 1.2 shows examples of different types of accidents, incidents and near misses in three domains.

Further down the scale is the category of unsafe acts, i.e., actions that in some way break a principle for safe behaviour, for instance as a minor violation (Reason, 1991). In most theories and models of human performance, unsafe acts are seen as an important – or even necessary – link between actions and failures. For the three domains listed in Table 1.2, the corresponding unsafe act would be not wearing a hard hat, walking against a red light, or trying to reach something standing on a chair instead of a ladder. It is obvious to anyone that such unsafe acts are very common, although they rarely lead to unwanted consequences.

Table 1.2: Examples of failure types

Type of failure	Place of occurrence		
	At work	In the traffic	At home
Accident	Being injured or killed	Being killed or seriously injured	Fire or water leakage
Incident	Being hit but not injured	Being hit by a vehicle	A blown fuse; breaking a window
Near miss	Something falling down close to person	Almost colliding with a vehicle	Forgetting to lock the door

(This raises an interesting semantic issue. In the case of traffic and home, the unsafe act can in some sense be said to lead to the unwanted outcome, since the person exposes him/herself to a risk, or indeed makes the accident more likely. The same is not the case for failing to wear a hard hat or helmet. The probability that something falls down and hits a person on the head is independent of whether or not s/he wears a hard hat, i.e., wearing a hard had is not a causal factor. The probability of being seriously injured, on the other hand, increases if a hard hat is not worn. Crossing against a red light exposes a person to a greater risk, although it does not as such cause other cars to hit you. Standing on a chair (instead of on a ladder) will increase the probability of falling or stumbling, in the sense that the probability would be zero if the person did not stand on the chair but remained on the floor.)

One difference between near misses and incidents / accidents has to do with how conspicuous they are: the occurrence of an incident or accident is quite obvious and is intersubjectively verifiable, in the sense that two or more people may easily notice it. The consequences are usually also quite evident and are normally impossible to overlook – unless done deliberately so. Near misses, on the other hand, are much less obvious both in how they appear and in their consequences. They may, indeed, often be noticed only by the person to whom they happen. A second difference has to do with the clarity of the criterion or definition. Although the classification of incidents and accidents may differ and vary among domains, the existence of a manifest outcome means that there rarely is any doubt when an incident/accident has occurred. In the case of near misses, the definition is less precise and much is left to personal judgment.

The basic point of this discussion is to emphasise that failures come in many forms and degrees of severity, and that there may be much to learn from failures that are less severe than incidents and accidents. The difference among failure types is often represented by the pyramid shown in Figure 1.5, which illustrates the relationship of accidents to other types of unsafe situations. One type is incidents with consequences that could have resulted in injury or damage meeting accident report thresholds but which for some reason failed to do so. Another type is near misses, or almost incidents, which raised the danger of an accident or incident, but which due to fortunate circumstances failed to develop further. A final type is unsafe acts, i.e., actions where the performance variability almost reached the threshold of the near miss classification.

The numbers in Figure 1.5 are the outcome of an analysis of 1,753,498 reported accidents from 21 different industrial groups (Bird, 1974; from Heinrich et al., 1980). Assuming, for the sake of discussion that the 1:10:30:600 ratios are correct, it is clearly insufficient to direct the total effort at the relatively few events terminating in serious or disabling injury when in addition there are 640 property damage or no-loss incidents that provide a much larger basis for more effective control of total accident losses. Firstly, one need not wait so long between opportunities to learn. Secondly, the learning would be less costly because the experience is direct and the consequences smaller. In order for this approach to be effective it is, however, necessary that the study is confined to the minor incidents and near misses that are directly related to the accidents at the top of the pyramid. As pointed out by Hale et al. (2000, p. 26), the fact that all serious accidents are preceded by many minor incidents and near misses with the same general components does not mean that all minor incidents are precursors of 'death and destruction'.

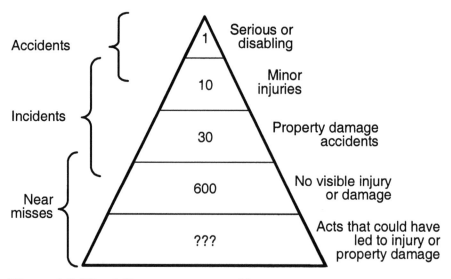

Figure 1.5: The failure types pyramid

The 1:10:30:600 ratios have achieved an almost mythical status, often quoted as 'studies show approximately 300 near misses occur for every accident.' The numbers may nevertheless be very different in reality and the importance lies not in the actual numbers, but in their meaning. Although it is nearly impossible to get reliable numbers for the occurrence of near misses, recent statistics of work injuries in the UK show that in 1999/2000 there were 220 fatal injuries and 28,652 non-fatal injuries, which gives a ratio of 1:130 for the first two categories alone. If we, just for the sake of illustration, scale up the ratios derived from Figure 1.5 with a factor 13, the result is that there should be 8,320 lesser events – and that number may not even include the true near misses.

A further reason to be careful is that the number of cases in each category depends on the definitions used by the event reporting or data collection system, i.e., the reporting threshold, which partly is tied to whether the manifestations of the events are unique or not. While we can be fairly certain about the number of accidents, failures with lesser consequences are reported with less consistency and reliability. Bourne & van Ours (2002), for instance, found that reported workplace accident rates, with the exception of fatal accidents, were inversely related to both the level of unemployment and the change in unemployment. Near misses are only rarely reported, and unsafe acts are as a rule not reported at all.

The Search for Causes

Whenever an accident happens there is a natural concern to find out in detail exactly what happened and to determine the causes of it. Indeed, whenever the result of an action or event falls significantly short of what was expected, or whenever something unexpected happens, people try to find an explanation for it. This trait of human nature is so strong that we try to find causes even when they do not exist, such as in the case of misleading or spurious correlations. For a number of reasons humans seem to be extremely reluctant to accept that something can happen by chance. One very good reason is that we have created a way of living that depends heavily on the use of technology, and that technological systems are built to function in a deterministic, hence reliable manner. If therefore something fails, we are fully justified in trying to find the reason for it. A second reason is that our whole understanding of the world is based on the assumption of specific relations between causes and effects, as amply illustrated by the Laws of Physics. (Even in quantum physics there are assumptions of more fundamental relations that are deterministic.) A third reason is that most humans find it very uncomfortable when they do not know what to expect, i.e., when things happen in an unpredictable manner. This creates a sense of being out of control, something that is never desirable since – from an evolutionary perspective – it means that the chances of survival are reduced. The condition was perfectly described by the philosopher Friedrich Nietzche (1844-1900) when he wrote that:

> (t)o trace something unknown back to something known is alleviating, soothing, gratifying and gives moreover a feeling of power. Danger, disquiet, anxiety attend the unknown – the first instinct is to eliminate these distressing states. First principle: any explanation is better than none ... The cause creating drive is thus conditioned and excited by the feeling of fear. Nietzsche (1990, p. 62)

A well-known example of this is provided by the phenomenon called the *gambler's fallacy*. The name refers to the fact that gamblers often seem to believe that a long row of events of one type increases the probability of the complementary event. Thus if a series of 'red' events occur on a roulette wheel, the gambler's fallacy lead people to believe that the probability of 'black' increases. Or conversely, that a positive outcome makes it less likely that another one will follow soon. Rather than accepting that the underlying mechanism may be random, people invent all kinds of explanations to reduce the uncertainty of future events. The general tendency to attribute rare events to causal factors is furthermore not the prerogative of gamblers, but may be found even scientifically sounding statements such as 'Given all the logically possible combinations of which DNA molecules are capable, the odds against human life evolving are staggering. The fact that we are here proves that some intelligence guided the process to make our appearance inevitable.' As Nietzsche said, any explanation is better than none.

Facts and Explanations

This book is not about error, neither the dreaded individual 'human error' nor organisational errors. The basic reason is that a focus on errors takes for granted that this is the most important thing to look at. It also implies that a simple cause-effect model is the only reasonable one, instead of keeping an open mind. As will be argued in Chapter 2, there are several ways in which an accident can be described and understood and the cause-effect assumption is perhaps the least attractive option. A further reason is that a number of works have already been published which go into discussions of errors at great length, although often with widely diverging views and opinions. Examples are Reason (1990a; 1997), Senders & Moray (1991), Rasmussen et al., (1987), Hollnagel (1993 & 1998); Woods et al. (1994) and many, many others. So rather than attempting yet another analysis of error, this book will focus on accidents in their own right and keep an open mind as far as the possible causes go.

The explanation of accidents, or the search for explanations, is often based on the assumption – incorrect as it turns out – that explanations can be deduced from the facts. Thus accident explanations and the search for causes are very often just trying to fit all the facts together, in the belief that there is some kind of objective truth to be found. Explaining an accident is seen as a detective story where the great detective tries to fit all the facts together. But first of all, we may not have all the facts and something may be missing. Also, some data may not be facts but just spurious observations that are causally unrelated although temporally contiguous. Finally, the facts such as they are, are not independent of the accident model. Indeed, facts are not found but sought out.

The Difference between Explanations and Causes

An accident investigation is an attempt to find out both *how* the accident happened and *why* it happened. An investigation should preferably be done in a systematic and rational fashion, so that the account of the accident neither is biased by premature assumptions or pet hypotheses nor invoke *ad hoc* psychological or organisational causes, which in effect only substitute one term for another. To ensure this, human factors researchers and safety conscious practitioners have over the years developed a set of accident analysis methods and classification systems. All methods necessarily imply an accident model, i.e., a mutually agreed and often unspoken understanding of how accidents occur. While there have been several changes to our understanding of accidents over the last couple of decades, such changes have mostly addressed the nature of the causes. We have gone from focusing on technological deficiencies, to focusing on the negative impact of human performance failures, to focusing on the role of organisational factors. Yet all of these explanations rely on the same tacit accident model, which usually is taken for granted and is shared among the people involved in the analysis. Chapter 2 will go into further details of the common accident models.

The tendency to look for causes rather than explanations is often reinforced by the methods that are used for accident analysis. The most obvious example of that is the principle of Root Cause Analysis (RCA), e.g., Cojazzi & Pinola (1994), which is commonly applied in many different domains. As the name implies, the principle entails that it is possible to find a basic cause that is the root or origin of the problems, specifically of the incidents and accidents that occur. It is thus an expression of a strong principle of causality, derived from the Axioms of Industrial Safety (Heinrich et al., 1980; org. Heinrich, 1931). The responses to the accident with the space shuttle Columbia on February 1, 2003, are a good illustration of how pervasive the root cause idea is. The initial reaction from NASA officials was that they wanted to find the root cause of the accident, but after a while the more considerate view prevailed, namely to find likely explanations of what happened. This is probably more the reluctant acceptance that the root cause could not be found for technical reasons, than an acknowledgement of the fact that the root cause is a meaningless concept. (More will be said about the root case concept in Chapter 2.)

Most root cause analysis methods propose a number of rules for how the analysis shall be carried out. One rule may be that causal statements must clearly show a 'cause and effect' relationship. This advice is deceptively simple and seemingly innocent. But it hides the assumption that it is possible to establish a 'cause and effect' relationship, which means: (1) that nothing happens without a cause *and* (2) that it is possible to find that cause from knowledge of the effect. It further implies, though more subtly, that if the cause is found and eliminated in some way, then the accident will not happen again. This is practically synonymous with the First Axiom of Industrial Safety, which states, '(t)he occurrence of an injury invariably results from a completed sequence of factors – the last one of these being the accident itself' (Heinrich et al., 1980). Both the rule and the axiom correspond to a simple model of an accident as a sequence of events, most vividly represented by the Domino model of accident causation.

The futility of this kind of reasoning is easily demonstrated by a small example. In this case a nurse who worked alone on a night-shift had to leave a ward in the middle of the night in response to a distress signal from another ward. She did that assuming that the alarm system for the patients was activated, so that she would be alerted if one of them suddenly became ill. When she returned to her ward twenty minutes later she found that one patient had died, and that the alarm system was not active. (The patient was an 86 years old woman who two days earlier had undergone heart surgery.) We may polemically ask whether the reasons that the patient died (apart from her serious heart condition, of course) were that the alarm system was turned off or that there was only a single nurse on duty. Hindsight reasoning suggests that if there had been two nurses on duty instead of one, then the patient's rapidly deteriorating condition could have been noticed, leading to a different outcome. Likewise, that if the alarm system had not been turned off, then the nurse could have been alerted to the situation and might have been able to intervene in some way. Yet one cannot reason the other way and say that the failure of either of these conditions was the cause. It would be equally absurd to say that a single nurse on duty or the alarm that had been turned off were in any way the cause of the patient's death. Nevertheless, the investigation into this case was started because it was felt that the nurse had made an error by leaving the patient with the alarm system turned off.

What we can say is rather that the accident happened because a number of factors came together or aligned at a specific time (the alarm turned off, etc.), but not that the accident was caused by any of them. Seen together, the several factors and conditions constitute an explanation, in the sense that we can understand *how* the accident happened. Yet this does not mean that the explanation is the cause and it does not tell us *why* the accident happened. The cause, if any, is in the concurrence or coincidence of these various factors, something that will be discussed further in Chapter 5. Yet since it is impossible to eliminate coincidences in any practical sense, it is also impossible to eliminate causes of accidents as such. The difference between looking for explanations and for causes is therefore crucial. If accidents have causes, then it makes sense to try to find them and to do something about them once found. If accidents have explanations, then we should rather try to account for how the accident took place and for what the conditions or events were that led to it. The response should not be to seek out and destroy causes, but to identify the conditions that may lead to accidents and find effective ways of controlling them.

From Technological Failure to 'Human Error'

Throughout the history of accident investigation there has been a strong and natural tendency to look for explanations or causes in those parts of the systems that fail most frequently or which in some ways are conspicuous. In the early phases, i.e., until the late 1950s, those were the technological or mechanical parts of systems. People knew from their everyday experience that technology on the whole was prone to fail or malfunction. When therefore an accident – and in particular a spectacular accident – happened there was a natural tendency to look for causes that could be expressed in terms of technological failures.

As time went by technology became more reliable, and therefore receded into the background as a possible cause of accidents. In its place came the human action – infamously known as 'human error'. Finding the explanation in human actions rather than in a technological malfunction is, of course, not enough, since that is a wholesale description almost on the level of acts of nature. Furthermore, since no system creates or maintains itself, the search for a human action is bound to succeed if it only goes on for long enough. When human action as such was identified as a cause, then little could be done except censure or punish the person in some way. There was a clear need to go further, i.e., to find an explanation beyond the explanation of 'human error'. Here human factors and information processing psychology came to help because they provided a powerful analogy from which explanations could be constructed.

The development of human factors took a big step forward when psychologists in the late 1950s discovered the computer metaphor and realised that the human mind could be described as an information processing system. The computer metaphor made it possible to decompose human behaviour into a set of basic structures and associated processes in complete analogy with the description of technological systems. Just as for technological systems, human information processing components could fail, if not directly break, and such failures could be seen as the cause of accidents through more or less well-defined cause-effect relations. The analogy was even taken as far as proposing the existence of a 'human error mechanism' although this ill-advised practice later has fallen into well-deserved disrepute.

The early enthusiasm for 'human error' as a universal source of accident causes has now waned, one reason being that it became rather obvious how easily new 'error categories' could be invented to fit a situation. (It is indeed a convenient feature of the human mind that it is always possible to suggest a new intermediate function or link, hence the plethora of 'human error' categories and cognitive functions.) And while explaining one problem by substituting it with another may be great fun, it is a rather futile exercise in the long run. In its place the focus was turned to the relation between organisational factors and accidents (Reason, 1997), although organisational factors in themselves at some level require an explanation on the level of the individual. Curiously enough, this development has been horizontal rather than vertical, in the sense that organisational factors have been seen as yet another link in the causes-effect relations, rather than as a transition to a qualitatively new level of explanation. The reason for that is probably that the underlying accident model has remained the same, namely the sequential accident model (Hollnagel, 2002). Yet it is clear, according to the above line of argument, that the concept of 'human error' is an artefact of a theoretical development coupled to a technological development. It is therefore time to reassess the term and hopefully take a step further.

Causality and Time

One of the most important, and possibly most overlooked, relations in accident analysis is between causality and time. As already discussed it is a general axiom of causality that the cause must exist prior to the effect – barring exotic fields such as quantum physics. There is, however, another consequence or effect of time, namely that events are ordered in time.

In relation to accident analysis this means that any description of the events that occurred before the accident – regardless of whether they were relevant for the accident or not – imposes a sequence or order. This is a consequence of the simple fact that time progresses in one direction only. However, the fact that event A occurs earlier than event B is a necessary condition for A being a cause of B, but not a sufficient one. This was pointed out already by Scottish philosopher David Hume (1711-1776) who in *Treatise of Human Nature*, published in 1739, provided a ground-breaking analysis of causality. Despite that, we have a deplorable tendency to equate temporal ordering with causality, particularly if the two events seem to have something in common.

What is more, and worse, is that we are misled by the fact that we can describe past events as a sequence to believe that we can describe future events in the same way. We cannot only describe past events as a sequence, but also as a tree, using the fallacious counterfactual reasoning. In this way we can examine or speculate about hypothetical developments that did not take place, either the ones that would have been beneficial or better, or the ones that would have been detrimental or worse (and hence praise ourselves, thankful that they did not obtain).

This possibility creates the incorrect belief that we can describe hypothetical future events in the same way. The reason why it is possible to describe past events in a sequence is that they did occur, and that therefore the temporal relations between the events are manifest. Hypothetical events can also be positioned relative to the manifest ordering of the real events. The same is not the case for future events. It is, of course, possible to consider alternative ways of development for a single future event, such as failure or error modes, but it is not possible to assume an order of two or more events in a sequence. Although it may indeed be reasonable to assume that in most cases event A will occur before event B – due to the physical laws, for instance – the order is not immutable. And it is precisely the unexpected reversals of order or breaking of the temporality that are the ones that create the serious accidents.

Evolving Concepts of Causes

Even though finding and eliminating the causes cannot always prevent accidents, it is still instructive to look for causes as parts of the explanations, rather than as root causes. It is also instructive to see how the categories of causes have developed through the years, reflecting a development from simple accident explanations to complex ones – from simple causality to complex coincidences (Figure 1.6). This is, of course, not unrelated to the *de facto* growth in the complexity of technological systems.

Going back to the early days of industrial accident analysis, which means the first half of the 20th Century stretching into the 1970s, the main categories of causes were technical failure, 'human error', and 'other'. (This rough characterisation obviously does injustice to a number of people who were far ahead of their time. It is nevertheless a fair rendering of the views of the mainstream, particularly the views of the engineering community as a whole, i.e., the non-specialists.) The reason is not difficult to find, since technical systems on the whole were less reliable than today. As an illustration, just consider a car from the 1950s and one from 2000. Despite the considerably larger number of components in a modern car, it is not only better performing but also more reliable.

Over the years there have been periodic developments within each of the three main categories either because new failure types arose or because of developments in the corresponding theories and models. As far as 'human error' is concerned, a major boost began in the mid 1970s when mainstream human factors specialists and psychologists adopted the human information processing view and used that both to enrich their understanding of the nature of human action and to produce a flourishing vocabulary. This development was initially focused on 'human errors' during operation or actual work at the sharp end, but soon grew to include other categories of human work, specifically maintenance, management, and design. The considerable literature on 'human error' mentioned above is testimony of that.

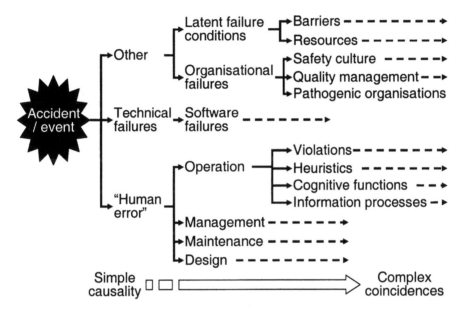

Figure 1.6: Developments in types of causes

The categories for technical failures have seen less of a development, due in the main to more reliable systems. One notable exception is the category of metal fatigue, which became known to the general public after two British de Havilland Comet airliners crashed in 1954, two years after their introduction in commercial flight. The cause turned out to be the weakening of a metal part due to repeated cyclical movement such as bending or twisting. Since then the technology has improved to the extent that metal fatigue has almost disappeared from sight.

Another kind of technical cause, which seems to be more difficult to get rid of, is software failures or software errors. Although these usually are seen as a kind of technical failure, they might equally well be considered as a human or organisational failure. Leveson (1995) has provided an excellent treatment of software failures, and there is therefore no reason to go further into this topic here.

Finally, the category of 'other' has undergone a remarkable development. During the 1980s and onwards there has been a significant development in our understanding of causes that have to do with the working environment, especially the organisation. One development has been the introduction of the concept of latent conditions – or latent failure conditions – due not least to the work of Reason (1990b). Another has been the growing understanding of the importance of organisational factors, leading to the emphasis on safety culture and quality management. This field is still developing, and more will be said about that in Chapter 2.

The large number of candidates for causes means that the root cause concept clearly is inadequate, and also that the construction of strict causal models is nearly impossible. In the end, of course, we still need the category of 'other' for the situations where we cannot really explain what has happened, or not easily find a satisfactory cause.

A Cynical Definition of Causes

The above discussion has hopefully made it clear that it is no simple matter to define what a cause is. Philosophers have been working at that at least since the days of David Hume and have more recently been joined by practitioners, although with the pragmatic aim simply to be able to do something about accidents.

In line with the arguments contained in this book and the whole line of reasoning that permeates current behavioural science studies of accidents and failures, a cause can be defined as the identification, after the fact, of a limited set of aspects of the situation that are seen as the necessary and sufficient conditions for the observed effect(s) to have occurred. The cause, in other words, is constructed rather than found just as the label 'human error' is a judgment made in hindsight (Woods et al., 1994, p. 210).

In consequence of this definition, a 'cause' has the following characteristics:

- It can unequivocally be associated with a system structure or function (people, components, procedures, etc.). That is, the cause can be associated to something tangible or something that we concretely can think about.

- It is possible to do something to reduce or eliminate the cause within accepted limits of cost and time. This is important from a pragmatic point of view, since there is little value in causes that we cannot do anything about. Knowing that there is a cause but that it is beyond control makes us uncertain, and in some cases no cost is spared to remove the uncertainty. The analysis of the TWA 800 accident is a good example of that, lasting close to four years (NTSB, 2000).

- It conforms to the current 'norms' for explanations. This is perhaps the most important aspect, since it means that the search for causes stops when an acceptable one has been found. Therefore, what is an acceptable cause at one point in time may not always remain so. Indeed, the developments in the types of causes illustrated by Figure 1.6 should be sufficient proof of that.

The bottom line is that the determination of the 'cause' is a relative (pragmatic) rather than absolute (scientific) process. The value of finding the correct cause or explanation is that it becomes possible to do something constructively to prevent future accidents. That, in a nutshell, is what this book is about.

Chapter 2

Thinking about Accidents

The quest for certainty blocks the search for meaning.
Uncertainty is the very condition to impel man to unfold his powers.
Erich Fromm (1900–1980), U.S. psychologist. *Man for Himself,* ch. 3 (1947).

Introduction

The quotation from Fromm is very relevant for the study of accidents, although it was not written with accidents in mind. It has been known since the days of Aristotle that humans have a thirst for knowledge, a need to find out about things. This has been pointed out an endless number of times since then, and often with considerable pride. It is, indeed, because of the never-ending search for knowledge, the eternal curiosity, the incessant need to ask 'what' and to find out 'why' – as every parent knows to his or her despair – that humankind has raised itself over the animals and has achieved the current level of development. (Though we need of course not be equally proud of every achievement.)

The view of Erich Fromm, however, puts a damper on the initial enthusiasm. Fromm points out that we in many cases seek certainty rather than knowledge. We want to know, not because of a thirst for pure knowledge, but to drive out the demons of uncertainty. (See also the quotation from Friderich Nietzsche in Chapter 1.) As a species, we tend to feel insecure and apprehensive if there is something for which we cannot find an explanation. It does not really matter of which type the explanation is, whether it is rational and scientific, emotional, religious, irrational and superstitious, etc. An explanation is needed and an explanation we must have.

Faced with unsettling and initially unexplainable events such as accidents, people have a strong need to find out why an accident has happened, more specifically expressed as a need to find its causes – or even better THE CAUSE in the singular! (The same argument can in various degrees be applied to incidents and untoward events of lesser importance.) Although we may think that we are looking for the meaning, in the sense of the explanation of the accident, we are in fact more often looking for certainty in the form of a cause. In other words, finding an acceptable cause is more important than finding out why the accident really happened.

This kind of arguing obviously implies that people are dishonest, at least some of the time. The dishonesty is, however, not deliberate, i.e., we are not trying to delude ourselves (which would also be logically impossible). It is rather that we often are satisfied with a quick explanation, something that can be seen in the strong tendency to look for confirming evidence. This is a feature of human thinking, which has been much discussed in the philosophy of science. In itself it can be seen as an example of the Efficiency-Thoroughness Trade-Off (ETTO) principle that will be described in Chapter 5. For the moment, the argument is simply that in order to save time and effort, we rarely look beyond the first explanation we find. That explanation, or rather the acceptability of it, is furthermore determined by psychological and sociological rather than logical factors. As argued in Chapter 1, there is no absolute criterion for what constitutes a correct explanation or a correct cause. The decision about that is a social judgment rather than a logical deduction – the 'wisdom' of rational reasoners like Sherlock Holmes notwithstanding.

In the case of most accidents and incidents we do manage to find explanations that not only get rid of the dreaded uncertainty but also are proper explanations in the sense that they increase our knowledge a little bit – at least about the particular event. The latter is proven by the fact that we can do something to reduce the likelihood of occurrence of a similar event in the future (a.k.a. accident prevention) or that we can protect ourselves against the outcomes should it occur nonetheless. The main purpose of trying to understand accidents and other untoward events is to be able to do something about them, to be ready to respond and to remain in control. An added bonus is that this may also eradicate some of the uncertainty in our lives. In some cases, commonly ascribed to acts of god or acts of nature, there is unfortunately little that can be done – also because such events usually are on a scale where precautions and protections in most cases are woefully ineffective (examples being earthquakes, tsunamis and epidemics).

The Search for Causes in Science and Philosophy

The search for causes is not confined to the investigation of accidents but is rather a pervasive trait of Western thinking. This is easily seen in the way in which we pursue science, as illustrated by the following examples.

In psychoanalysis, the basic principle is the existence of a dynamic unconscious that influences every action. This has entered into popular fiction and the foundations of the modern Western culture, so that we now – jokingly – know that in order to understand how people behave we have to look for the underlying drive. Indeed, a major element of psychoanalysis is the doctrine of psychic determinism, which holds that nothing is a matter of chance but that everything has a deeper cause. The best example of that is the so-called Freudian slip, which is the term used to describe a verbal mistake that is thought to reveal an unconscious belief, thought, or emotion. A recent example is when the 43rd President of the United States, in a television address to the nation's teachers, allegedly started by saying 'First I'd like to spank all the teachers ... '.

Another way in which this thinking shows itself is in the popularisation of criminal investigations (and probably also in the real investigations) where there always is a search for the motive to a crime. Without a motive, the action becomes meaningless or senseless, and it is assumed that this is only rarely the case. Indeed, if we cannot find a plausible reason for what people do, we classify them as psychologically disturbed or even psychotic.

The search for causes is also exemplified by the reductionistic trend to explain everything in terms of neurological functions. There is a certain logic to that, in the sense that human functioning is based on what happens in the brain, or rather that without the brain we would be unable to do anything. We acknowledge that the centre of our thoughts, memories, emotions, etc., is the brain and not any other organ of the body (despite associating emotions with the heart). Since everything can be traced back to the brain, and since the brain is made up of neurons, it makes some kind of sense to explain everything in terms of the functioning of neurons. (It is, of course, also possible to go even further back and try to understand how the neurons work on a chemical or molecular level. But an explanation on that level would be so far removed from the initial phenomenon that it would hardly explain anything at all. It would, in the words of Scriven (1964, p. 168), be an explanation that existed 'after the grave' in the sense that it would no longer have anything to do with the original phenomenon.) Two recent examples of that are the proposed disciplines of neuroergonomics, which is the application of neurophysiological concepts and methods to human factors and ergonomics (Parasuraman, 1998), and neuroeconomics, which aims to understand human social interactions through every level from synapse to society (Grimes, 2003). The former tries to reduce ergonomics to the neural level, the latter hopes to do the same for economics. While there is a kind of unreasonable logic to it, in the sense that without the brain we would be unable either to work or trade, this argument does not mean that the phenomena that are considered by ergonomics and economics, respectively, can be explained by a reduction to simpler functions. The problem is the same as in the use of the popular 'abstraction hierarchies' that abound (e.g., Lind, 2003). The real significance of descriptions at different levels of abstraction is that they are *different* descriptions, and that one therefore cannot be reduced to the other.

The Big Bang. The premier example of causal thinking is found in cosmology, in the big-bang theory. Reasoning backwards to the beginning of the universe and time must simply be the ultimate case of reverse causal thinking. The big-bang theory states that all of the matter and energy in the universe was concentrated in a very small volume that exploded about 15 billion years ago. Everything – all matter, energy, even space and time – came into being at that precise instant. Starting with the big bang, the universe expanded. The evidence for that comes from astronomical observations going as far back as the 1920s, which show that most galaxies are receding from the Milky Way. Indeed, the universe is still expanding.

If the expansion of the universe is run backwards from where we are now, there comes a point in time when the universe was confined to an extraordinarily small volume with infinitely high density and temperature, known as a singularity. While cosmology can take us back until the universe was a mere 10^{-35} seconds old, the singularity is a big problem for physicists. One reason is that it requires some way of explaining how space and time, matter and energy could have come out of absolutely nothing.

One of the dominating ideas is that the universe went through a brief period of exceedingly rapid expansion or inflation right after the big bang. Assuming that inflation did happen, and there seems to be data to support that, what remains is to explain why inflation happened. True to the tradition of physics, some scientists have proposed that a special particle, appropriately called an *inflaton*, is needed. This 'solution' is very illustrative of this way of thinking and reflects the strong belief in the causality assumption: if there is an effect (inflation, in this case), then there must also be a cause. Not knowing of what type the cause is, we can at least give it a name. Although no one (probably) believes that there is such a particle, the very fact that it has been proposed illustrates the strength of causal thinking.

This way of thinking is so deeply ingrained in the Western approach to science, that we are practically unaware of it. It often seems as if the most important thing is to put a name to something, as the example of the inflaton illustrates. As another example, consider the world 'electron'. To a scientist this word represents a unique subatomic particle with specific properties. It is furthermore accepted – or believed – that all of the zillions of electrons in the universe are identical and that all of them can be described by the same equation, the Dirac equation. The ability to name something gives us comfort, a sense of power, and a feeling of control. In behavioural sciences and the study of accidents we find exactly the same tendency in the enthusiasm for our own 'elementary particle' – the 'human error'.

The cosmological thinking about the big bang is really not very different from the idea about a first cause, which in philosophy is the self-created being (i.e., the deity) to which every chain of causes must ultimately go back. Many philosophers and theologians in the Judeo-Christian tradition have formulated an argument for the existence of god by claiming that the world we observe with our senses must have been brought into being by god as the first cause. Indeed, every civilisation seems to have produced an explanation of creation, e.g., Boorstin (1993). The classic Christian formulation of this argument came from the medieval theologian St. Thomas Aquinas, who argued that the observable order of causation is not self-explanatory. It can only be accounted for by the existence of a first cause; which is not simply the first in a series of continuing causes but rather a first cause in the sense of being the cause for the whole series of observable causes. In philosophy, this became known as the principle of sufficient reason, usually attributed to the German philosopher Gottfried Wilhelm von Leibnitz, although it can also be found in earlier medieval thinking. Put simply, the principle says that nothing can be so without there being a reason why it is so. This was later disputed by the 18th-century German philosopher Immanuel Kant, who argued that causality cannot legitimately be applied to a transcendent cause beyond the realm of possible experience.

Causality

In Western philosophy, David Hume is known for his analysis of causality. He argued that the concept was a complex one and that it involved three components. The first was that the cause must be prior in time to the effect. The second that cause and effect must be contiguous in time and space. And the third that there must be a necessary connection between them, i.e., that there is, or has been, a constant coincidence of cause and effect such that the same cause always has the same effect. In *A Treatise on Human Nature*, Hume wrote that:

> (t)he necessary connexion betwixt causes and effects is the foundation of our inference from one to the other. The foundation of our inference is the transition arising from the accustomed union. These are, therefore, the same.

In other words, causation is inferred from observations but is not something that can be observed directly. This corresponds to the contemporary view that the cause is constructed from an understanding of the situation, rather than found. Even more precisely we can say that the cause is selected from a set of possible causes, hence that it is the result of an act of inference rather than an act of deduction.

Even without wanting to be philosophical about it, we usually take for granted that if there is a cause, then there must be an effect (Figure 2.1). It is, of course, perfectly sensible to do so, and we find constant proof of that almost every moment when we are awake. On a macroscopic level it is the basis for all our sciences, as well as the foundation for the technology without which we would soon perish. In fact, whenever the effect is missing we become worried and look for an explanation, which ironically is usually expressed in terms of cause and effect. That is, if something fails, we look for the reason why it failed, i.e., a cause of the unexpected rather than of the expected effect.

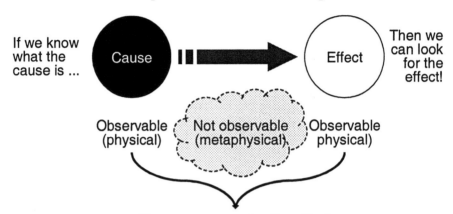

The cause precedes the effect.
Cause and effect are contiguous in space and time.
Cause and effect have a necessary connection.

Figure 2.1: The principle of forward causality

Mercury mission MR-1 is a good example of that. On November 21, 1960, well before the first manned flight with Alan Shepard on May 2, 1961, a Redstone rocket with a Mercury capsule was launched and began lift-off. However, after a 'flight' of a few inches, lasting a mere 2 seconds, the motor cut off and the vehicle settled on the launch pad. The escape tower rockets fired to separate the Mercury capsule from the rocket, which deployed the re-entry parachutes and landed 1,200 ft. away. The whole area was cleared for 28 hours both because the reason for the engine shutdown was unknown and to allow the Redstone batteries to drain down and liquid oxygen to evaporate.

Since the actual outcome was a far cry from the expected outcome, every effort was made to find the effective cause. In the end it was realised that the rocket's engine cut-off because of an unintended sneak path. (A sneak circuit or sneak path is defined as an unintended current, which causes an unwanted function to occur or which inhibits a wanted function.) In this case the sneak path existed because the tail plug that connected the rocket to the launch assembly was prematurely pulled out before the control cables. It turned out that the tail plug was rebuilt after every launch by cutting back the burned wire and insulation and reinstalling the connector. As a result of this, the cable one day became too short and pulled out as soon as the rocket lifted off the pad while the control cables were still connected.

In this case the missing effect found an efficient explanation, which not only made it clear why the launch had failed but also enabled effective countermeasures. (The incident is famous because it gave rise to the practice of sneak path analysis. It is also interesting because it shows the consequences of a lack of foresight or requisite imagination, cf. Adamski & Westrum (2003). It should really not have been that hard to figure out what the consequence of constantly shortening the wire would be. More will be said about requisite imagination in Chapter 6.)

While people usually are very successful in reasoning from cause to effect, this unfortunately tricks them into believing that the opposite can be done with equal justification. This is something that has been studied intensely by psychologists interested in human reasoning (e.g., Wason & Johnson-Laird, 1972). Knowing how well people are able to draw logically valid conclusions, and in particular which mistakes they are prone to make when doing so, is obviously of great interest for accident investigations. Without going into any details a few examples illustrate the scope of the problem.

Consider the following statement, known as an implication: 'If the pressure drops, then the warning light is turned on'. When people are told that the pressure has dropped, then most will be able correctly to conclude that the warning light will turn on. If told that the warning light does not turn on, some people find it hard to draw the correct conclusion that the pressure has not dropped. On the other hand, if told that the warning light was turned on, then many people will conclude that the pressure has dropped, although this is not necessarily so. (The light might have come on for other reasons, for instance.) This particular kind of reasoning is called 'affirming the consequent', and is illustrated in Figure 2.2.

It has been argued that affirming the consequent, i.e., concluding that the antecedent is true because the consequent is, may be a plausible inference to make even though it is logically invalid. Most people will probably agree with the following chain of statements: 'If something is of good quality, then it is expensive' $\Rightarrow$ 'It is expensive' $\Rightarrow$ 'Therefore it is of good quality'. In practice this is a plausible inference to make, but we also know that there are exceptions. However, in accident analysis it is not sufficient to be plausible, and it is therefore important to avoid logically incorrect conclusions. There must, of course, in all cases be a cause for something and the causality principle is true in the sense that nothing happens spontaneously – at least not in the type of systems we are thinking about here. This is nevertheless not the same as saying that we can always go back and find the cause. Indeed, there may often not be a cause (in the singular) but rather a set or complex of causes, in the plural.

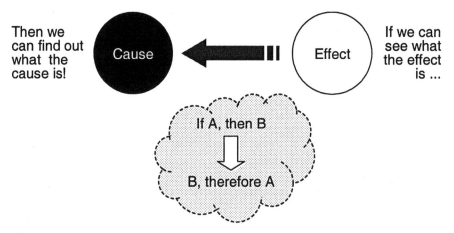

Figure 2.2: Reverse causation

The Need for Accident Models

It is a truism that we cannot think about something without having the words and concepts to describe it, or without having some frame of reference. Quite often the frame of reference represents an unspoken but commonly held view that is part and parcel of a specific technical culture. The advantage of having a common frame of reference is that communication and understanding become more efficient, because a number of things can be taken for granted. The disadvantage is that it strongly favours a single point of view, which rarely is questioned once the frame of reference has become established. This makes it more difficult to be sufficiently thorough in an analysis, in the sense of considering alternative explanations. The frame of reference is particularly important in thinking about accidents, because it determines how we view an accident and in particular how we view the role of humans. I shall refer to this frame of reference as the *accident model*, i.e., a stereotypical way of thinking about how an accident occurs.

If we look at the results from accident analyses over a period of about 40-50 years, it is possible to summarise the development as shown in Figure 2.3. Of the three curves in the figure, the one showing the number of accidents where human performance was found to be the cause is based on a number of studies representing various fields of application. (The data sources are described in Hollnagel, 1993, p. 4. As argued in that book, the curve represents the cases where the analysis attributed the cause to human performance – specifically 'human error' – although this does not necessarily mean that human performance failure was the actual or 'true' cause.) For instance, two studies published in 1960 gave 20% resp. 23% as low estimates of 'human error', and 50% resp. 45% as high estimates. Similarly, studies from the beginning of the 1990s estimated the contribution to around 90%. Indeed, official EU reports from as recently as 1999-2000 suggests that over 90% of road accidents are due to driver error!

The two other curves, one for technological or equipment causes, and the other for organisational causes, are theoretical rather than empirical. Since the graph as a whole shows the attribution of causes for accidents in general, and since practically no accidents go unexplained, it follows that the causes must sum up to 100%. Going back to 1960, it would have been unusual to attribute the cause of an accident to organisational factors, which means that the estimate of the contribution from technological factors must be about 70%.

Following the same argument, and noting that the estimates of the human contribution continued to increase during the last half of the 20th Century, it is easy to suggest how the curves for human and technological causes should look. There is some obvious sense to this, since technology during the same period became increasingly reliable, as discussed in Chapter 1. If evidence is needed, just think of the average computer in the 1950s and in the 2000s. Despite the fact that the latter contains about 10,000,000 times as many components as the former – using Moore's Law as the basis for calculations – it is both far more powerful and infinitely more reliable. The first commercial computers had a mean time before failure of about 4 hours, whereas we now expect them to run for at least 10,000-20,000 hours without breaking down. Indeed, were it not for the emergence of the dreaded 'software error', basic technological systems would on the whole give little cause for concern. (Unfortunately, that the same cannot be said for complex socio-technical systems, cf. Perrow, 1984.)

% Attributed cause

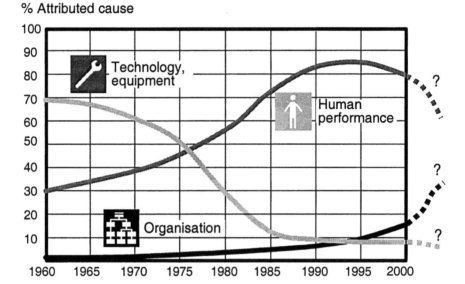

Figure 2.3: Trends in attributed accident causes

While people involved with accident analysis, either as researchers or practitioners, on the whole were happy with having either humans or technology as their main categories of causes – not forgetting, of course, the catchall cause of 'other' – a third category of organisational causes began to emerge in the early 1980s. The seminal event was the nuclear accident at Three Mile Island on March 28, 1979, which clearly demonstrated the need to go beyond human and technological cause types. This led to a revision of accident analysis, as seen in the growing number of cases where the cause was attributed to organisational factors. This is shown in Figure 2.3 as a change in the overall distribution of attributed causes: technology-related causes continued to drop slowly due to steady improvements in engineering and manufacturing, and organisation-related causes increased while human-related causes decreased. That there was a real change in emphasis is obvious from the technical literature, where reports and books about organisational accidents and safety culture became quite common since the middle of the 1990s.

On closer inspection the change shown by Figure 2.3, however, only concerns the nature of the attributed causes. Using examples from the domains of rail transport and nuclear power generation, Reason (1991) illustrated how incident investigations and the preferred preventive measures in the early stages of any new technological development focus mainly on technical failure as the cause of incidents. After that the focus switches to 'human error' (i.e. human failures) and human-machine mismatches, and finally to organizational factors. The way of thinking about accidents – the accident model – is, however, more or less the same. The situation can be shown as in Figure 2.4, where we still think about accidents in the same way, but have new categories as favourites.

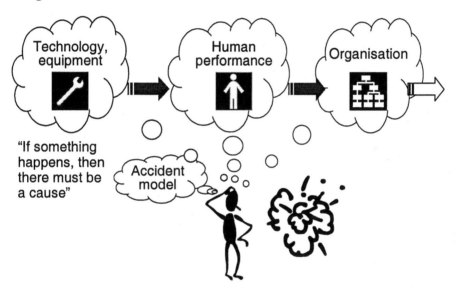

Figure 2.4: The 'constant' accident model

This description is admittedly a little unfair, since there has been some development in accident models in parallel to the changes in cause types. Indeed, over the years a great many accident models have been proposed with at least formal differences. When looked at from a distance, taking a step back so to speak, they nevertheless seem to correspond to one of the three types characterised below.

Sequential Accident Models

The simplest types of accident models describe the accident as the result of a sequence of events that occur in a specific order. This corresponds to the description in the First Axiom of Industrial Safety, which reads:

The occurrence of an injury invariably results from a completed sequence of factors – the last one of these being the accident itself. The accident in turn is invariably caused or permitted by the unsafe act of a person and/or a mechanical or physical hazard. (Heinrich et al., 1980, p. 21)

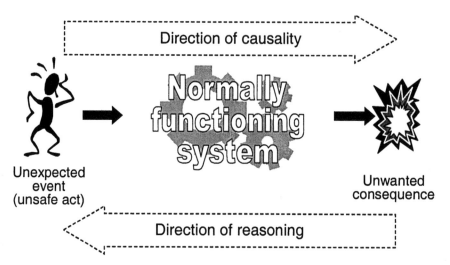

Figure 2.5: The sequential accident model

The sequential accident model embodies the main defining characteristics of an accident that were discussed in Chapter 1: an unexpected, and unintentional, event leading to an unwanted outcome. According to this model, an accident can happen when the system seemingly is working normally. A sudden, unexpected event initiates a sequence of consequences where the last one is the accident. As shown in Figure 2.5, the unexpected event has often been taken to be an unsafe act, in line with the emphasis on 'human error' as a predominant accident cause. It can, of course, equally well be something else, such as the failure of a component.

Figure 2.5 also indicates that the sequential accident model has a clear assumption about causality, specifically that there are identifiable cause-effect links that propagate the effects of the unexpected event. The aim of an accident analysis is therefore to identify these cause-effect links, which is indicated as a direction of reasoning going from the accident to the underlying causes. This way of thinking is quite consistent with the First Axiom of Industrial Safety, which corresponds to the domino theory. This offers a way of visualising an accident as a set of domino blocks lined up in such a way that if one falls it will knock down those that follow. Figure 2.6 shows one version of the domino theory, based on the description in Heinrich et al. (1980). Here the domino blocks represent different accident factors, and the model shows how these factors constitute a sequence of events where the linking of cause and effect is simple and deterministic. (Note that the label on the leftmost domino block, *social environment*, indicates that the importance of the work environment was acknowledged, even though it was not obvious from the wording of the First Axiom.) According to the logic of the domino theory, an accident can be prevented if one or more of the domino blocks is removed or in other ways stopped from falling.

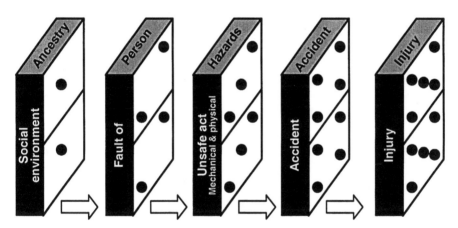

Figure 2.6: The Domino theory (after Heinrich, 1931)

(The domino theory was not limited to issues of industrial safety but for many years provided the basis for US foreign policy. The term was coined by President Eisenhower in 1954 to describe the belief that the fall of one nation to a communist regime would lead to the fall of its neighbours. In the 1960s it was used to justify American involvement in Vietnam. It was probably just as misapplied there as in industrial safety.)

A more recent example of a sequential model is the Accident Evolution and Barrier (AEB) model (Svenson, 1991, 2001), which describes an accident in terms of a sequence of events – or rather in terms of barriers that failed. (The AEB model will be presented in more detail in Chapter 3.) This description directs the focus to what went wrong, but in doing so leaves out additional information that may be potentially important. More generally, sequential models represent the accident as the outcome of a series of individual steps organised according to their order of occurrence.

Sequential models need, of course, not be limited to a single sequence of events but may include a representation of multiple sequences of events in the form of hierarchies such as the traditional event tree and networks, such as Critical Path models (Programme Evaluation and Review Technique or PERT) and Petri networks. They may represent either the scenario as a whole, or only the events that went wrong. Figure 2.7 shows a typical example of a sequential model known as the 'anatomy of an accident' (Green, 1988). The representation is that of a tree, which shows how the top event – the accident – is the result of a sequence of combinations of other events or conditions. In this case the explanation of the accident starts from the left with a normal condition that is perturbed by an unexpected event leading to an abnormal condition. The unexpected event can be a component that fails, an external disturbance, the incorrect execution of an action, or simply an unexpected combination of unsafe actions and latent conditions. If the abnormal condition is not properly controlled it may lead to a loss of control. If that is exacerbated by a lack of defences or barriers, the accident becomes a reality. Technically this kind of logical tree is known as a fault tree, of which more will be said in Chapter 4.

Sequential models are attractive because they encourage thinking in causal series rather than causal nets (cf. Dörner, 1980). As everyone knows, it is much easier to follow a line of reasoning step by step than to keep track of several parallel lines at the same time. Sequential models are furthermore easy to represent graphically, which facilitates communication of the results. In order to be adequate for accident descriptions, sequential models unfortunately require that the events correspond to the model assumptions, i.e., that the cause-effect relations underlying the accident are relatively simple. So while sequential accident models were adequate for socio-technical systems up until the middle of the 20th Century, they turned out to be limited in their capability to explain accidents in the more complex systems that became common in the last half of the century. The need for more powerful ways of understanding accidents led to the class of epidemiological accident models to be described next, which began to gain in popularity in the 1980s.

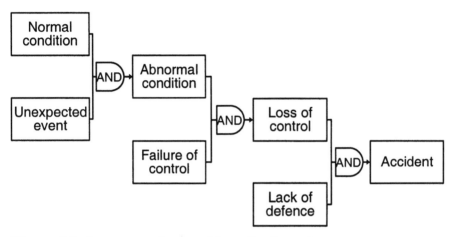

Figure 2.7: Anatomy of an accident (fault tree)

In practical terms, accident analysis based on sequential models is usually a search for specific causes and well-defined cause-effect links. The underlying assumption, as illustrated by the domino model, is that an accident is the result of a sequence of events and that causes, once they have been found, can be eliminated or encapsulated, thereby effectively preventing future accidents. It is, with all due respect, a little like the inebriated gentleman who looks for a lost key under the streetlamp, not because the key was lost there but because the light is better.

The Root Cause. It is consistent with the principle of the sequential accident model that there is a final cause, commonly referred to as the root cause. Just as there must be a first domino that makes the others tumble, so there must be a first event or occurrence that makes the accident happen. Although this metaphor is highly attractive, it is also fallacious as illustrated in the following.

The root cause is usually defined as the combinations of conditions and factors that underlie accidents or incidents, or even as the absolute beginning of the causal chain. In the Safety Glossary of the International Atomic Energy Agency (IAEA) a root cause is defined as 'the fundamental cause of an initiating event which, if corrected, will prevent its recurrence'. This corresponds to the common meaning of a root as a primary source or an origin, the root cause of an accident thus being the origin of the accident. The common representation of an accident makes use of a tree diagram, i.e., a graphical structure that illustrates the lineage among component events, e.g., Figure 2.7. If we rearrange lightly the components of Figure 2.7 the result may be a diagram such as Figure 2.8, which shows the lineage among events starting by the initiator, the unexpected event or the point at which the accident comes into existence and from which it is derived – or in other words the 'root' cause.

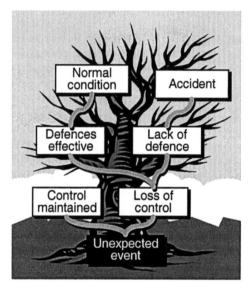

Figure 2.8: Trees, events, and the root

Yet as everyone knows a tree does not have a root in the same sense as, e.g., a carrot does (and, strictly speaking, the carrot *is* the root). The root of a tree is quite complex with a structure of branching shots that in many ways is as intricate as the branches and twigs above ground. The point is, however, that we cannot see the root since it is underground, and we are therefore prone to disregard it. The tree ends in the stem and looks deceptively as if it continues in the same way underground. So once we hit the 'root' cause, which more properly should be called the stem cause, we assume that there is nothing further to find.

In reality the situation is, however, quite different. The unexpected event is not where the accident begins, but can itself be seen as the outcome of a complex set of causes, cf. Figure 2.9. Just as a real tree has a kind of symmetry between what is above ground and what is below, so has an accident. If the root cause therefore is interpreted as suggested by Figure 2.9 it is, ironically, an entirely acceptable concept. However, it does not make accident analysis any simpler.

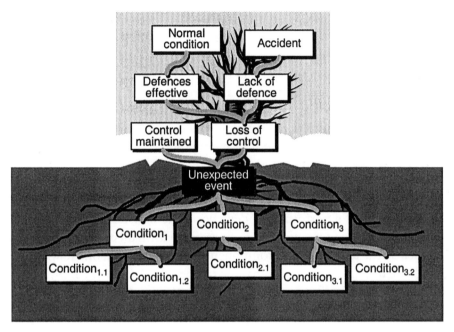

Figure 2.9: Symmetric complexity between tree and root

Since the unexpected event at the 'root' does not come about spontaneously it is an arbitrary point for stopping the analysis, as shown by Figure 2.9. The analysis can always be taken one or more steps further back to explain why the unexpected event occurred. This brings out an important point about accident analysis, namely the definition of the stop rule, i.e., the criterion for when the analysis stops. This ought to be well-argued and systematic, but is in practice often rather arbitrary and likely to be determined more by, e.g., constraints on time and other resources rather than by the completeness or correctness of the explanation. This rendering of the accident analysis also means that the whole procedure becomes relative, in the sense that any step or event can be seen as the starting point both for going forwards to find the consequences and for going back to find the causes. This makes it clear that the notion of a root cause is not only an abstraction, but also an artefact of a specific analysis principle.

Epidemiological Accident Models

Epidemiological models, as the name implies, describe an accident in analogy with the spreading of a disease, i.e., as the outcome of a combination of factors, some manifest and some latent, that happen to exist together in space and time. Beginning in the early 1980s, the analyses of a number of major industrial accidents, first and foremost Three Mile Island, made it clear that more powerful, and therefore also more complex, accident models were needed. The epidemiological models can be seen as a response to this demand and differ from the sequential accident models on four main points.

Performance Deviations. The notion of an unsafe act, which often was treated as synonymous with a 'human error', gradually became replaced by the notion of a performance deviation. The new term was first of all neutral with regard to its object, since a performance deviation could happen for a technological component as well as a person. It was also less loaded than the term 'human error' since a deviation simply was a normal action that for one reason or the other had gone wrong rather than a separate category or function.

Environmental Conditions. As if to emphasise that, the epidemiological model also considered the conditions that could lead to the performance deviation. In relation to the discussion of the root cause above, the concept of the environmental conditions was used as a way of making the analysis more open-ended. Environmental conditions exist for humans and technology alike, although in the former case they often are referred to simply as working conditions.

Barriers. A third new feature of the model was the barriers that could prevent the unexpected consequences from occurring, and which in a sense could stop the development of the accident at the last moment. In the illustration of the epidemiological model (Figure 2.10), the barriers are shown at the right hand side. The thinking in terms of barriers can obviously be expanded to cover protective barriers, as well as barriers at all stages of the accident development, as envisaged already by the domino model. The nature and functioning of barriers will be treated in detail in Chapter 3.

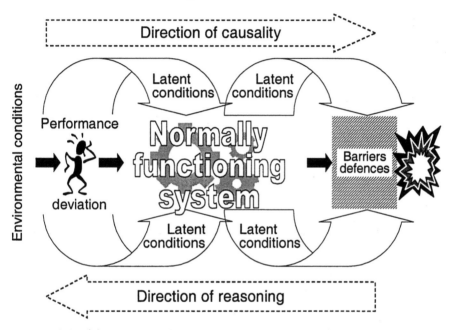

Figure 2.10: The epidemiological accident model

Latent Conditions. A final feature, and in many ways the most important one, was the introduction of the concept of latent conditions. Latent conditions, which in the beginning were called latent failures and later latent failure conditions, sprang from a distinction between latent and active failures that gained widespread recognition in the scientific community during the late 1980s. One of the early discussions took place at the NATO ARW in Bad Windsheim in August 1986 (Reason, 1987a). The notion that latent or dormant conditions could contribute to the development and signature of an accident is, however, much older and may be traced back to Heinrich's (1931) domino model or Turner's (1978) analogy of an incubation period in the build-up to man-made disasters.

The defining feature of latent conditions is that they are present within the system well before the onset of a recognisable accident sequence. The influence of these factors in complex, high-hazard systems, such as nuclear power plants, chemical process plants, modern aircraft, etc., gives rise to multiple-failure accidents. These can in turn be attributed to basic organisational processes such as design, construction, procedures, maintenance, training, communication, human-machine interfaces and the like (Reason, 1990b). Whereas active failures – and especially 'human errors' – denote the local triggering events that usually are seen as the immediate causes of an accident, latent conditions do not trigger accidents as such, but may rather themselves be brought into the open by a seemingly innocent performance deviation. Similarly, latent conditions may also render ineffective the barriers in the system.

Latent conditions can have several different causes, such as organisational or managerial decisions, design failures or deficiencies, maintenance failures or deficiencies, and the undetected, slow degradation of system functions or resources (e.g., corrosion, small leaks). Latent conditions can exist in several forms that combine with active failures to produce an accident. These conditions typically belong to one of the following three categories:

- Lack of barriers so that a designed prevention against an accident either is missing or dysfunctional; barriers can be physical or functional (procedures, rules).
- Lack of resources so that the necessary means to counter or neutralise an event are missing. A simple example is that the pressure of a fire extinguisher may be too low; a more complex one is that there may be insufficient energy to start the emergency diesels or to power emergency lights.
- Finally, precarious conditions, which means that parts of the system have become unstable so that a small active failure is sufficient to release a latent condition; the analogy is that of an avalanche or any other supercritical system.

The term 'epidemiological accident model' was used as far back as 1961, when Suchman proposed that an accident phenomenon is 'the unexpected, unavoidable unintentional act resulting from the interaction of host, agent, and environmental factors within situations which involve risk taking and perception of danger' (Suchman, 1961; quoted in Heinrich et al., 1980, p. 50). According to this view an accident will have observable and measurable effects, but the accident itself results from a combination of 'agents' and environmental factors that create an unhappy setting, subsumed under the labels of predisposition and situational characteristics, respectively (Figure 2.11). This also corresponds to the general model of an epidemic, which tries to account for the effects of an agent on a host in a specific environment.

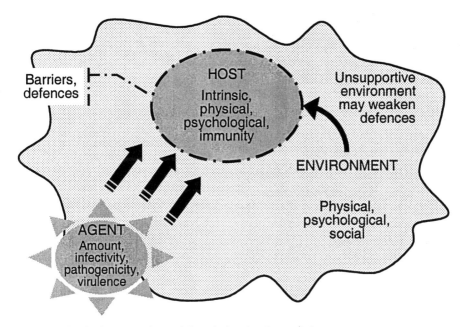

Figure 2.11: A generic epidemiological model

The epidemiological accident model was alluded to in the analysis of the Chernobyl accident, which contained the following passage:

> All man-made systems have within them the seeds of their own destruction, like 'resident pathogens' in the human body. At anyone time, there will be a certain number of component failures, human errors and 'unavoidable violations'. No one of these agents is generally sufficient to cause a significant breakdown. Disasters occur through the unseen and usually unforeseeable concatenation of a large number of these pathogens. (Reason, 1987b)

The concept of a pathogen or a specific causative agent is clearly taken from medical terminology, and so is the notion of the pathogen being resident. It corresponds to the notion of latent conditions as proposed by Reason (1990a). Other examples are models that consider barriers and carriers such as the well-known Swiss cheese analogy (Reason, 1997), models of sharp end – blunt end interactions (Woods et al., 1994), and models of pathological system (organisation) states. Real-world examples of epidemics are distressingly easy to find, the most recent being the case of the Severe Acute Respiratory Syndrome (SARS) that erupted in the spring of 2003. This illustrated the typical traits of an epidemic, including also the reliance on barriers, since the main remedy was to isolate anyone who was suspected of having caught the disease.

Epidemiological models are valuable because they provide a basis for discussing the complexity of accidents that overcomes the limitations of sequential models. The notion of latent factors simply cannot be reconciled with the simple idea of a causal series, but requires a more powerful representation – at least that of a causal network. This means that the analysis cannot be a search for simple causes, but must involve an account of more complex interactions among different factors. Yet despite the added details, epidemiological models still follow the principles of the sequential models, i.e., a propagation of effects from a beginning to an end, as indicated by the direction of causality. The added complexity certainly makes them better suited to account for many different types of accidents, but unfortunately also makes them more cluttered in the graphical representation. Epidemiological models are, however, never stronger than the analogy behind them, i.e., they are difficult to specify in further detail, even though the concept of pathogens allows for a set of methods that can be used to characterise the general 'health' of a system (Reason, 1997).

In the case of epidemiological models, the accident analysis is usually a search for 'carriers' and latent conditions, as well as for reliable indicators of general system 'health'. On a more general level the search is for characteristic performance deviations, with the recognition that these can be complex phenomena rather than simple manifestations. Remedial efforts consequently are focused on two major issues, which both reflect the common response to an epidemic in the medical sense of isolating the carrier in order to hamper further spreading of the disease. One is to isolate the task, situation and systemic factors that, in combination, are known to promote performance deviations. These are collectively referred to as error-promoting conditions. The other is to erect or reinforce the barriers and safeguards that mitigate or block the adverse consequences of errors and violations. These are often classified according to the functions they serve (i.e., alarms, warning, protection, recovery, containment, escape and rescue) and by the various systemic modes in which they are implemented (i.e., engineered safety features, supervision, safety briefings, administrative controls, rules and regulations, personal protective equipment, etc.).

Systemic Accident Models

The third type of models is the so-called systemic model. As the name denotes, these models endeavour to describe the characteristic performance on the level of the system as a whole, rather than on the level of specific cause-effect 'mechanisms' or even epidemiological factors. Instead of using a structural decomposition of the system into components and their associated functions, the systemic view considers accidents as emergent phenomena, which therefore also are 'normal' or 'natural' in the sense of being something that must be expected. This is consonant with Perrow's notion of normal accidents (Perrow, 1984), although it is applicable to simple as well as complex systems.

Systemic models are on the one hand structurally simpler than epidemiological models, but on the other functionally more complex. The simpler structure is obvious from Figure 2.12. Compared with the epidemiological model, the two features of performance deviations and environmental conditions have been replaced by the sharp end – blunt end depiction of how failures may arise. Indeed, every event that contributes to an accident rather than just the last one can be seen as being at the sharp end. This is described in more detail below, as well as in Chapter 6. Although there obviously still must be a temporal progression from the beginning to the end of the development, the view of accidents as emergent phenomena means that the steps or stages on the way are seen as parts of a whole rather than as distinct events. Events can still be ordered *post hoc* either temporally or in terms of causal relations. But in the systemic model each event may be preceded by several events (temporally or causally), as well as be followed by several events. Another consequence of this view on accidents is that the arrow indicating the direction of causality has gone.

Accidents do, of course, still happen for a reason, but it is misleading to suggest the simple progression that originated in the sequential models. The arrow indicating the direction of reasoning remains, since accident analysis as a process still traces the development of events back in time, starting from the accident as it occurred.

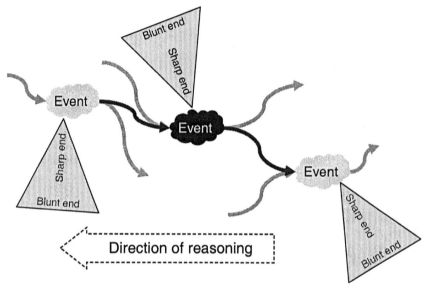

Figure 2.12: The systemic accident model

Systemic models have their roots in control theory (Sheridan, 1992), in chaos theory, and most recently in the idea of stochastic resonance that will be explained further in Chapter 5. The concept of emergence itself goes further back and is usually ascribed to the 19th-century English philosopher of science George Henry Lewes, who proposed a distinction between resultant and emergent phenomena, according to which the former were predictable from their constituent parts and the latter were not. An analogical form of systemic models is the Brownian motion model. Brownian motion refers to the random movement of microscopic particles suspended in a liquid or gas, caused by collisions with molecules of the surrounding medium. The analogy is that while the particles can be seen to move around in an unpredictable way, the underlying cause – being the statistical fluctuation in the bombardment by the molecules of the suspending medium – remains hidden. More distinct exemplars are found in supervisory control models, which provide an account of how the complexities of human-machine interaction may lead to function failures. An example of that is a model depicting the hierarchy of feedback loops in human performance shown in Figure 2.13. Based on a proposal from Sheridan (1992), the model shows how a number of factors must work together to produce a correct performance. Conversely, performance failures can arise from instabilities in any of the control loops or from the interactions among them.

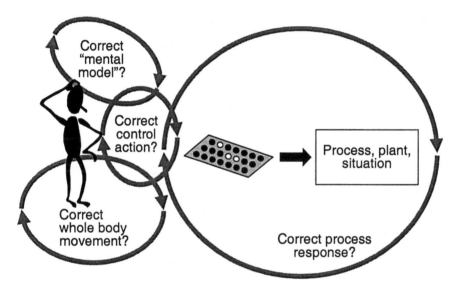

Figure 2.13: Hierarchy of feedback loops

Another analogical form is found in chaos theory, specifically the so-called butterfly effect. In a scientific context the word chaos refers to an apparent lack of order in a system that nevertheless obeys particular laws or rules. A chaotic system is one that meets these conditions, rather than one that is just in a state of disorder. The two main ideas in chaos theory are (1) that even complex systems rely upon an underlying order, and (2) that very simple or small systems and events can cause very complex behaviours or events (Lorenz, 1993). This latter idea is known as the butterfly effect, but is more technically a case of sensitive dependence on initial conditions. The study of chaotic systems was started by the meteorologist Edward Lorenz in the early 1960s, but the sensitivity dependence was described already by the French mathematician Henri Poincaré, who noted that for some systems '...

small differences in the initial conditions produce very great ones in the final phenomena. ... Prediction becomes impossible, and we have the fortuitous phenomenon' (Poincaré, 1912, p. 2). Because of this sensitivity such systems over time become unpredictable so that it is impossible to know what the outcome of a particular initiating event will be. This was vividly illustrated by the suggestion that a butterfly flapping its wings in Brazil could set off a tornado in Texas (Lorenz, 2003, p. 181). The contrast to the domino effect could hardly be more striking. In both models an initiating event may lead to serious consequences, but in the case of a chaotic system each iteration amplifies the effects of the previous step. Technically speaking, the responses of the system are non-linear, which means that the effect (output) is not proportional to the cause (input). This is quite different from sequential accident models where the system responses are linear. It is in this sense that accidents from the systemic point of view are emergent rather than resultant phenomena.

The Sharp End and the Blunt End. One of the important changes between the epidemiological and the system model is the use of the sharp end – blunt end description to account for the events leading to the accident. The idea was already present in the thinking about latent conditions and can therefore be seen as a bridging concept between the epidemiological and systemic model types. The earliest reference is probably in the foreword to Reason (1990a), although the terms here were front end and blunt end. The sharp end refers to the people who 'actually interact with the hazardous process in their roles as pilots, physicians, space controllers, or power plant operators' (Woods et al., 1994, p. 20). In other words, these are the people who are working at the time and in the place where the accident takes place.

Since it had become generally accepted during the 1980s that most, if not all, of the failures made at the sharp end were determined by the working conditions and the nature of the tasks, there was a need to be able to describe how this influence came about. This was done by defining a corresponding blunt end as being the people who affected safety 'through their effect on the constraints and resources acting on the practitioners at the sharp end' (*ibidem*). In other words, the constraints and resources acting on the practitioners at the sharp end do not arise out of the blue but are assumed to be determined by what other people have done at an earlier time and in a different place.

Graphically, the relation is often illustrated by a triangle where the sharp end is put at the apex and the blunt end at the base. Figure 2.14 shows a different version, which maintains the left-right temporal orientation used in the previous figures.

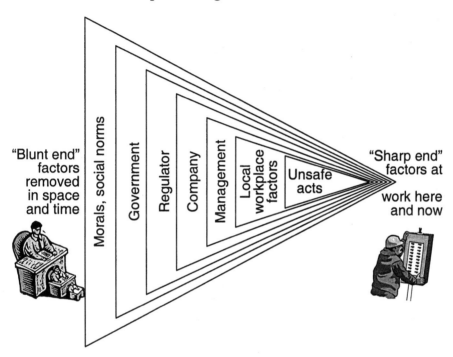

Figure 2.14: The sharp end – blunt end relations

The main implication of the sharp end – blunt end view of accidents is that the performance variability of people at the sharp end, and in particular the failures they may make, are determined by a host of factors. This means that the backwards search for causes is more likely to find a complex network than to reveal a simple cause-effect chain. By reasoning backwards from the unsafe acts at the sharp end we come first to the local workplace factors, which are determined by what (local) management does. The performance of (local) management is in turn affected by what happens at the company level – or levels. For many fields of activity, such as nuclear power production, aviation, and healthcare, the company works under conditions set by national and /or international regulating authorities as well as by the government. What the government decides to do is in turn influenced by the public opinion and the reigning norms for acceptable safety. (The reader may see a certain similarity between this rendering and the nursery rhyme used in Chapter 1.)

The sharp end – blunt end representation does not imply that all unsafe acts can or should be traced this far back. Indeed, it may in many cases make little sense to go much beyond the local workplace and the local management. There may, for instance, be little information available about what shaped past decisions with regard to, e.g., working instructions, safety procedures, human-machine interface structure and functionality, communication channels, etc. At the sharp end it may sometimes be difficult to understand why things have to be done in a certain way, or why a piece of equipment requires a specific set of operations. Yet trying to find answers to questions of 'why' may be difficult, e.g., because the reasons for such decisions never were properly documented or because those who might know are unavailable. There is therefore a pragmatic limit to how far back the reasoning can go. Neither does the representation in Figure 2.14 imply that the intervening layers always are necessary to mediate the effects of blunt end actions and decisions. On the contrary, many higher-level decisions, rules and regulations may affect the sharp end directly – as well as propagate through the several layers in between.

Finally, the definition of what is the sharp end and what is the blunt end is relative rather than absolute. If we look at a workplace accident that has happened, the people directly interacting with the process represent the sharp end, whereas a decision taken somewhere in the production department represents the blunt end. However, if we consider the actions by the people who in this way are designated as being at the blunt end – assuming that these actions in some way were found to be faulty – then these people represent the sharp end relative to the new focus of the investigation. They still have to act under the conditions set by some other blunt end, which now is to be found elsewhere, for instance in company policy, product legislation, insufficient distribution capacity, etc. It is very important to understand this relativity in the sharp end – blunt end relations, which often is emphasised by pointing out that 'everybody's blunt end is someone else's sharp end'. Everyone, from the front-line operator to the company manager and beyond, must carry out their tasks in a local workplace with specific constraints and resources. The differences lie in, e.g., the nature of the constraints, the resources and tools available, the variability of the environment and the predictability of effects, the scope and consequences of decisions, the possibilities for detection and recovery, the time horizon of the work, etc. The nature and conditions of work at different levels of an organisation can obviously be very dissimilar but in some sense everyone is at the sharp end in their own line of work and at the blunt end relative to others.

Consequences of Systemic Models. The overriding advantage of systemic models is their emphasis that accidents analysis must be based on an understanding of the functional characteristics of the system, rather than on assumptions or hypotheses about internal mechanisms as provided by standard representations of, e.g., information processing or failure pathways. An accident can be described neither as a causal series nor as a causal net, since either representation is incapable of accounting for the dynamic nature of the interactions or the non-linearity of the effects. Systemic models deliberately try to avoid describing an accident as a sequence or an ordered relation among individual events or even as a concatenation of latent conditions. Unfortunately, that makes it a little difficult to represent them graphically.

In terms of accident analysis, the systemic models advocate a search for unusual dependencies and common conditions that, from experience, we know are associated with accidents. This reflects the belief that there always will be variability in the system and that the best option therefore is to monitor the system's performance so that potentially uncontrollable variability can be caught early on. Unlike the performance deviations that were part of the epidemiological models, the performance variability of the systemic models is not inherently bad and the aim should therefore not be to eliminate it at any cost. Quite to the contrary, performance variability is necessary for users to learn and for a system to develop; monitoring of performance variability must therefore be able to distinguish between what is potentially useful and what is potentially harmful.

Comments to the Models

The three main types of accident models presented in this chapter are summarised in Table 2.1. As the presentation has shown, each type carries with it a set of assumptions about how an accident analysis should take place and what the response should be.

The distinction between the three types of accident models proposed above does not imply that one is unequivocally better than the others. Although it is inadvisable to rely on a sequential accident model as the only basis for analysis and explanation, models of this type need not be discarded outright. Indeed, events such as the blackout in the US and Canada on August 15, 2003, can adequately be explained as a 'domino' phenomenon because of the way in which the electrical grid is constructed. In other cases where there also are easily distinguishable causes it obviously makes sense to try to eliminate them. Similarly, in cases where there is a multitude of contributing factors it may be better to apply preventive and protective barriers or to monitor closely the system to detect impending instabilities and coincidences. Although complexity is difficult to handle, both in theory and in practice, it should not be shunned.

Table 2.1: The main types of accident models

	Model type		
	Sequential models	Epidemiological models	Systemic models
Search principle	Specific causes and well-defined links	Carriers, barriers, and latent conditions	Tight couplings and complex interactions
Analysis goals	Eliminate or contain causes	Make defences and barriers stronger	Monitor and control performance variability
Examples	Chain or sequence of events (domino) Tree models Network models	Latent conditions Carrier-barriers Pathological systems	Control theoretic models Chaos models. Stochastic resonance

Both the sequential and the epidemiological accident models represent thinking in terms of clear cause-effect links. In these models accidents are resultant phenomena, in the sense that the consequences are predictable – at least in principle – from knowledge about their constituent parts. In contrast to that, the systemic models see accidents as emergent phenomena, as something that arises out of the complex of conditions but which cannot be predicted in a similar manner. This difference in views has important consequences for how accident analysis is done, as described in this chapter. And since the way in which we understand and explain accidents determines how we respond, the differences are also important for accident prevention. The remaining chapters of the book will develop these issues in much more detail.

Finally, it should also be noted that the choice of accident model has consequences for how risk assessment is done, for instance the approach to probabilistic safety assessment. Most of the methods in this field of practice are based on the traditional event tree, but as we have seen this may not be adequate to account for the complexity of modern socio-technical systems. This raises an important question of where alternatives can be found, but this topic will not be considered further here.

Chapter 3

Barrier Functions and Barrier Systems

One, a robot may not injure a human being, or through inaction, allow a human being to come to harm; Two, a robot must obey the orders given it by human beings except where such orders would conflict with the First Law; Three, a robot must protect its own existence as long as such protection does not conflict with the First or Second Laws.
Isaac Asimov (1920 – 1992), Laws of Robotics from *I, Robot*, (1950)

Introduction

The purpose of accident analysis is to look for the events and conditions that led to the final outcome, which is the same as finding the set of probable causes (Woods et al., 1994). The outcome of an accident analysis is usually a description of one or more combinations of causes that together constitute a satisfactory explanation, cf. the cynical definition of causes in Chapter 1. Complementary to that, an accident can also be described as one or more barriers that have failed, even though the failure of a barrier only rarely is a cause in itself. A barrier is, generally speaking, an obstacle, an obstruction, or a hindrance that may either: (1) prevent an event from taking place, or (2) thwart or lessen the impact of the consequences if it happens nonetheless. In the former case the purpose of the barrier is to make it impossible for a specific action or event to occur. In the latter case the barrier serves, for instance, to slow down uncontrolled releases of matter and energy, to limit the reach of the consequences, or to weaken them in other ways. These simple considerations suggest that it is useful to make a basic distinction between barriers that *prevent* and barriers that *protect*.

Barriers are important for the understanding and prevention of accidents in two different, but related, ways. Firstly, the very fact that an accident has taken place usually means that one or more barriers have failed – either because they did not serve their purpose adequately or because they were missing or dysfunctional. The search for barriers that have failed must therefore be an important part of accident analysis. Secondly, once the aetiology of an accident has been determined and a satisfactory explanation has been found, barriers can be used to prevent the same or a similar accidents from taking place in the future. In order to facilitate this, the consideration of barrier functions must be a natural part of system design.

Origin of Barriers

In Chapter 1, a barrier was tentatively defined as something that stops the passage of something or someone, usually in a physical sense. Throughout the history of civilisation barriers can be found everywhere, even at the very beginning. For instance, the earliest examples of urbanisation in Mesopotamia (Iraq) around 3,500 B.C. typically included a citadel (a stronghold) walled off from the rest of the city. A wall is indeed a prototypical example of a barrier and humans have always used walls, natural or constructed, as a way of preventing unwanted visitors to get access. The construction of the most famous wall in the world, the Great Wall of China, was started as early as the 7th Century B.C. More modest examples are Hadrian's Wall between England and Scotland, built from A.D. 122 and onwards, or the Dannevirke (Dane's Bulwark) between Denmark and Germany where construction began around A.D. 808. For comparison, the Great Wall of China at one time ran for about 7,300 kilometres East to West, while Hadrian's Wall was about 130 kilometres miles long, and Dannevirke stretched the 17 kilometres from east to west.

A wall obviously needs some kind of opening through which to pass from one side to the other and an opening furthermore needs something akin to a door to control the passage and prevent unwelcome persons from entering (or leaving). A door in turn needs some kind of mechanism so that it can stay closed or be opened and locks and keys are therefore among the oldest artefacts. Although the Greek sculptor Theodorus of Samos (around 550 B.C.) usually is credited with inventing the lock and key, an even earlier reference is in the Bible in the book of Judges, Chapter III, which means that locks must have been in use in Palestine as early as the 13th Century B.C.

The more systematic use of barriers is well illustrated by the Roman army camp or *castrum*, which always had a rampart of ditches, earth walls, and wooden palisades to guard a well-organised interior. This probably represents the high point in the use of a single barrier or line of defence. In the Middle Ages the building of castles, not least in connection with the crusades, developed the single line of defence into multiple lines or levels of defence. A castle would consist of the *enceinte* or outer wall, defended by one or more lines of moats crossed by drawbridges in front of gateways. The gateways themselves were defended by *barbicans* (small fortifications), *portcullises* (sliding gates), doors, and *machicolations* (openings in the gateway roof through which unpleasant objects could be dropped on attackers). The focal point of the castle was the keep or the *donjon*, which itself was carefully fortified with thick walls – as well as a line of escape.

The use of multiple lines of defences has in more recent times become institutionalised as the principle of defence-in-depth. The principle means that there must be a number of precautions and barriers that all must fail before an unwanted event occurs. In nuclear power plants, the defence-in-depth principle has the following concrete realisation (INSAG, 1996):

- The plant must be constructed such that it provides unperturbed functioning and includes few sources of disturbance.
- There must be multiple physical barriers that protect against the release and dispersion of radioactive materials.
- There must be a multiple of safety systems that protect the physical barriers against damages during disturbances and accidents.
- The plant must have a verified technical / technological reliability, determined by approved programmes for control and testing. This must address the construction of the physical barriers as well as the functioning of the safety systems.
- The plant must be run and maintained by an organisation with a sound basic structure. This implies a clear structure of responsibilities and sufficient resources in terms of economy and qualified staff.
- The plant / organisation must have a verified quality in all processes that affect the man-technology-organisation interaction. This implies a distinct safety policy, clear management and follow-

up of events, clear instructions and procedures, recurrent training of staff together with exercises, and well-functioning internal safety investigations and quality assurance.

- The plant must have well-functioning systems and procedures to analyse operational experience, in-house as well as from other plants, as well as adequate research.

Whereas the barriers used to defend a medieval castle mostly were of a physical nature, the modern principle of defence-in-depth combines different types of barriers – from protection against the release of radioactive materials to event reporting and safety policies. In other applications, such as network and computer safety, new types of defence have completely replaced physical barriers. A few additional examples will show the diversity of barriers and also serve to introduce a systematic categorisation.

Barrier Examples

One example is an industrial robot on, e.g., a production line. Industrial robots are often surrounded by a fence or a cage, which prevents people from accidentally getting too close to the robot and possibly being hit by it. (The fence is necessary because robots today have no awareness of what takes place in their surroundings, except that which has been specified as part of their function. We are thus unable to rely on the Laws of Robotics as an effective barrier) At times it may, however, be necessary to enter the cage to maintain or reprogram the robot. In such cases the act of opening the door to the cage may stop the robot, either by abruptly switching off the power or by guiding it to a halt or a safe neutral position. Whereas the cage constitutes a material or physical barrier, the opening of the door constitutes a functional or logical barrier. Finally, there may be warnings or safety rules that forbid personnel to come close to a moving robot. This simple example illustrates how several types of barriers can be applied in the same situation, and also suggests that multiple barriers usually are necessary to prevent an unwanted event from taking place.

Another example is the railing or fence running along a road. The purpose of this barrier is to prevent cars from going off the road or crossing into the side of the road for the opposite direction. The barrier, which clearly is a physical structure, is effective to the extent that it is able to withstand the impact of cars that are neither too heavy nor move too fast. However, on minor roads the railing is often replaced either by cat's eyes or posts with reflective marks placed along the road boundary. Such posts are incapable of withstanding the impact of a car, hence preventing it from going off the road. Instead they serve as a way of showing drivers where the edge of the road is – especially at night. Although the purpose of this barrier is the same as for the railing, i.e., to prevent the driver from going off the road, it is achieved in a completely different manner. (The use of reflective posts may, however, sometimes have unexpected consequences, as discussed in Chapter 6.) Technically speaking, it provides a visual Gestalt of a line or an edge that serves as a perceptual demarcation. If, therefore, the posts are too far from each other the barrier will not work as intended. (Note that a railing combines the perceptual demarcation and the physical hindrance; if it cannot be seen, e.g., at night, it will therefore only partly fulfil its function.)

A third example is the launch control of an Inter-Continental Ballistic Missile (ICBM). It obviously is important that an ICBM is not launched by accident, and several barriers are therefore included in the system. Firstly, the command to launch may require independent authentication by two or more people. Secondly, the launch control has to be armed either by using separate keywords or keys. Thirdly, the launch requires the simultaneous pressing of two buttons that are so far apart that a single person cannot reach both at the same time. This barrier is interesting because it actually combines several different features into one, namely physical distance, synchronisation (the need to press both buttons at the same time), and communication or collaboration (the need to plan to work together). Clearly, if a larger number of barriers are combined into an aggregated barrier, it is less likely that it is broken or that it malfunctions in other ways.

Getting In and Out of Doors

A door has already been mentioned as an example of a barrier. Usually, we think of doors as something that will allow us to go into another room or an adjacent separate space, and the door is therefore a hindrance or a barrier if it is closed. Indeed, it is an essential function of a door that it can prevent a person from entering or leaving a room at will and all buildings usually have doors with locks to prevent people from entering freely – or, in the case of prison cells, to prevent people from leaving. In many cases it is deliberately made easier to go in one direction than in the other. In extreme cases there will be mechanisms to allow people to go only in one direction but not in the opposite, such as turnstiles.

While we think of doors as made for people, they obviously serve as barriers for any type of transportation between two adjacent spaces. For those who live in the Northern countries, doors are important to avoid cold air coming in and warm air leaving – and the converse in warm climates where houses have air-condition systems. Doors may also prevent fires, odours ('shut the door to the kitchen!'), sounds, and many other things.

An interesting case is doors in public transportation vehicles, such as buses and trains. The door is, of course, a barrier in itself but it is usually combined with additional barriers to prevent it from being opened while the vehicle is moving. In the case of Swedish buses, the doors can usually only be opened from the inside, either by the driver or by an automatic mechanism. The user therefore has little control of the movements of the door, and in particular cannot control when the door closes. Since the premature closing of a door may be inconvenient or lead to accidents, steps must be taken to prevent this from happening.

Accidents in Sweden. The following recent accidents / incidents from Sweden illustrate that it is not always unproblematic to get safely off a bus.

- In the winter of 1998, two boys were killed in an accident with a bus, because they had become stuck in the door when it closed, and the bus driver had started to drive the bus without noticing them.
- In the winter of 1999 (weekend of February 13-14), a 15 year old boy got stuck in a door in a bus. Again the bus started to move without the driver noticing the boy, who as a result was injured and broke a leg.
- Later in the same week, a three-year old girl got her head stuck in the door, and was caught for about three minutes before the driver noticed it. (Her mother noticed immediately, but apparently it took

some time to communicate it to the driver, the reason being that the mother had left the bus before the child.)

In a modern city bus, the doors open automatically when the bus stops. In a many cases this requires that the stop button has been pressed, and then only the door nearest to the button will open. There is usually a system of photocells to detect when a person leaves the bus, and to keep the door open as long as someone is standing by the door. After the person has left (according to the rules of the system), and presumably after some reasonable time interval, the door will automatically close. Since, however, it is possible that people for one reason or another may still be in the doorway when the door closes, doors are equipped with sensors that detect an obstacle and as a result force the door open again.

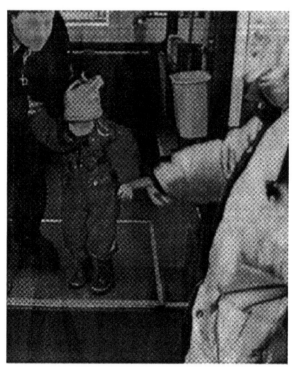

Figure 3.1: Getting through a bus door

The risks in closing a door too early are illustrated by the three cases mentioned above. The risks are due to the fact that the opening and closing of the door is automatic, and that the driver must wait at the bus stop until informed by the system that the doors have been closed (e.g., by an indicator on the dashboard). In order to reduce or eliminate these risks there must be some kind of barrier that can prevent the door from closing prematurely while someone is still in the doorway. The driver, of course, is supposed visually to inspect the doors by using the mirrors but this may not always be sufficient. There may, for instance, be obstacles in the line of sight, or he may rely too much on the indicators and simply drive away. Presumably there is also a need to keep to the timetable, as well as to pay attention to the traffic around the bus. This may in practice be more important from the driver's point of view, since the automatic systems are supposed to prevent a person from getting caught in a door. When there is insufficient time to attend to everything, the driver will invariably choose that which is considered most important and may therefore leave the bus stop before the unloading procedures have been fully completed.

When accidents with bus doors happen, they often involve children. There are several reasons for this. One is that children may hesitate when leaving the bus and step backwards before going out, hence behave differently than the automatic system 'assumes'. (The rules in the automatic system effectively constitute a model of the behaviour of a person leaving the bus.) Another is that children are smaller and lighter than adults, hence may be more difficult to detect by the sensors in the door edge. After one of the accidents in Sweden it was realised that the sensors did not cover the lowest part of the door (11 cm up from the bottom edge). Thus, a child that fell and got caught by the hand or the leg near the bottom of the door would not be detected. It was also realised (surprise, surprise) that whereas the sensors in the door worked correctly when tested in a warm and dry garage, they might fail during actual conditions, e.g., sub-zero temperatures, wind, snow, rain, dirt, etc. Drivers, of course, have manual controls that they can use when needed, e.g., when prams or wheelchairs have to board or leave the bus. But in general the manual override is used as sparingly as possible, since it is slower than the automatic system.

Barriers and Accidents

The few examples given above have illustrated the different ways in which the term 'barrier' can be used, referring to either the type or the nature of a barrier, its function, its purpose, etc. In daily language, the precise meaning of the single term 'barrier' is normally clear from the context. For the purpose of a more systematic use in accident analysis and system design it is, however, necessary to clarify the various meanings of the term 'barrier' and to introduce a more precise terminology.

Barriers, using the term in a general sense, may be characterised in several different ways. One is with regard to their temporal relation to an actual or hypothetical accident. Barriers that are intended to work *before* a specific initiating event takes place, serve as a means of *prevention*. Such barriers are supposed to ensure that the accident does not happen, or at least to slow down the developments that may result in an accident (cf. Svenson, 1991). Barriers that are intended to work *after* a specific initiating event has taken place serve as means of *protection*. These barriers are supposed to shield the environment and the people in it, as well as the system itself, from the consequences of the accident. Barriers may also be either *active* or *passive*. An active barrier entails one or more functions, the effects of which achieve the purpose of the barrier. A passive barrier fulfils its purpose just by being there rather than by actively doing something. In relation to protection, an active barrier serves to reduce or deflect the consequences, whereas a passive barrier contains or holds the consequences. (The definitions here differ somewhat from how the terms are used in current traffic safety research. Here an active safety system is one that works in the pre-crash phase, while a passive safety system works in the post-crash phase.) Finally, a barrier may be *permanent* or *temporary*. Permanent barriers are usually part of the design base, although they may also be introduced later, for instance as a response to an accident. Temporary barriers are restrictions that apply for a limited period of time only, typically referring to a change in external conditions. The most dramatic example in recent history is the ban on flying in the wake of the attack on the World Trade Center on September 11, 2001. In this case the temporary barrier was followed by a number of permanent – or at least long lasting – barriers.

Consider, for instance, a nuclear power plant, where there are multiple barriers to prevent an initiating event from taking place – specifically to prevent operators from taking an incorrect course of actions. This may include features of the interface design, procedures, organisational rules, etc. The commonly most dreaded result of such an initiating event is the uncontrolled release of radioactive material following damage to the reactor core. If such a release of radioactive material takes place, then the containment building serves as a passive protective barrier, hindering the radioactive material being spread to the environment. The difference between prevention and protection is illustrated in Figure 3.2.

As shown by Figure 3.2, the role of barriers is relative to the point in time when the accident happens. This is shown as the moment when control is lost or the moment where some function failed. (The concept of failure modes is discussed further below.) In accident and risk analyses this is sometimes called the initiating event. Before this happens, barriers serve to prevent the initiating event from taking place. The barriers can be either active or passive, an example of the former being monitoring and detection such as in an early warning system and an example of the latter being the restriction of access to a hazardous zone.

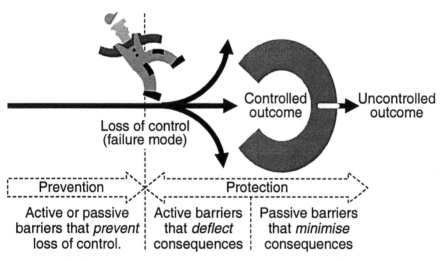

Figure 3.2: Prevention and protection

After control has been lost, barriers serve to protect against the possible outcomes, i.e., the possible consequences of the accident. Here it is possible to make a further distinction between barriers that serve to deflect consequences, and barriers that serve to minimise consequences usually by preventing them from spreading further. In both cases the consequences are controlled in some way. If neither of these works, the result is that the consequences are uncontrolled, leading to what in the domino model was called the injury. In terms of accident prevention, everything up to and including the controlled outcome falls under the category of design-base accidents (DBA), which means accidents that have been anticipated when the system was conceived and built, and for which adequate countermeasures have been provided. Cases where this fails are usually subsumed under the label of beyond design-base accidents (BDBA), which means that this specific development of events was unanticipated.

The determination of a barrier as being either preventive or protective is relative to the occurrence of the initiating event in the sense that the very same barrier in some cases may be preventive and in some protective. To take a simple example, a door leading into a room with dangerous equipment or materials may serve as a preventive barrier in the sense that it may hinder people from entering the room, and as a protective barrier in the case of an explosion or a fire. The barrier that prevents the transportation of physical matter, i.e., the door, is, of course, the same in both cases.

Use and Description of Barriers

The barrier concept must be considered both in relation to possible methods for identifying barriers and barrier failures, and in relation to a way of systematically describing or classifying barriers. The two aspects are dependent, since a classification scheme is a necessary prerequisite for a method, regardless of whether the analysis is a retroactive or a predictive one (Hollnagel, 1998). This chapter will consider the issues of the classification scheme, while Chapters 4 and 6 will describe the associated methods.

Despite the importance of barriers in accident analysis and prevention, there are surprisingly few systematic studies in the available literature. The main ones are described below in chronological order.

The Prevention of Accidents

In a chapter entitled 'The prevention of accidents', William Haddon Jr. discussed the role of barriers in relation to Class I injuries, which were defined as cases where 'damage is caused by the delivery to the body of amounts of energy in excess of the corresponding local or whole-body injury thresholds' (Haddon, 1966, p. 592). The discussion focused on transport accidents, recreational accidents, and work accidents. In order to prevent such injuries Haddon proposed that countermeasures should be applied in the following order of preference:

> (1) (T)o prevent the marshaling of the hazardous energy; (2) to prevent or modify its release; (3) to separate it and the susceptible structure in time or space; (4) to interpose a barrier that blocks or attenuates its action; (5) to raise injury thresholds so that damage is prevented or substantially reduced; (6) to provide as rapidly as possible the optimum in emergency care and transportation; and (7) if required, later to provide the clinical, corrective, and rehabilitative services necessary to reduce to the maximum possible extent the damage already produced. (Haddon, 1966, p. 594)

This is clearly a version of Heinrich's domino model, since it describes the accident as a sequence of events. The rationale behind the order of preference is that it is better if accident countermeasures are applied as early as possible. This is entirely sensible in relation to the specific accident model, although it may not be valid for other model types. According to Haddon, barrier characteristics were determined by the nature of the structures they protected and by the types of energy exchanges they were designed to block, where the latter aspect was considered particularly useful. Altogether, barriers were seen as just one type of countermeasure among several, and they were only considered as a way of separating the object or target from the hazard.

Barriers and MORT

Another treatment of barriers was part of the Management Oversight and Risk Tree (MORT) programme. The MORT approach (Knox & Eicher, 1983) described a technique for a comprehensive investigation of occupational accidents as well as a technique to analyse safety programmes. The MORT approach was based on the use of a formal decision tree that integrated a wide variety of safety concerns in a systematic fashion. The MORT chart described, in an orderly manner, all the potential causal factors for accidents that could occur in a system. An important part of this was obviously the relation between energy transportation (or energy releases) and barriers.

The MORT barrier analysis (Trost & Nertney, 1985) made a distinction between control barriers and safety barriers where control barriers related to the wanted or intended energy flows and safety barriers to the unwanted or unintended energy flows. Examples of control barriers were: conductors, approved work methods, job training, disconnection switches, pressure vessels, etc. Examples of safety barriers were: protective equipment, guardrails, safety training, work protection code, emergency contingency plans, etc.

In terms of the elimination of hazards in a system, MORT listed four approaches in order of importance. These were: (1) elimination through design; (2) installation of appropriate safety devices (barriers); (3) installation of warning devices (alarms); (4) development of special procedures to handle the situation. This ordering seems to reflect differences in the nature of barriers, for instance whether they are material or organisational.

Corresponding to the discussion above (cf. Figure 3.2), MORT made a distinction between three different barrier purposes, which were called *prevention*, *control*, and *minimisation*. This reflects a temporal view of systems and accidents, in the sense that preventive barriers are present in the system independent of the task, control barriers work as part of the task, and minimisation barriers work after the incident or accident. The latter category thus corresponds to the notion of protective barriers described in Figure 3.2.

MORT also proposed a distinction between several different types of barriers. These were: (1) physical barriers; (2) equipment design; (3) warning devices; (4) procedures / work processes; (5) knowledge and skills; and (6) supervision. Finally, the MORT barrier analysis discussed how barriers might be unable to achieve their purpose, either because they failed as such or for other reasons. It was pointed out that barriers could be impractical, that they could fail outright, or that they could be overlooked or ignored.

The Barrier Concept in Risk Analysis

Taylor (1988) provided a representative account of barriers as used by risk analysis practitioners. The context was a general discussion of the techniques applicable to assess the safety of weapon systems. A barrier was straightforwardly defined as 'equipment, constructions, or rules that can stop the development of an accident'. The examples provided included a distinction between three types of barriers called *passive*, *active*, and *procedural*. Passive barriers, such as firewalls and distance (spatial separation), would work because of their physical characteristics and would always be ready to use. Active barriers, such as safety switches and fire extinguishing equipment, would require some kind of activation before they could be used. Finally, procedural barriers, such as instructions for use of equipment, would require a mediating agent in order to be effective. The general concept of a barrier was illustrated by a diagram similar to the representation used by the AEB model, which is described in the following section.

Taylor also provided an extensive discussion of the requirements to barrier quality. The criteria were mixed in the sense that some of them, such as the adequacy requirements, were relevant for any kind of barrier, while others, such as the availability requirements, mainly applied to active barriers.

- *Adequacy.* The ability to prevent all accidents within the design-base (DBA). Barriers must meet requirements set by appropriate standards and norms. Capacity must not be exceeded by changes to the primary system. If a barrier is inadequate, additional barriers must be established.
- *Availability, reliability.* All necessary signals must be detectable when barrier activation is required. Active barriers must be fail-safe, and either self-testing or tested regularly. Passive barriers must be inspected routinely.
- *Robustness.* The ability to withstand extreme events, such as fire, flooding, etc. One barrier shall not be disabled by the activation of another. Two barriers shall not be affected by a (single) common cause.
- *Specificity.* The effects of activating the barrier must not lead to other accidents. The barrier shall not destroy that which it protects.

The classification of barriers – as passive, active, or procedural – and the pragmatic requirements to barrier quality, very much reflect the proactive use of barriers. As such it represents concerns that should be recognised by any serious attempt to classify barriers. Despite the obvious value of this line of work it has, unfortunately, received little attention outside the field of risk analysis, and the impact has therefore been smaller than deserved.

The Accident Evolution and Barrier (AEB) Model

Svenson (1991) described the evolution leading to an accident as a chain or sequence of failures, malfunctions, and errors in what was basically a sequential accident model. In the analysis of barriers he introduced the important distinction between barrier functions and barrier systems in the following way:

> A barrier function represents a *function* (and not, e.g., an object) which can arrest the accident evolution so that the next event in the chain is never realized. *Barrier systems* are those maintaining the barrier function. Such systems may be an operator, an instruction, a physical separation, an emergency control system, and other safety-related systems, components, and human factors-organizational units. (Svenson, 1991, p. 501)

More generally, a *barrier function* can be defined as the specific manner by which the barrier achieves its purpose, whereas a *barrier system* can be defined as the foundation of the barrier function, i.e., the organisational and/or physical structure without which the barrier function could not be accomplished. Compared to the distinction in system analysis between 'why', 'what', and 'how', the 'why' corresponds to the purpose of the barrier, the 'what' to the barrier function, and the 'how' to the barrier system. The use of the barrier concept should be based on a systematic description of various types of barrier systems and barrier functions, for instance as a classification system. This will help to identify specific barrier systems and barrier functions and to understand the role of barriers, in either meaning, in the history of an accident.

The Accident Evolution and Barrier function (AEB) model represented the development of an accident as a sequence of steps belonging to either the human factors / organisational system or the technical system. In the model, each step represented either, (1) the failure or malfunction of a component or, (2) an incorrectly performed function within each system, and barrier functions were used to indicate how the development of the accident could be arrested.

The AEB model proposed three different barrier systems, namely physical, technical, and human factors/organisational (Svenson, 1991, p. 501). Barrier functions were discussed in relation to a specific incident and also included an interesting discussion of the factors that could affect the strength of barrier functions, similar to Taylor's (1988) discussion of robustness. Although the AEB model is less elaborate than the six-way distinction made by MORT, there is a clear mapping between the two proposals. Of the three barrier systems defined by the AEB model, the technical barriers correspond to types 1-3 in MORT, the human barrier corresponds to type 6, and the human/organisational barrier corresponds to types 4 & 5. The notion of a barrier type in MORT therefore seems to correspond to the notion of a barrier function in the AEB model.

Barriers and Latent Failures

The development of accident models in the late 1980s to early 1990s was marked by the introduction of the concept of latent failures (e.g., Reason, 1993). The basic paradigm was still a sequential development of the accident starting with organisational processes, which via task and environmental conditions promoted unsafe acts at the level of individuals. The defences, or barriers, were added as a layer intervening between the unsafe acts and the accident. The models described how latent failure conditions coming from the organisational processes could degrade the defences, thereby leaving the way open for unsafe acts to become accidents.

An early description of this model described the defences as serving the following six distinct functions (Reason, 1993, p. 226).

- *Protection*: To provide a barrier between the hazards and the potential victims under normal operating conditions.

- *Detection*: To detect and identify the occurrence of an off-normal condition, an unsafe act or the presence of hazardous substances.
- *Warning*: To signal the presence and the nature of the hazard to all those likely to be exposed to its dangers.
- *Recovery*: To restore the system to a safe state as quickly as possible.
- *Containment*: To restrict the spread of the hazard in the event of a failure in any or all of the prior defensive functions.
- *Escape*: To ensure the safe evacuation of all potential victims after an accident.

It was noted that the defences comprised both technical and human elements, i.e., that the functions were implemented by systems, but the description did not provide further details of how this took place. In the order they are listed here the six defences correspond to three pairs (protection-detection, warning-recovery, and containment-escape) that provide a reasonable match to the purposes of prevention, control and minimisation described by MORT.

Barriers in Software Systems

Leveson (1995) has provided a more recent discussion of the barrier concept and presented three main approaches to hazard reduction, called controllability, barriers, and failure minimisation. Although the terms are the same as used by the MORT approach, Leveson seems to use the concept of barriers in a somewhat narrower sense. The difference may be due to the fact that MORT was developed to analyse hazards and barriers in systems with energy flows, whereas Leveson discussed barriers mostly in relation to software systems.

According to Leveson, a distinction can be made between three types of barriers, called lockout, lockin, and interlock, respectively. A *lockout* 'prevents a dangerous event from occurring or prevents someone or something from entering a dangerous area or state' (Leveson, 1995, p. 422). A lockout is thus a kind of shield or defence, which either prevents a specific initiating event from taking place, or prevents an agent from getting into the system. A *lockin* was defined as something that maintains a condition or preserves a system state. Lockins can be either physical, such as walls, doors, cages, safety belts, containers, or functional in the sense that they maintain a specific system state or condition. Finally, an *interlock* serves 'to enforce correct sequencing or to isolate two events in time' (Leveson, 1995, p. 426). An interlock can work by inhibiting (or preventing) an event from occurring by establishing a set of pre-conditions or execution conditions. An interlock can also work by enforcing a certain sequence of actions or events, which in principle is functionally equivalent to defining a pre-condition for an action. Interlocks are common in many systems, and may be implemented either by hardware or, increasingly, by software.

Compared to the earlier approaches, Leveson mainly described different types of barrier functions with the focus on prevention rather than protection. This may be because the domain was systems that included or were based on software. It is natural in such cases to be concerned with preventive rather than protective barriers, and to focus on barrier functions rather than barrier systems since the transportation of information is of greater concern than the transportation of mass or energy.

Classification of Barriers

The above examples have shown how an analytical description of barriers can be based on several different concepts, such as their origin, their purpose, their location, and their nature. Each of these is considered separately in the following.

Classification Based on the Origin of Barrier

In terms of their origin, barrier systems can be generated either by organisations or individuals. (Conceivably, a physical barrier system may also result from an act of nature, such as the Great Barrier Reef, although this is hardly the outcome of an intention on the human scale of events.) It is nevertheless the exception that barrier functions or barrier systems are created by an individual *qua* individual, except during abnormal conditions, emergencies, etc. In those cases barriers are typically *ad hoc* restrictions that serve a temporary need and therefore are discarded when conditions return to normal. Since barriers should preferably reflect a systematic and comprehensive analysis of the risks and weaknesses of the system as a whole and be able to serve their purpose in a wide range of conditions, it is unlikely that they will be based on the transitory needs and intentions of an individual. (If individuals feel compelled to introduce barriers for normal working conditions it is more likely an indication that the organisation does not function adequately.) In any case, since the notion of the origin of a barrier system is limited to very few categories, and since this does not say much about the type or nature of the barriers, it is not considered an appropriate basis for a comprehensive classification system.

Classification Based on Purpose of Barrier

It has already been mentioned that barriers may serve several different purposes, e.g., being preventive, controlling, protective or minimising. Kecklund et al. (1996) discussed how a barrier may serve to prevent a human failure, i.e., an incorrectly performed action by a human, or a technical failure. Another example is the ubiquitous confirmation dialogue box that is part and parcel of human-computer interaction. The dialogue box is a barrier to prevent people from making elementary mistakes, such as deleting the wrong file or neglecting to save a piece of work. The MORT approach also identified three different purposes of a barrier, as prevention, control and minimisation. As argued in the preceding, the purpose of a barrier system or function is relative to the onset and development of the accident or event, and it is therefore not the best criterion to use as the basis for a categorisation.

Classification Based on Barrier Location

The barrier analysis that was part of the MORT technique (Trost & Nertney, 1985), made a distinction between where in the system a barrier was located. In the terminology used here, this would be the location or focus of the barrier function. According to this, a barrier could either be placed on the source, between the source and the worker or the exposed targets, on the worker or the target, or work by means of a separation in time or space (cf. Haddon's classification above). For example, separating a source of combustion from a source of ignition is in time a very effective barrier that may prevent a fire or an explosion. This distinction of barrier locations is, of course, only applicable to barriers that have some kind of physical reality, and is therefore not adequate as the basis for a more comprehensive classification.

A Classification of Barrier Systems

This leaves the nature of barriers as a possible starting point for developing a classification. The nature of barriers is independent of their origin, their purpose (e.g., as preventive or protective), and their location. In terms of their nature, barrier systems can range from physical hindrances (walls, cages) to ethereal rules and laws. One proposal to classify barrier systems is to use the following four categories.

- *Physical or material barrier systems.* These physically prevent an action from being carried out or an event from taking place, and correspond to the physical barriers in the MORT analysis. Material or physical barrier systems may also protect by blocking or mitigating the effects of an unexpected event, cf. Figure 3.2. Examples of physical barrier systems are buildings, walls, fences, railings, bars, cages, gates, containers, fire curtains, etc. A physical barrier system presents an actual physical hindrance for the transportation of mass, energy or information from point A to point B and although it may not prevent it under all circumstances, it will at least slow it down or delay it. A physical barrier system can withstand forces up to a certain maximum beyond which it is no longer effective. A door or a wall may be broken down, a dike may be flooded, a tank may explode, etc. An important characteristic of physical barrier systems is that they do not have to be perceived or interpreted by the acting agent in order to work. (This can be testified by anyone who has walked into a glass door.) They can therefore be used against energy and material, as well as against people.
- *Functional* (active or dynamic) *barrier systems.* A functional barrier system works by impeding the action to be carried out, for instance by establishing an interlock, either logical or temporal (cf. Leveson, 1995). A functional barrier system effectively sets up one or more pre-conditions that have to be met before an action can be carried out. These pre-conditions do not always require interpretation by a human but may be interrogated or sensed by a technological

artefact, for instance an automatic safety device such as an airbag system. A functional barrier system may not always be visible or discernible to a human user, although its presence often is indicated in one way or another. This is clearly necessary if it requires one or more actions to be overcome. A lock is a good example of a functional barrier system, whether it is a physical lock that requires the use of a key or a logical lock that requires some kind of password or identification. Functional barrier systems correspond to the categories of equipment design and supervision proposed by the MORT analysis.

• *Symbolic barrier systems.* The defining characteristic of these is that they require an act of interpretation in order to achieve their purpose, hence an 'intelligent' agent of some kind that can perceive and respond as intended. (Alternative terms may therefore be conceptual or perceptual barrier systems.) Whereas the railing along a road is both a physical and a symbolic barrier system, the reflective posts are only a symbolic barrier system: they indicate where the edge of the road is, but unlike the railing they are insufficient to prevent a car from going off the road. Symbolic barrier systems are ubiquitous and we are everywhere surrounded by all kinds of visual and auditory signs and signals. Other examples are warnings (by text or by symbol), warnings devices, interface layout, information presented on the interface, visual demarcations, etc.

Whereas a functional barrier system works by establishing an actual pre-condition that must be met by the system or the user before an action can be carried out, a symbolic barrier system indicates a limitation on performance that may or may not be respected. The indication of maximum speed on a road sign is a symbolic barrier, which only works if the drivers notice it and slow down. In contrast, if a train driver passes a red signal 'in danger' the automatic braking activated by the ATC is a functional barrier system. Even though a functional barrier system may include a pre-condition, that pre-condition need not be interpreted in the same sense that a symbol is.

• *Incorporeal barrier systems.* The final class of barriers comprises the incorporeal barriers. An incorporeal barrier lacks material form or substance in the situations where it is applied and instead depends on the knowledge of the user in order to achieve its purpose. Incorporeal barrier systems can exist or be represented in a physical form such as a book or a memorandum, but are usually not physically present when their use is mandated. Typical incorporeal barrier systems are: rules, guidelines, safety principles (safety culture), restrictions, and laws. In industrial contexts, incorporeal barrier systems are largely synonymous with organisational barriers, i.e., rules for actions that are imposed by the organisation, rather than being physically, functionally or symbolically present in the system. Incorporeal barrier systems correspond to the MORT types of procedures / work processes, knowledge and skills.

(When the four barrier systems were first proposed, the fourth system was called the immaterial barrier system. The term immaterial was used in the sense of 'non-material' rather than 'irrelevant'. Although the great Samuel Johnson argued against the second meaning, stating that 'this sense has crept into the conversation and writings of barbarians; but ought to be utterly rejected,' the risk of confusion suggests that the less ambiguous term incorporeal be used.)

It is clearly possible to combine several barrier systems and functions in the same physical artefact or object. Figure 3.3 shows an example, which includes a cage, a locked door, and a warning sign. Here, the door and the cage are physical barrier systems, the written warning is a symbolic barrier system, and the lock requiring a key is a functional barrier system. It may, indeed, be the rule rather than the exception that several different barrier systems and functions are used together to achieve a common purpose.

A Classification of Barrier Functions

The basic purpose of a barrier is to stop something from happening. Consider, for instance, two different ways of preventing traffic from entering a street (cf. Figure 3.4). One way is to put a traffic sign at the entrance, such as the internationally recognised 'no entry' sign. If this turns out to be insufficiently effective, as well it may, another way is to block the entry to the street by a physical barrier. Obviously, the two solutions can also be combined.

Figure 3.3: A combination of barrier systems

In both cases the barrier provides the same function, i.e., preventing vehicles from going into the street. But they do it in different ways. According to the terminology proposed here, one is a physical barrier system while the other is a symbolic barrier system. Although the purpose or function is the same, the means are quite different. The same argument can be applied to any other example and it is therefore reasonable generally to make a distinction between barrier functions and barrier systems. (The two barrier systems clearly differ in their efficiency, etc., something that will be discussed at length below.)

The following four tables present a classification of the barriers that are commonly found in practice. Each barrier is described with regard to the underlying barrier system, i.e., one of the four main types as defined above, and the specific barrier function, i.e., the more precise description of what the barrier does. The lists of barriers functions in Tables 3.1 – 3.4 are unlikely to be exhaustive, but are hopefully sufficiently extensive to be of some practical use.

Figure 3.4: No entry

A physical barrier system concretely prevents an event from taking place or mitigates the effects of an unexpected event by blocking the transportation of mass, energy or information from one place to another.

Table 3.1: Barrier functions for physical barrier systems

Barrier function	Example
Containing or protecting. Prevent transporting something from the present location (e.g., release) or into the present location (penetration)	Walls, doors, buildings, restricted physical access, railings, fences, filters, containers, tanks, valves, rectifiers, etc.
Restraining or preventing movement or transportation of mass or energy	Safety belts, harnesses, fences, cages, restricted physical movements, spatial distance (gulfs, gaps), etc.
Keeping together. Cohesion, resilience, indestructibility	Components that do not break or fracture easily, e.g., safety glass.
Separating, protecting, blocking	Crumble zones, scrubbers, filters, etc.

A functional barrier system effectively sets up one or more preconditions that have to be met before an event can take place. A functional barrier system can either be in an active (= ON) condition or an inactive (= OFF) condition. For some functional barrier systems a user accomplishes the transition from one state to the other. For example, people usually control locks in doors by means of keys, radio signals, voice commands, and the like. Other functional barrier systems are autonomous in the sense that they can change state according to the conditions. To do so they must be equipped with detection and activation mechanisms.

Table 3.2: Barrier functions for functional barrier systems

Barrier function	Example
Preventing movement or action (mechanical, hard)	Locks, equipment alignment, physical interlocking, equipment match, etc.
Preventing movement or action (logical, soft)	Passwords, entry codes, action sequences, pre-conditions, physiological matching (iris, fingerprint, alcohol level), etc.
Hindering or impeding actions (spatio-temporal)	Distance (too far for a single person to reach), persistence (dead-man-button), delays, synchronisation, etc.
Dampening, attenuating	Active noise reduction, active suspension
Dissipating energy, quenching, extinguishing	Air bags, sprinklers, etc.

Whereas a physical barrier system can fulfil its purpose by itself, e.g., a wall prevents movement of matter or energy just by being a wall, functional barrier systems in most cases only work if they are combined with a physical barrier system. (The issue becomes arguable in the case of software systems and other logical barriers.) In a sprinkler system, for instance, it is the water spray that extinguishes the fire. Similarly, in an airbag it is the inflated bag that absorbs the energy from the driver or passenger. They are nevertheless classified as functional barrier systems because they can be in two (or more) states, e.g., either 'ready' or 'activated'. Yet such systems should only start to function when a specific condition exists, and their effectiveness therefore requires both that the triggering conditions can be reliably detected and that the function can be activated. For a sprinkler system, water should only be let out when a fire, or smoke, has been detected. Similarly, an airbag should only inflate in case of a collision. The issue of reliably detecting the activation conditions is far from trivial, and involves considerations of signal validation, detection thresholds, sensor reliability, etc. In many cases the detection and activation are structurally part of the same mechanism, as in the case of a sprinkler system. In other cases they may be separate, as when a remote sensor activates a defensive function. (In all cases the detection and activation must obviously functionally be parts of the same system.) From a human factors point of view, interesting combinations arise when humans function either as detectors or activators of a joint system.

A symbolic barrier system works indirectly through its 'meaning', and hence requires an act of interpretation by someone. Symbolic barrier systems are ubiquitous in a modern society. In a symbolic barrier system humans always provide the detection function and will continue to do so barring the development of 'real' artificial intelligence. Humans usually also serve as the means by which the corresponding barrier function is implemented, although a combination of humans and machines can be relevant.

Table 3.3: Barrier functions for symbolic barrier systems

Barrier function	Example
Countering, preventing or thwarting actions (visual, tactile interface design)	Coding of functions (colour, shape, spatial layout), demarcations, labels & warnings (static), etc. Facilitating correct actions may be as effective as countering incorrect actions
Regulating actions	Instructions, procedures, precautions / conditions, dialogues, etc.
Indicating system status or condition (signs, signals and symbols)	Signs (e.g., traffic signs), signals (visual, auditory), warnings, alarms, etc.
Permission or authorisation (or the lack thereof)	Work permit, work order
Communication, interpersonal dependency	Clearance, approval, (on-line or off-line), in the sense that the lack of clearance etc., is a barrier

Finally, an incorporeal, or non-material, barrier system also requires interpretation and furthermore relies on the acting person to recognise its existence in the first place.

Although it is analytically correct to maintain a strong distinction between barrier systems and barrier functions, it quickly becomes cumbersome since it leads to clumsy expressions. For practical purposes it is often easier just to talk about barriers. In the rest of the book the term barrier is therefore used to denote a barrier function implemented by a barrier system. In most cases this should not create problems, but whenever it may lead to ambiguity the more specific terms barrier systems or barrier functions will be used instead.

Table 3.4: Barrier functions for incorporeal barrier systems

Barrier function	Example
Complying, conforming to	Self-restraint, ethical norms, morals, social or group pressure
Prescribing: rules, laws, guidelines, prohibitions	Rules, restrictions, laws (all either conditional or unconditional), etc.

Composite Barrier Systems

The classification of barriers is not always a simple matter, as pointed out above. A wall is, of course, a physical barrier system and a law is an incorporeal barrier system. But what about something like a procedure? A procedure by itself is an instruction for how to do something, hence not primarily a barrier, except in the sense that performing the correct actions rules out performing the incorrect ones. From a performance point of view this is an issue of facilitation, i.e., making something easier to do, rather than preventing something from happening. In that sense facilitators and barriers may be seen as two sides of the same coin. Procedures do, however, often include warnings and cautions as well as conditional actions (if-then rules). Although the procedure may exist as a physical document, other formats are also possible, such as a flowchart or a computerised presentation. The procedure therefore works by virtue of its contents or meaning rather than by virtue of its physical characteristics. To the extent that a procedure is a barrier, it represents a symbolic barrier system since its warnings, cautions, and conditions require an act of interpretation in order to work.

Incorporeal barrier systems are often complemented by symbolic barrier systems. For instance, general speed limits given by the traffic laws (highway code) are supplemented by road signs (a symbolic barrier system) and at times enforced by traffic police (acting as a symbolic barrier system if they are seen and as a functional one if they are unseen) perhaps supplemented by physical barrier systems such as roadblocks or speed bumps. Physical barrier systems may also be complemented by symbolic barrier systems to encourage their use. Seat belts are physical barrier systems, but can only serve their purpose if they are actually used. In commercial aviation signs (text, icons), signals (seat-belt lights), verbal instructions, demonstrations, and visual inspection support the use of seat belts. In private cars the physical barrier system is normally only supported by the incorporeal barrier system, i.e., the traffic laws, although some models of cars also have a warning signal if the driver forgets to put on the safety belt. On the whole, the result is less than perfect, especially since the use of a safety belt seems to be strongly influenced by cultural norms.

For physical and functional barrier systems, the respective barrier function is provided by the system itself. In a containment building of a nuclear power plant, the walls as such are the barriers against a release of radiation. Similarly, in a car, the anti-blocking brake system is also the barrier against skidding. In these cases there is therefore no need of an external agent to carry out the barrier function; detection and activation are part of the same physical system. The situation is, however, completely different for symbolic and incorporeal barrier systems. Here, the barrier systems cannot themselves provide the barrier function. It requires an action by someone (or possibly something) to realise the barrier functions. In some sense one might say that the action is the barrier, but it would be more proper to say that the action implements the barrier function, which in turn is provided by a barrier system. This is more than a play with words since knowing which barrier functions the actions serve and whether the actions came from an instruction (a symbolic barrier system) or a sense of duty (an incorporeal barrier system) can have significant consequences.

The examples given earlier in this chapter can now be re-examined to illustrate the proposed classification of barrier systems.

- The cage around an industrial robot is a physical barrier system that contains the robot and prevents people from coming near it. The door in the cage is also a physical barrier system and has the same purpose. The lock on the door, which stops the robot when the door is opened, is a functional barrier system that serves to render the robot inactive. (The lock is a lockout in the terminology used by Leveson, 1995.) Finally, the safety rules that forbid personnel to come close to a moving robot represent an incorporeal barrier system. The safety rules may be supported by a symbolic barrier system, such as a written warning or a sign, or a painted separation line on the floor.
- The railing or fence running along a road is a physical barrier system that restrains the cars and stops them from going off the road (provided the cars do not go too fast or are too heavy). Since

seeing or observing the railing is used by car drivers to stay on the road, the railing is also a symbolic barrier system. Reflective posts or markers used on minor roads are a symbolic barrier system, although the function (preventing) is the same.

- The launch control of an ICBM includes several barrier systems and functions. The rules for authorisation of the launch command represent an incorporeal barrier system (monitoring), whereas the authorisation code itself represents both a functional barrier system (preventing) and a symbolic one (permission). The need to use separate keywords or keys is a functional barrier system that prevents an action. The spatial separation of the firing or launch buttons represents a physical barrier system that also prevents an action from taking place. Note, however, that this is only effective because two actions must occur simultaneously. The need for synchronisation represents a functional barrier system and the barrier function is that of prevention.

Bus Doors Revisited

The use of multiple barrier systems and functions is a way to ensure that a single failure does not lead to an unwanted event or accident in a system. Barrier systems and barrier functions may be combined in various ways, for instance according to the defence-in-depth principle. These concerns, which were addressed by the requirements described by Taylor (1988), become very important when barriers are used proactively in the design of safety functions. The discussion below, however, considers another aspect, namely how to address the issue of barriers in accident analysis. (More will be said about that in Chapter 4.)

In the case of the bus door, the barrier functions that were supposed to prevent the door from catching or capturing a person depended on a number of conditions, and hence could not be counted upon to work appropriately when one or more of these failed. This illustrates one problem with functional barrier systems, i.e., the robustness during different conditions and the ability to work when the triggering conditions deviate from the design cases (children instead of adults, prams, etc.). For the bus doors it turned out that a certain procedure should be followed in order for the barrier to work properly. (Needless to say, this procedure was never made explicit.) In the case of adults with children, the child should leave the bus first, while the adult waits. In this way the adult will both block the light of the photocell and be able manually to intervene with the door mechanism if needed, e.g., by sticking an arm in between the doors or using the manual override. If the adult leaves first, a child will sometimes hesitate before leaving the bus, hence 'trick' the automation. The parent, being outside the bus, and possibly a few feet away, will also have less possibility of intervening in the automation. In reality the parent may nevertheless often leave the bus first in order to be able to watch for other traffic or help the child to get out, e.g., to lift him/her down to the ground.

As an interesting aside to the bus door accident, the response was to issue a new instruction to the bus drivers, namely to take special care when parents with children or prams were leaving the bus. This is a classical example of relying on an incorporeal barrier system as a first response – and often also as the only one. A new instruction is cheap to produce and quick to implement. One may nevertheless have some doubts about how efficient this kind of response will be, especially in the long term. As long as the accident is fresh in the mind of the drivers, the instruction will work – and it will hardly be needed. But complacency soon sets in and the need to keep to the timetable will be more important than the need to follow the instruction. *Plus ça change ...*

Barrier Analysis and Barrier Design

Barrier Quality

Since barrier systems are an important means to achieve safety goals, it is useful also to describe them in terms of how they are applied. This can be based on a set of pragmatic criteria that address various aspects of barrier quality, cf. Hollnagel (1995).

- *Efficiency* or *adequacy*. This refers to how efficient the barrier is expected to be in achieving its purpose, i.e., how well it can meet its intended purpose.
- *Resources required*. The resources are those needed to implement the barrier (to design and develop it) rather than the resources needed to use it. This also includes the resources needed to maintain the barrier. The most important resource is usually money, i.e., the cost

of the barrier system. Efficiency is never considered without also thinking of the cost and safety always has a price.

- *Robustness (reliability)*. This refers to how reliable and resistant the barrier is, i.e., how well it can withstand the variability of the environment (working practices, degraded information or noise, unexpected events, wear and tear, etc.).

- *Delay in implementation*. The time from conception to implementation of a barrier, i.e., the delay in implementation. It always takes time to implement a barrier, which may conflict with the need to act quickly in the wake of an accident.

- *Applicability to safety critical tasks*. Safety critical tasks play a special role in socio-technical systems. On the one hand they are the occasions where specific barriers may be mostly needed; on the other hand they are usually subject to a number of restrictions from either management or regulatory bodies.

- *Availability*. This refers to whether the barrier can fulfil its purpose when it is needed. This is an issue for functional barrier systems in particular, since it requires some way of assuring that the function will work when so required. Examples range from whether a smoke detector will sound if the toast gets too burnt to whether an emergency diesel will start when external power is lost. Assuring availability and reliability is often more difficult, but also more critical, for barriers intended to be used under rare conditions.

- *Evaluation*. Evaluation is important in order to determine whether a barrier works as expected and to ensure that it is available when needed. The evaluation can be considered with regard to how easy it is to carry out (in terms of, e.g., money, man-power, time) and in terms of whether suitable methods are available. Evaluation should address barrier quality both during design and during actual use (inspection, readiness verification).

- *Dependence on humans*. This is the extent to which a barrier depends on humans in order to achieve its purpose. The dependence refers to the effectiveness of the barrier system in use rather than, e.g., the need for maintenance.

It would clearly be desirable to have barriers that were efficient, robust, fast and cheap to implement, applicable to all kinds of tasks, and easy to verify. As the evaluation in Table 3.5 shows, this is not easy to achieve. Rather, the choice of a barrier invariably represents a compromise between different criteria.

Table 3.5: Evaluation of barrier system quality

	Physical	Functional	Symbolic	Incorporeal
Efficiency	High	High	Medium	Low
Resource needs (cost)	Medium – High	Low – Medium	Low – Medium	Low
Robustness (reliability)	Medium – High	Medium – High	Low – Medium	Low
Implementation delay	Long	Medium – Long	Medium	Short
Applicable to safety critical tasks	Low	Medium	Low (uncertain interpretation)	Low
Availability	High	Low – High	High	Uncertain
Evaluation	Easy	Difficult	Difficult	Difficult
Dependence on humans (during operation)	Nil	Low	High	High

The use of the criteria listed in Table 3.5 is illustrated in the following by some examples. As an overriding concern, it is important to be able to assess how vulnerable barrier systems are and how they may fail. This is done in accident analysis by determining which barriers failed and why they failed. In system design and risk assessment it is the identification of how barriers may potentially fail, i.e., what the weaknesses of the system are. The descriptions of vulnerabilities may be further developed into an assessment of the reliability of the different barrier systems. Such an assessment may be a valuable input to system design.

Physical Barrier Systems. An example could be a building constructed to prevent the release of a substance to the environment, or equally well the entry of something from the environment (e.g., 'clean rooms' or shielding against electromagnetic interference). The extreme case is probably the containment building of a nuclear power plant or a biohazard facility. If we take a nondescript protective building as an example, the efficiency is usually high provided the building is well constructed. The resource needs are usually also high. The robustness or reliability is good for design-base accidents but unknown for beyond design-base accidents. The delay in implementation can be very long, in the order of months or years, since it may take considerable time to design and erect a building. The applicability to safety critical tasks is low in the sense that a physical barrier system rarely can be tailored to specific tasks. The availability is high, since a physical barrier system works just by being there, even if it is temporary. The evaluation is relatively easy and the dependence on humans is nil apart from maintenance. Indeed, both efficiency and robustness depend on regular and effective maintenance, which in general is the Achilles' heel of physical barrier systems.

Functional Barrier Systems. A good example is a lockout (Leveson, 1995), or more generally a lock that prevents someone or something from entering a protected zone. (In relation to a protective building, an airlock is a functional barrier system.) Consider, for instance, a password protected system or function. The efficiency of a password can easily be made very high, and the resource needs are often low. The reliability is medium-high, although difficulties in remembering passwords may lead to counterproductive shortcuts. In practice, functional barrier systems of the mechanical or spatio-temporal type require reliable construction and regular maintenance while functional barrier systems of the logical type require a verified implementation and adequate security. The delay in implementation is usually acceptable, although it can be long. The applicability to safety critical tasks is medium. The availability depends on the complexity of the barrier system, but also on the quality of construction and maintenance. It may be difficult to evaluate how well a lockout works, since it requires data from actual practice rather than a simple functional test. Finally, the dependence on humans is low, as a functional barrier system usually comprises its own 'mechanism'. This, however, refers to the dependence during operation only, i.e., when the barrier function is activated. As discussed below, all barrier systems depend on humans when it comes to test and maintenance. For functional barrier systems that are only used rarely, it may be quite difficult to verify that they will work when the need arises.

A recent example of a functional barrier system is the zero-speed category of functions for automobile navigation information systems. A major concern with such systems is that their operation requires effort, and hence may interfere with driving. For navigation systems it is common to distinguish between 'pre-drive' and 'in-transit' functions. The former consists of the complex planning and attention demanding tasks needed to define a route and a travel. The latter consist of the tasks that are necessary to use the system efficiently while travelling. In addition there are the zero-speed functions, which become available when the car is stopped (speed = 0) but are unavailable whenever it is in motion.

Symbolic Barrier Systems. Symbolic barrier systems are everywhere, usually in the form of warnings, signs and symbols of various kinds. As illustrated by Figure 3.5, signs and symbols are used liberally and often combined in an *ad hoc* manner. The design of warnings has grown into a field of specialty of its own, and is indeed a major concern for ergonomics (e.g., Wogalter et al., 1999.) As an example of a symbolic barrier system, consider any of the signs shown in Figure 3.5. Putting too many symbols together on a single warning placard may, however, be counterproductive.

The efficiency of a symbolic barrier system is in the medium range, but can vary considerably. There is a certain degree of habituation in the use of signs, both in the sense that the interpretation becomes easier with practice and in the sense that frequently encountered signs tend to be neglected. (A good example of that is the health warning on a pack of cigarettes.) The resource needs are relatively low for each sign, but may be significant if many signs are to be used (e.g., in a large organisation or across a geographical region). The robustness is mostly also low since symbolic barrier systems depend on how they are interpreted. The delay in implementation is short to medium; handmade signs can be produced in a matter of minutes or hours, while professionally made signs will take longer. Symbolic barrier systems are not well suited for safety critical tasks because there is only limited control over how they are interpreted, hence what their effect will be. Availability is usually high, since signs or symbols often are permanently in place. The evaluation of the sign in use is often difficult, and may demand lengthy periods of observation. The evaluation of the sign as such, e.g., in terms of the ergonomic qualities, is usually easy, but of limited value. Finally, symbolic barrier systems depend completely on the people who use them.

Figure 3.5: Examples of symbolic barrier systems

On the whole, symbolic barrier systems are vulnerable in many ways. Interface design, for instance, requires valid design specification, verified implementation, and systematic updating. In their use signs, signals and symbols require regular maintenance, systematic modification and reliable functioning. The latter is especially important for symbols that are state dependent, such as alarm indications. And to be really effective they require a high degree of compliance by users.

Incorporeal Barrier Systems. Finally, incorporeal barrier systems can be illustrated by considering the introduction of a new rule or procedure. As mentioned above, this is often a first reaction after an accident in order to stop or suspend all related activities until a suitable cause or explanation has been found. For example, when a shipment of radioactive iridium (Ir-192) from Sweden arrived in New Orleans on January 2, 2002, the transportation container was found to emit a high dose-rate. Two days later, on January 4, the Swedish Radiation Protection Authority, awaiting the results of an investigation into the incident, banned all further shipments. (The transportation ban was partly revoked on February 28.)

Another example is provided by the Swedish Jas 39 Gripen, an advanced combat aircraft equipped with a digital fly-by-wire system. As a highly sophisticated and complex technological system it has unsurprisingly had its share of minor and major problems. Since being taken into use by the Swedish Air Force in 1993, there have been two crashes but in both cases the pilots escaped unharmed. The more numerous problems that are encountered during daily operations are carefully reported, investigated and dealt with to ensure continued safe and efficient operation. In this respect the Gripen is similar to most other high-performance and complex technological system. In such systems it is also common to impose operational restrictions or precautions, which serve as temporary safeguards for problems that are serious but which cannot be immediately resolved. In the case of the Gripen, fifteen such operational restrictions were introduced during 2003, and three of these remained in force by the end of the year.

- A relay in a missile attachment had proven to be unreliable. Restriction: check the relay before a missile is attached.
- The volume of the aircraft's internal radio system could suddenly go into a high setting. Restriction: check that the settings of the radio system are correct before a mission.
- The ground proximity warning system gave too many warnings. Restriction: Ensure that the pilots are aware of this condition.

All three restrictions rely on an incorporeal barrier system to prevent an unwanted occurrence. The first and the second refer to a specific task, checking, that must be carried out as part of a larger procedure. It is therefore possible to complement it by a set of written instructions or by symbols and warnings, i.e., by a symbolic barrier system. The third restriction is different, since it puts the burden on the pilot to keep in mind that some – but probably not all – warnings may be false alarms. From a reliability point of view that is not really an optimal solution. All three restrictions well illustrate both the advantages and disadvantages of incorporeal barriers as summarised by Table 3.5.

Since incorporeal barriers depend on the users' willingness to abide by them, they score low in terms of efficiency, robustness, applicability to safety critical tasks, and ease of evaluation. Their availability is also uncertain since it depends on whether the user remembers them in the situation. They also completely depend on the users' compliance. They may nevertheless be attractive because the resource needs are low, as is the delay in implementation. Unless the population of users have unusually high moral standards, incorporeal barrier systems are not recommended, except as a temporary remedy. There may possibly be a relation between incorporeal barrier systems and safety culture, but this discussion must be saved for another time.

Barriers and Failure Modes

The practical application of barriers to accident analysis and accident prevention requires that the barrier concept be combined with the notion of failure modes. For accident prevention and risk assessment in particular it is important to be able to anticipate how barriers may fail. Although it has been common to look at human failures first and system failures second, the systemic accident model makes it advisable to reverse the order, hence to consider the system failure modes first. Table 3.6 presents a list of ten possible system failure modes, derived from a previous analysis of basic human failure modes (Hollnagel, 1998). The failure modes refer to what has been called the phenotypes of consequences failures, i.e., the ways in which failures manifest themselves. The phenotypes are objective in the sense that they do not depend on a single person's interpretation of what goes on but can be verified either by other observers or by measurements. This also means that it is possible to propose clear criteria for when a failure mode has occurred.

The descriptions in the cells of Table 3.6 can be used directly as a checklist in accident analyses. It would, however, be inefficient to do this in a mechanical or unreflective fashion, since it is unlikely that the failure modes apply equally well to all four barrier systems. Based on the definition and characteristics of each of the four barrier systems, it is possible to propose how susceptible each barrier system may be to a certain failure mode. A physical barrier system, for instance, cannot fail in terms of timing, duration or speed since it is a fixed structure. Following the same line of reasoning, an incorporeal barrier system can only fail in terms of timing (e.g., when the rule is to be applied), object and sequence. The susceptibility of the barrier systems relative to the ten failure modes is summarised in Table 3.7.

Table 3.6: System and human failure modes

	System failure mode	Human failure mode
Timing (time of onset)	A position/location is reached too early or too late. Equipment not activating as required	An action is started too early or too late
Duration (time of cessation)	A function is performed too briefly or for too long. System state held too briefly or for too long	An action is performed too briefly or for too long
Distance / length	System or object transported too short or too far. An object is too short or too long	An object or control device is moved too short or too far
Speed	System moving too slowly or too fast. Equipment not responding as required	An action performed too slowly or too fast
Direction	System or object (mass) moving in the wrong direction	An action or movement is in the wrong direction
Force / power / pressure	System/component exerting too little or too much force, or having too little or too much pressure or power. Equipment not calibrated correctly	An action is performed with too little or too much force
Magnitude	The extent or amplitude of a movement is too large or too small	The extent or amplitude of an action or a movement is too large or too small
Object	Function targeted at wrong object	An action is performed on wrong object or target
Sequence	Two or more functions performed in the wrong order	Two or more actions are performed in the wrong order
Quantity and volume	System/object contains too little or too much, is too light or too heavy	None

Table 3.6 and Table 3.7 are also useful to select the right barrier system as a part of accident prevention. Consider, for instance, the failure mode of distance. Here a physical barrier system can be highly efficient in preventing a movement from being taken too far (although not for preventing too short a movement). A functional barrier system may also be highly efficient, but symbolic and incorporeal barrier systems are both likely to be of little use.

As Table 3.7 makes clear, incorporeal barrier systems are normally rather inefficient even though they are cheap and fast to implement (cf. Table 3.5). This is in agreement with the ordering of approaches to hazard elimination in the MORT technique, where incorporeal barrier systems such as the development of special procedures to handle the situation came last. The other barrier systems may be efficient in different ways and establishing an effective barrier in practice usually requires a combination of several barrier systems. The following chapters will present some principles for how this may be done.

Table 3.7: Relative susceptibility of barrier systems to failure modes

	Physical	Functional	Symbolic	Incorporeal
Timing	None	High	Medium	Medium
Duration	None	High	Low	None
Distance	High	High	None	None
Speed	None	High	High	None
Direction	High	High	Medium	None
Force	Medium	High	None	None
Magnitude	Medium	High	None	None
Object	High	Medium	Low	Medium
Sequence	None	High	High	High
Quantity and volume	Medium	Medium	None	None

Other Types of Barriers

As shown above, barriers have in the past been named in a variety of ways. Most of the barriers can rather easily be subsumed under the four barrier systems proposed here, either as a single system or a combination of systems. The one that may require a little more discussion is the concept of organisational barriers, since it is often used in the context of discussing organisational accidents. As the following sections will show, an organisational barrier is however not a separate category but rather an example of a symbolic barrier system.

In an application of the AEB model, an extensive study looked for the barriers that existed in a given system (the refuelling process in a nuclear power plant) and analysed the reliability of the existing barrier functions (Kecklund et al., 1996). The analysis found a considerable number of barriers and proposed that they be assigned to one of the following three groups: human, technical, and human/organisational. (Note that this differs from the three barrier systems proposed by Svenson, 1991.)

Human barriers were all related to visual inspection or checking of the conditions of the system, or device, to be used. These are all cases of a functional barrier system, where the human operator serves in the role of verifying that a pre-condition has been fulfilled. The human operator was thus not a barrier as such. (A doorman or a bouncer might possibly be.) An example of a technical barrier was that two systems should be aligned before a process could be started, for instance in terms of a mechanical interlock. This clearly corresponds to a functional barrier system as the term is used here. Finally, three human/organisational barriers were identified: (1) permission to work, (2) check of information consistency between two persons, and (3) an administratively forbidden zone. According to the proposal made here, a work order is a symbolic barrier system, a check of information consistency is a pre-condition, and hence a functional barrier system, while an administratively forbidden zone is an incorporeal barrier system.

Hale et al. (2004) proposed that behaviour should also be considered as a barrier. They proposed that a distinction was made between hardware barriers and behavioural barriers. The former corresponds to what here is called physical barrier systems, while the latter seemingly corresponds to the three other classes put together. There can be no disagreement that human behaviour, at both the sharp and the blunt ends, is essential to implement various barrier functions. Indeed, it is only a limited number of barriers that can work completely on their own, and even in these cases humans are needed for periodic inspection and maintenance. Yet human behaviour in all cases serves to implement a specific barrier function relative to a barrier system, rather than as a barrier in and of itself. The distinction between barrier systems and barrier functions is therefore essential fully to understand human behaviour and its role in safety and accident prevention.

Organisational Barriers

We have already seen several references to concept of organisational barriers. Yet an organisation cannot usually be a barrier in itself. The metaphorical example is, of course, the organisation in Franz Kafka's novel 'The Trial'. Here Joseph K. finds himself arrested but is unable to find out what the charge against him is. In a sense the organisation is a barrier that prevents Joseph K. from finding the truth. Yet going beyond the metaphorical sense, it is the functioning of the organisation (or perhaps the lack of functioning), rather than the organisation itself that is a barrier.

If we return to the real world, barriers may be initiated and implemented by an organisation but the barrier is actually in the form of rules or procedures that are carried out by people. The implementation is by an organisation, by people working according to rules, norms, and procedures, but the barrier is not the organisation itself.

Consider, for instance, the issue of getting permission to do something, such as getting the approval of an ethical committee for a research project, or getting the permission of a superior to begin a specific task. In the existing classification, a permission to do something, such as a permission to work, is classified as a symbolic barrier system. The permission is the symbol or token that is required before an activity can be started. The absence of the permission (or token) does not in itself make the work impossible. As a matter of fact, there are many cases where work and activities start before permission is given, either because the permission is anticipated to be granted, or because it is hoped that a *fait accompli* in the end will lead to the permission being issued. Such examples clearly show that this is not a functional barrier system, i.e., there is nothing in the executing system itself that prevents the actions from being carried out, short of ethics or morals (or fear of punishment).

Chapter 4

Understanding the Role of Barriers in Accidents

'I've got my facts pretty clear,' said Stanley Hopkins. 'All I want now is to know what they all mean.'
Arthur Conan Doyle, *The Adventure of the Golden Pince-Nez,* (1904)

Introduction

The first three chapters of this book have put forward the conceptual basis for accident prevention by discussing the nature of causes, providing an outline of the ways in which we can think about accidents, and introducing the principles of barrier systems and barrier functions. The three remaining chapters will use this basis to look at what can be done in practice either to prevent accidents or to protect against their outcomes or consequences.

As the preceding discussions hopefully have shown, the failure or malfunctioning of a barrier cannot in itself be the cause of an accident, although it may have an effect on the further development thereof. A barrier system exists to prevent something from happening but the harmful influences that it is expected to guard against are obviously different from the barrier as such.

In trying to understand the role of barriers in accidents, three issues require attention. The first has to do with how barrier functions can be represented in accident descriptions, either verbally or graphically. This leads to two subsidiary considerations, namely how barrier function analysis can be integrated into accident analysis, and how barrier functions can be used as a part of accident prevention, i.e., in the selection and implementation of effective countermeasures. Put differently, the issue is whether any of the common forms of accident representation – such as event sequences, event trees, and fault trees –

easily can be used to represent barrier systems and barrier functions. This will be discussed using the AEB model and the variation tree diagrams as examples. They represent two common forms – sequence and tree, respectively – and have both been proposed explicitly as the basis for representing barrier functions.

This leads rather naturally to the second issue, which is the complexity of barrier systems and barrier functions. Until now, we have in the main discussed barrier functions in isolation or one by one. A few examples will, however, suffice to show that barrier functions may not always be straightforward to use, that they can have both intended and unintended effects, and that there easily may be interactions among barrier functions that require thorough consideration before they are put to use.

The third issue has to do with barriers and accident prevention. This includes considerations of the responses to accidents seen from the barrier perspective. The predictive aspects have to do with how barriers can be used to prevent future accidents or protect against their consequences, or more generally how barriers can be used to reduce or eliminate identified risks. Here any kind of network or graphical representation is practically an invitation to suggest barriers, since the breaking of a link between two nodes signifies the basic nature of a barrier. The downside is that such representations are static, hence cannot show the possible ways in which barriers may interact or influence each other.

Representation of Barriers in Accident Analysis

Whereas accident analysis deals with events that have happened, risk analysis looks at events that may happen in the future. Risk analysis is an important part of building both technological and social systems, and a considerable number of specialised methods have been proposed over the years. In order to carry out a risk analysis it is necessary to have some description or representation of how an event may develop. This representation is obviously also important for accident analysis, but is somewhat easier to produce here since the event already has happened, i.e., a concrete and known development has taken place. The problem in accident analysis is mainly to get sufficient data and information about what took place; the corresponding problem in risk analysis is to generate plausible but hypothetical combinations of conditions and events that can describe possible future accidents.

In Chapter 2 we looked at a generic accident description known as the 'anatomy of an accident'. This showed how an accident could be described as the result of a component failure, an external disturbance, the incorrect execution of an action, or just an unforeseen combination of states and events that lead to an unwanted consequence. This approach comprises most of the possible causes although only as general categories. More detailed analyses require more specific theories and better methods.

The starting point in accident descriptions is obviously the accident that has happened, specifically the evident consequences or main manifestations. In technical terms, the starting point is usually referred to as the top event, and the analysis is strictly speaking a top-down – or backward chaining – analysis, which in a systematic manner tries to identify the specific combinations of events and conditions that shaped the accident. Among these are, of course, the barriers that failed in one way or the other.

As discussed in Chapter 2, it is important to realise that we cannot conclude that event A is the cause of event B just because A precedes B. It is worthwhile to emphasise this, since it is unavoidable that events of the past are ordered in time when looked at from the present. The reason for this is that time is one-dimensional; anything that has happened necessarily did so at a specific time. Events will therefore inevitably fall into a sequence if they are organised according to their time of occurrence, i.e., one event will necessarily precede the other. (The problem of two events occurring at the same time can be resolved by increasing the resolution of description, i.e., using smaller time intervals. In this way there need never be two simultaneous events, at least in the non-quantum world.) Yet the fact that one event occurred (shortly) before the other may have nothing to do with their causal relations. There is thus more to an accident analysis than simply listing events in the order in which they took place.

Whereas accident analysis by necessity must start from the observed consequence, risk analysis can take place in two principally different ways. One approach, the fault tree, is similar to the accident analysis, in the sense that it begins by a specific, hypothetical outcome or top event and tries to develop all the logically possible combinations of prior events that may lead to that. The second approach, the event tree, starts from a chosen event, usually called the initiating event, and considers the various ways in which this can possibly develop.

Fault trees

The fault tree was first proposed in 1961 to evaluate the launch control system for the Minuteman ICBM (cf. Leveson, 1995) and is now a basic technique in risk analysis for technical systems. The starting point of a fault tree is a possible (unwanted) outcome, which is called the top event. In the example shown in Figure 4.1, the top event is a traffic accident, i.e., the collision of two cars. The analysis goes backwards step-by-step from the top event to find all the possible conditions that could lead to it. This produces a tree of events rather than a simple sequence because there normally is more than one prior condition that may lead to a certain outcome.

In the example shown in Figure 4.1, car A may collide with car B for a number of reasons. (The readers are encouraged to develop a different set of conditions, perhaps based on their own experience.) One condition might be that the road friction is reduced due to aquaplaning or sudden frost (undercooled rain). Another, that there is insufficient time to reduce speed or change direction in order to avoid the collision. A third condition could simply be that the brakes fail, and so on. In technical terms, the top event – that the two cars collide – may come about because of a number of conditions, any of which is sufficient. The or-node in the first level of analysis (shown by the shaded area) means that the collision happens if either condition A *or* condition B *or* condition C, and so on, obtain. (The or-node was already discussed in Chapter 1.) In other words, just one of these conditions will be sufficient. (Note that in the case of an actual accident, it would only be necessary to include those conditions that actually existed at the time. It would thus be known whether the friction was reduced or whether the brakes had failed, hence if one condition was the case, the others could be excluded. For this reason an accident analysis would generate a less complex tree than a risk analysis.)

Either of the conditions found in the first level of analysis may themselves be subject to further analysis. A proper analysis, specifically a risk analysis, needs to understand why each of the conditions preceding the final consequence could occur themselves. (An accident analysis would again be simpler since only the conditions that actually were present would have to be examined.) In Figure 4.1 this is done only for the conditions 'time too short'. In this case it is assumed that time was too short because the other car was detected too late and because the speed was too high. (The two conditions may sometimes affect each other, but they may also genuinely be separate as when the other car suddenly appears from a hidden passage.) This is shown in Figure 4.1 as an *and*-node, which means that both conditions must exist at the same time for the effect to obtain.

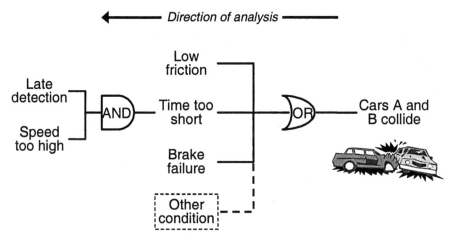

Figure 4.1: A simple fault tree for a collision of two cars

In a risk analysis, the same procedure should be applied to all the conditions found by the previous step and should be repeated for each new set of conditions, as many times as it is reasonable. In practice the risk analysis stops either when it comes to the end of the process under consideration, or when it reaches some action or event for which it is not reasonable to consider an antecedent – although, in principle, the analysis may go on forever. (In an accident analysis, the same principles apply except that there will be fewer conditions to consider and that the stopping point will be easier to identify.) Since there generally will be more that one possibility to analyse for each step, the graphical representation will resemble a tree, although one where the top event is the 'root'. The tree is often drawn horizontally with the top event to the right.

Wrong Drug Dispensed. To show how a fault tree for a real event may look, consider the following incident. On a busy January afternoon, a customer at a local pharmacy somewhere in Sweden gave the pharmacist several prescriptions, including one for a cough medicine for her daughter. On returning home, she realised that she had been given a prescription lotion for skin treatment rather than a cough medicine. The case was reported and the incident thoroughly investigated.

A fault tree based on these events is shown in Figure 4.2. Generally speaking, a wrong drug can be handed out if the pharmacist picks the wrong drug and if the subsequent control of the drug fails. (In the actual case, both of these events occurred.) The and-node means that the top event, the dispensing of the wrong drug, cannot happen if either the pharmacist picks the right drug or if the final control works correctly. The control can fail for a number of reasons, of which three are listed in Figure 4.2. One is that there is a software error in the system (assuming that the control is computerised, as it was in this case). Another, that the staff, due to high workload conditions, may not perform the control procedure correctly. Finally, the interface of the control tool may be inadequate or misleading. In the current case the main reason for the inefficient control was high workload. The pharmacy was understaffed on a day when there was a flood of customers due to the miserable January weather. There was furthermore only one computer terminal available to carry out the medicine control, and the staff was constantly waiting to get access to it. In order to reduce the time needed to handle a transaction, the pharmacist simplified the procedure by entering the numerical code for the drug rather than the name.

Continuing the analysis, there are also several reasons why a pharmacist may pick the wrong drug. One is that the packaging for different drugs may be similar. Another, that drugs are placed in a way that reflects criteria such as manufacturer or product code rather than differences in use. Clearly, if drugs were placed according to their use a cough medicine and a skin lotion would not be next to each other. A further condition, which in itself may be sufficient, hence the or-node in the upper branch of Figure 4.2, is that the names of the drugs are similar. In the present case the two drugs were named *Ephedrinhydroklorid* and *Estradiol,* and were therefore not easily confused by name. On the other hand they did come from the same manufacturer, had very similar packaging, and were placed close to each other because both began with an 'E'. Altogether it is therefore no big surprise that a mistake occurred. The fault tree description can, of course, be extended to include other possible conditions, and readers are encouraged to try that. Yet even from the simple version shown in Figure 4.2 it is clear both that there are several ways in which the top event can occur, and that there also are a number of ways in which the likelihood of this can be reduced or the event even outright be prevented. This example also illustrates how the fault tree can represent the results of an accident analysis as well as of a risk analysis.

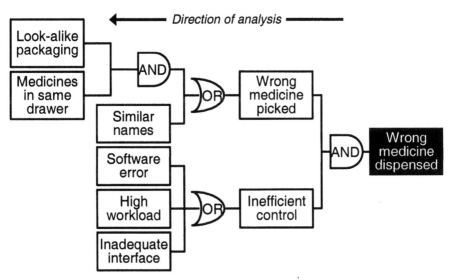

Figure 4.2: Fault tree for wrong drug dispensed

Event Trees

The second main approach to risk analysis starts from an initiating event and considers how this may possibly develop. This approach is rarely applied to accident analysis, for the simple reason that the possible initiating event – or events – is where the analysis ends rather than where it starts. If event trees are used in accident analysis, it is often to support a what-if analysis, i.e., a reconsideration of the accident including hypothetical changes but based on an identification of the likely causes. This is obviously a useful way to consider how potential accidents can be prevented from happening, but in this case it is

practically indistinguishable from a risk analysis – although the flavour
is qualitative rather than quantitative.

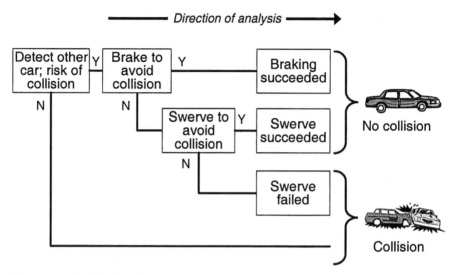

Figure 4.3: The initial steps of an event tree

If we take the same simple example as above, we can define the
initiating event to be that the driver of car A detects car B and believes
that the two cars are on a potential collision course. The driver of car A
therefore responds by braking. In the simplest case there are two
possible outcomes: one is that the braking succeeds and that the
collision is avoided, the other is that the braking fails, in which case the
two cars collide. The two outcomes, success and failure, create a binary
branching from the initiating event. By tradition – or convention – the
'success' branch is shown as the upper branch, while 'failure' is shown
as the lower. Note that there is no concern for why the braking failed,
at least not in the first instance. Just as for the top-down analysis,
further steps can be added by considering the possible developments
following the failure to brake. (There is clearly no need to expand the
success branch.) In this example a possible further action is swerving,
i.e., trying to steer away from car B. (In principle, braking and swerving
might be reversed, although this rarely is the case in practice.) Swerving
can again either succeed or fail, leading to a representation shown in
Figure 4.3, which now begins to resemble a tree, although it is a very
small one.

In practice, the steps that are considered – the nodes of the event tree – are not thought of one by one but are prepared as a whole in advance, for instance in the form of a procedure or a task description. The analysis is then applied for all steps of the task description, in each case considering success and failure as the two possible outcomes. This will gradually produce a binary branching tree where the 'root' is the initiating event and the leaves are the possible outcomes of which some are wanted and others unwanted. (In probabilistic safety assessment, the event tree is further elaborated by assigning probability values to each step, so that the probability of the final outcomes can be calculated.)

To illustrate more clearly the difference between a fault tree and an event tree, the example of wrong drug dispensed (Figure 4.2) is shown as an event tree in Figure 4.4. Notice how this describes the event as developing through a series of steps that may be performed either correctly or incorrectly. If all steps are performed correctly, the result is 'success', i.e., the correct drug is delivered to the customer. Similarly, if all steps go wrong, the result is a failure because the wrong drug will be handed over to the customer. In between are a number of different outcomes. In cases where the correct drug was fetched but where one or more of the subsequent checks failed, the outcome is either a near miss or a serious near miss. The reason is that the right drug was handed over to the customer despite checks that failed rather than because of checks that succeeded. In cases where the wrong drug was fetched but where one or more of the subsequent checks succeeded, the outcome is classified as recovery, i.e., the failure was detected and presumably corrected.

Fault Trees and Event Trees Compared

In relation to the models discussed in Chapter 2, the event tree corresponds to a sequential accident model while the fault tree corresponds to an epidemiological accident model. While both representations rely on a tree structure and therefore superficially look identical, there are some important differences. One is that the fault tree can include the effects of latent conditions (as and-nodes), while the event tree cannot. Another is that the event tree refers to a single sequence of events that are temporally ordered, whereas the fault tree can represent multiple, parallel paths. For example, in Figure 4.2 'wrong medicine picked' and 'inefficient control' both happen prior to 'wrong medicine dispensed', but the tree does not define a relative ordering of these events. A third difference has to do with the position of the 'root'. The two representations can be seen as mirror images of each other, i.e., trees that are (expanding) either to the left or to the right (at least if they are drawn horizontally). But where an event tree node is restricted to binary branching or or-nodes, fault tree nodes can have one, two or more inputs in any combination of or-nodes and and-nodes.

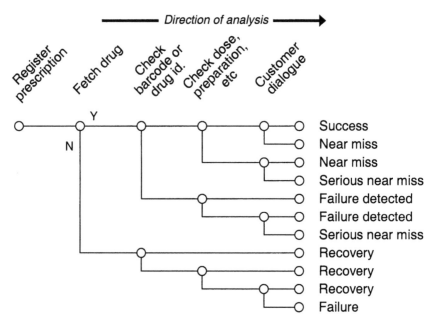

Figure 4.4: Event tree for wrong drug dispensed

Both representations, as graphical renderings, are nevertheless useful to think about barriers. Since barriers serve to block the transport of mass, energy, or information between two points in the system, a barrier can simply be represented by blocking a path in the diagram in some way, for instance by introducing a test or check. This will be illustrated by a number of examples in the following sections.

The AEB Model. We have already looked at the AEB model (Svenson, 1991), which represented the development of an accident as a sequence of steps belonging to the human factors / organisational system or the technical system. As shown by Figure 4.5, each step represents either (1) the failure or malfunction of a component or (2) an incorrectly performed function within each system. Barrier functions, shown by two parallel lines '//', are used to indicate how the development of the accident could be arrested. The comments to the right of the diagram describe in more detail the contents of the barrier.

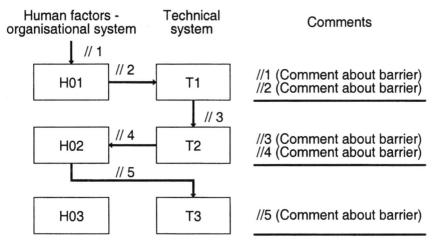

Figure 4.5: The Accident Evolution and Barrier (AEB) function model

The AEB model is basically a single, i.e., non-branching, sequence of actions or events, although these may be grouped to show how they relate to different main categories. The AEB model, as well as the event tree, is well suited for identifying barriers that may possibly prevent a specific development from taking place. But since it only describes what went wrong (Svenson, 2001), it is arguable whether this representation is sufficient for accident prevention where it is necessary to represent actions that fail as well as actions that do not. So while it is easy to represent barriers in the AEB model, it is not sufficiently detailed to serve the purposes of accident prevention.

Variation Diagrams. Another proposal for representing barriers in accident analysis is the variation diagram or 'variation tree' method, proposed by Leplat & Rasmussen (1987). The basis for the variation diagram is the variation tree – or cause tree – originally developed at the Institute National de Recherche et de Securitè (INRS) by Meric et al.,

(1976). The method is based on the recognition that operator 'errors' can be seen as changes to a normal sequence of events, rather than as unique events in themselves. This means that the accident arises from 'variations' relative to the normative or required performance.

Whereas a fault tree is intended to show all the possible ways in which a specific top event can occur, the variation tree mainly refers to an accident that has happened and provides a summary of what the causes were. However, rather than showing only what did go wrong, the variation tree also tries to capture things that could go wrong and thereby lead to the same outcome. The variation tree represents the accident as 'the consequence of a chain of events released and/or conditioned by a number of 'variations' with respect to a normally successful performance' (Leplat & Rasmussen, 1987, p. 162).

Figure 4.6 shows a variation tree for an accident with a lorry. The basic sequence is that the lorry is loaded, driven via the normal route to the destination, and unloaded upon arrival. This can clearly go wrong in many different ways, of which Figure 4.6 represents the following:

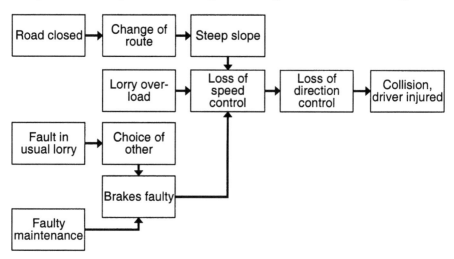

Figure 4.6: Variation tree of a driving accident

- The driver's own lorry is not available due to a mechanical malfunction, and he therefore has to use a replacement lorry.
- The brakes of the replacement lorry are not in good working condition, although the driver is not aware of that.

- The cargo is too heavy for the replacement lorry, leading to a condition of overload.
- The normal driving route is closed due to roadwork, and the driver therefore has to take a different, less familiar route.
- On the detour the driver comes to an unexpected steep slope. In combination with the overload and the deficient brakes, this leads to a loss of control of the speed of the lorry, which in a curve runs off the road and hits a wall, thereby severely injuring the driver.

The purpose of the variation tree is to represent the events and conditions leading to the accident in such a way that it becomes easier to decide where safety measures may be introduced. This can be done either by cancelling a node or by breaking the accident sequence. A variation node can be cancelled by changing the conditions so that the node no longer is active, i.e., so that it no longer exists in the variation tree. The accident sequence can likewise be broken or disrupted in several places. For instance, a break may be introduced between 'change of route' and 'steep slope on route' so that the driver avoids this particular alternative route. This could be done by examining route characteristics before beginning the drive, and deciding not to use the new route if it was dangerous. (Note the similarity to the AEB model on this point.)

It is clear that both 'cancelling nodes' and 'breaking the sequence' constitute barriers in the general sense of preventing something from happening. The description of the variation tree method does, however, not go into details about different types of barriers except by warning against *ad hoc* solutions that may apply only to a single case. This warning is even more important because the variation tree represents an accident that has occurred, and which therefore cannot be undone. At the time of writing, the technique still needs to show its practical worth.

Representing Barriers in Accident Descriptions

Due to their nature, barriers must always be seen in relation to a potential flow of mass, energy, and information – or control. It is therefore natural to base barrier analysis on a representation of possible sequences of functions or successions of events such as time-lines or tree diagrams. A time-line description is a representation of events according to their time of occurrence, usually represented as positions on an axis stretching from past to present. The advantage of a time-line description is that it clearly shows the order in which the events occurred. The main disadvantage is that it usually only shows a single line of action, hence making it more difficult to see how concurrent or parallel paths came together in the accident. The time-line also misrepresents causal or functional relations, since events are ordered by the time in which they occurred rather than by how they affected each other. For that reason alone it is probably advisable not to use a time-line as the basis for thinking about barriers.

As described above, the event tree can effectively represent potential future accidents – and is, indeed, the *de facto* standard approach as of today – but is ill suited to represent accidents that have occurred, for the simple reason that it cannot show combinations of events or actions. Is it technically possible to use an event tree as the basis for deciding about barriers, since it clearly shows which paths may result in unwanted outcomes (cf. Figure 4.4). As barriers represent how failures can be prevented, every 'failure' branch of an event tree is a potential location for one or more barriers. There is, however, a serious limitation with the event tree, namely that the sequence of events is fixed before the analysis. Any variation – such as a reversal of two steps, the omission of a step, or the insertion of a new step – requires that a new event tree be constructed. Since it is quite unlikely that the actual development of events will always match the pre-defined sequence, it very quickly becomes impractical to use the event tree as a basis for realistic accident prevention.

The fault tree is an effective form of representation for both accident analyses and risk assessments (i.e., future accidents). When used for accidents analysis it is usually structurally simpler than for risk assessment, as discussed above. Barriers can be shown as nodes in the fault tree, and in this manner a failed barrier represents a condition that contributes to the accident. If, for instance, the braking of the car in the example used above (Figure 4.1) had been automatic rather than manual (e.g., triggered by a forward sensing radar), then the automatic braking would be a functional barrier system. This could, for instance, be shown by removing the existing brake failure node and inserting a new node for the automatic braking system between the or-node and the collision node. A barrier could also be introduced as an additional condition (input) to an and-node, as that would effectively prevent the propagation of events. Since the fault tree is not limited to representing a single sequence of events and since it allows the insertion of new conditions when needed, it is clearly a better candidate for a representation of barriers in accidents than either the time-line or the event tree.

The Limitation of Graphical Representations

As argued in Chapter 2, accident analysis in many cases requires models that can describe the events on the level of the system as a whole, rather than on the level of system components and their associated functions. The strength of a graphical representation is that it can show a number of things simultaneously, whereas texts or verbal descriptions can only present them sequentially. In order for humans to grasp the relations between structures and functions from a verbal or sequential description, they must somehow 'translate' them in their heads. Although this is entirely possible, and has been developed into a highly specific skill in disciplines such as logic and mathematics, the fact remains that most people find it far easier to grasp the overall relations within a system – and among systems – if they are presented visually rather than verbally, i.e., if graphical representations rather than textual descriptions are used.

Unlike the sequential and epidemiological accident models, the essence of a systemic model cannot be captured by any of the tree-based representations or by simple graphs such as a Petri net. The reason is that these representations all embody the notion of a sequential development, which is inadequate to show the functional dependencies that are so important to the systemic view. The obvious alternative is instead to use a complex graph such as a network. The practical problem is, however, that a representation on a two-dimensional surface is limited in two important ways. The first, and potentially the most serious, is that it is visually misleading. This is a consequence of the fact that it is impossible to place more than three items on a surface without two of them being closer together than the others. The physical proximity of two items, i.e., that they are closer together than the rest, invariably makes them stand out from the rest as described by the Gestalt principle of proximity. The advantage of a graphical representation is that the human brain can easily grasp it and detect patterns, but the disadvantage is that it may also recognise patterns that are neither intended nor meaningful. It is, however, unavoidable that this happens since pattern recognition is a perceptual feature beyond the control of consciousness.

The second limitation is that a graphical representation in two dimensions makes it difficult to draw connections between components that are not neighbours. (This difficulty obviously also exist for a higher number of dimensions, although the number of possible connections increase proportionally. It is nevertheless impractical to go beyond three dimensions, and even that requires sophisticated computer-based visualisation tools.) Yet a functional representation does require that such connections can be shown. While this can be achieved using nothing more complex than pencil and paper, the result soon becomes a mess even if good ergonomic principles are applied. The intuitive grasp of the overview is thereby lost, and the limit is soon reached where a textual description is more efficient.

The Systemic View. Since we do not have access to *n*-dimensional paper to write on (and even if we had it would be very difficult to look at it due to the limitations of our perceptual system), one alternative is to use a graphical representation without connections. (The other alternative, a purely textual description, is not very effective for communication, as argued above.) The advantage of not connecting the nodes is that their position on the representation plane becomes less important. Effects would furthermore no longer have to propagate uniformly from left to right or from top to bottom, but could connect individual nodes according to explicitly defined criteria.

This solution requires some discipline in choosing the form and in the definition of the semantics of the connections. That is actually an advantage, since the normal practice of drawing a line between two boxes (as in most of the figures used in this book so far) leaves the nature of the connection unspecified. Yet in the systemic accident model the nature of the connections or relations is quite important.

A useful basis for such a representation is found in the Structured Analysis technique (Ross, 1977). As seen from Figure 4.7, the basic principle is to characterise a function in terms of what the nature of the function is and what the relations or dependencies to other functions are. These are then specified as:

- *Inputs*, which are the necessary conditions to perform the function and which constitute the link to previous functions. Inputs can be either transformed or used during the performance of the function in order to produce the outputs.

- *Outputs*, which show the outcome produced by the function and thereby constitute the link to subsequent functions.
- *Resources*, which represent items (hardware, procedures, software, etc.) that are used to carry out the function.
- *Controls* or constraints, which describe items such as physical laws, work organisation, control and protective systems that exist to supervise or restrict the function.

This technique was developed within the field of software engineering but has also been used to model the functions of a power plant in a safety analysis (Rasmussen & Petersen, 1999).

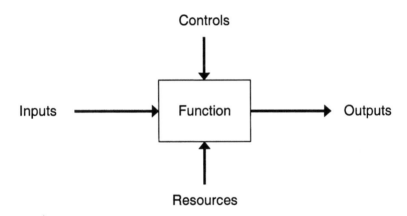

Figure 4.7: Structured analysis diagram

For the purpose of supporting a systemic accident model it is necessary to modify the basic structured analysis representation. The result is a unit with six rather than four possible connectors as shown in Figure 4.8, resembling a hexagon or snowflake. *Inputs* (*I*) and *outputs* (*O*) remain as the two main connectors through which inputs are transformed into outputs, usually with increasing order or decreasing entropy as a result. For example, patients come to an emergency ward in a helter-skelter fashion but come out 'sorted' in categories, if not completely treated. Data to a market analyst comes in scrambled but comes out as comprehensive – or at least ordered – graphs and tables.

Parts come into an assembly line but come out as gadgets. Food ingredients are the input to cooking and the output is (hopefully) a delicious meal.

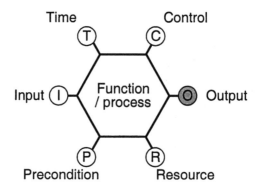

Figure 4.8: The hexagonal function representation

The processing or treatment of the input requires some *resources* (R), often as energy but also as manpower. More formally, the processing consumes either mass, energy, or information. The processing can, however, usually not begin before one or more *preconditions* (P) are satisfied although these need not be fulfilled during the process of transformation. (A further connection could be to a set of execution conditions, but this normally is not necessary.) Examples of such conditions are checklists, availability of resources, plans, backups, etc. The most important precondition is probably that another step or process has been completed (as in event B following event A), or that a specific system condition has been established (as in 'tank level is greater than 21% and less than 90%'). As we shall discuss in Chapter 5, one of the ways in which things can go wrong is if the preconditions are disregarded, which means that the action is carried out even though it should not have been.

The function or process requires some kind of *control* (C) to supervise or restrict the activity (to monitor it and adjust it when it goes astray). Controls can be active functions or just plans, procedures and guidelines. Finally, all processes take place in *time* (T) and are governed by time. Time is in some sense a resource, but it is a resource of a special kind. It is, for instance, not possible to provide more time in the same way that it is possible to provide more money or more electrical power. Indeed, time seems to come in a steady flow and not discrete chunks of different sizes. Time can also be a constraint in the sense that there is a time window for an activity (a duration), for instance defined by an earliest starting time or latest finishing time (Allen, 1983). If there is too little time, one way of saving time is to be less thorough either with the control of how the function is carried out or in verifying the preconditions.

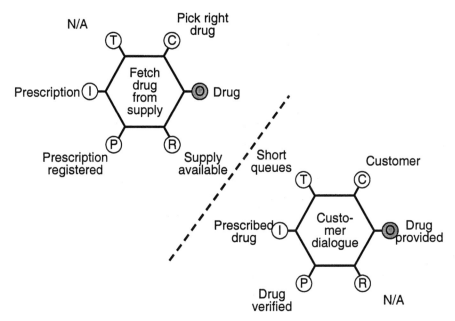

Figure 4.9: The hexagonal function representation for part of 'wrong drug dispensed'

To illustrate how this way of representing an event may work, two of the functions from the procedure for effectuating a drug prescription are shown in Figure 4.9. For each of these, the six connectors are characterised; note, however, that in both cases one connector is seen as being unimportant for that specific function, hence marked as not applicable (N/A). The two functions are not connected in the diagram and do not even follow each other in the formal procedure (which can be gleaned from the upper row of Figure 4.4). However, should the pharmacist for some reason skip the checks of the drug as prescribed by the procedure ('Check barcode or item identification' and 'Check dose, preparation, etc.'), the two functions would suddenly become connected. The output from 'Fetch drug from supply' would effectively become the input to 'Customer dialogue' rather than to 'Check barcode or item identification'. Since, however, 'Customer dialogue' has some preconditions defined, this function could only be carried out if the precondition was skipped, for instance because it was really urgent that the customer got the drug quickly or because the pharmacist did not question the correctness of the drug.

Figure 4.9 only shows two functions, and it is quite obvious that this is a laborious way to show a larger number of functions (in addition to the limitations of graphical representations discussed above). In practice it would be more convenient to provide the same information in a tabular form, and then perhaps use tokens for functions in the graphical representation. If we use the two functions from Figure 4.9 as an example, the result might look like this:

Function	Fetch drug from supply (cabinet of drawers)
Input	New prescription
Output	Drug has been taken from supply
Preconditions	Prescription has been registered by drug name
Resources	Drug is available in supply
Time	Not applicable
Control	Correct drug is taken from supply (name, dose, etc.)

Function	Customer dialogue
Input	Prescribed drug has been verified
Output	Customer has received prescribed drug
Preconditions	All customer items have been handled
Resources	Not applicable
Time	Sufficient time for dialogue, no pressure from queues
Control	Customer understands what pharmacist says

The systemic view emphasises how functions depend on each other and can therefore show how unexpected connections may suddenly appear. The analogy is that the individual 'snowflakes' may come together and create an 'avalanche', i.e., an uncontrolled outcome. Since the representation is at the level of individual functions, there is no explicit description of the overall structure of the system. Instead it is implicitly given, as it can be derived from how the connections between functions are defined. This structure, however, represents the normative organisation of functions, i.e., how events should develop if everything goes according to plan. Since it is unreasonable to assume that this will always be the case, it is preferable to use a representation that makes it possible to account for how events may develop in reality.

Since we cannot be certain that functions will always be connected in a specific way, barriers must be considered in relation to individual functions rather than in relation to an overall structure. In the format shown here, barriers can be associated with any of the five incoming connectors by adding conditions using an and-node. Barriers can furthermore themselves be described as functions, which make it easy to account for the effects of latent conditions and common failures. Event trees and fault trees both require that there is a predefined order among events, temporal in the one case and logical in the other. By relinquishing this requirement the systemic model leads to a representation that is both more flexible and more robust, as we shall see in Chapters 5 and 6.

Complexity of Barrier Functions

So far in this chapter, and indeed in this book, we have talked about barrier functions as if they had a single effect and were independent of each other. In practice, however, barrier functions have multiple effects, of which some are unintended, and may also affect each other, thus making the result less than straightforward. A few examples will suffice to illustrate that.

Reciprocity

Consider, for instance, a modern train equipped with an Automatic Train Control system (ATC). The purpose of this system is to stop the train automatically if it goes through a red light. This is something that happens often enough to be a concern, and indeed so often that it has acquired its own acronym – SPAD, which means 'Signals Passed at Danger' (May & Horberry, 1994). According to the terminology proposed here the ATM is a functional barrier system, whereas the red light (signal) is a symbolic barrier system because it requires that the train driver sees and interprets the signal.

With the exception of a few subway systems, no trains are completely automated. The train driver remains in the train for a number of reasons, one of which is to take over the control of the train in case the ATM does not function. This may happen because the automation itself malfunctions, but is more often due to line maintenance. So whereas the ATM is a barrier in case the train driver fails, the driver can similarly be seen as a barrier in case the ATM fails. This creates the situation shown in Figure 4.10.

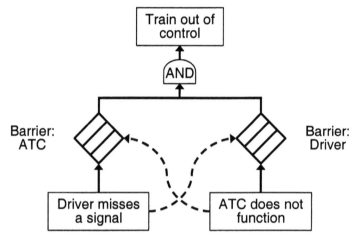

Figure 4.10: Reciprocity between two barrier systems

This relation can be called reciprocity. It means that system A is a barrier (protection) against failures in System B, while at the same time System B is a barrier (protection) against failures in System A. This creates a dependency between the two barrier systems that makes their application non-trivial. There have, for instance, been cases where train drivers for one reason or another turned the ATC off and then missed a signal.

Barrier Bypass

As another example, consider the issues related to getting access to a website or a directory on a computer. Since access can be restricted for one reason or another, a functional barrier in the form of a password or access code usually protects the system. (The same goes, e.g., for doors into many buildings.) Without knowing the password, it is impossible to get access. This lockout (Leveson, 1995) is a basic barrier function and a functional barrier according to the definitions used here.

The downside of this approach is that the user needs to remember the password. Since passwords often can be difficult to remember – partly because some systems put minimum demands to password complexity in order to overcome the human preference for simple passwords – the systems may kindly offer to help. Many web browsers, for instance, offer to keep the password for the user after the first access. Thus, the second time the user tries to access the site, the password is no longer required but is retained by the system. This can be called a bypass or a facilitator, since it relieves the user of having to remember the password. It makes it easier to use the system, but it also goes against the purpose of having the password in the first place.

In cases where such help is not available users often overcome the memory problem by defining passwords that are easy to remember. A concrete example of that is shown in Figure 4.11, which shows a navigation system on a vessel. The Swedish text says 'Network password: 12345678'. Not only is this a password that is easy to remember but it is also written on a piece of paper that is glued onto the monitor. The users would probably have preferred to do without the password altogether, but the system obviously did not permit that.

Figure 4.11: Easy password

The problem with a barrier bypass is that it neutralises the barrier. Anyone who comes to the computer and tries to log in to the site, only needs to guess the user name to be provided automatically with the password. And guessing a user name is usually a lot easier than guessing a password, which is exactly why passwords are needed in the first place. (The problem is also known from trapdoors into systems, i.e., hidden passageways that, if found, bypass all barriers.) The question is whether it is possible to reconcile the two requirements, i.e., to find a single system, which at the same time demands a password, hence provides a protection function, but also allows a simple passage through it. The situation is shown graphically in Figure 4.12. This also illustrates the physical analogy, as when people hide the key to a door near the door – so they can find it if they have forgotten their own key.

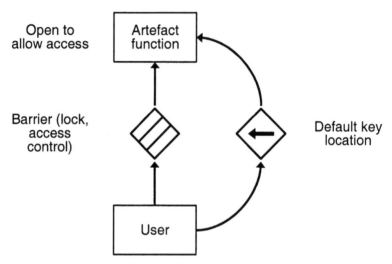

Figure 4.12: Barrier with built-in bypass

One possible solution is to dispense with the password altogether and instead rely on another type of personal identity that does not require the user to remember anything. Examples of that are various types of biometrical data, such as fingerprint recognition, analysis of typing rhythm, iris recognition, speech and voice recognition, etc. Another solution is to consider whether it is sufficient to rely on a single lockout, or whether there are other ways of achieving the goal of protecting the access to data.

Unintended Barriers

The Russian Zarya control module for the International Space Station was plagued by a very high level of noise. This came from the equipment onboard the module, such as fans, air filters, dust collectors and pumps. The noise level could be as high as 72.5 dBA, and even the quietest parts of the space station exceeded the design requirements of 50 to 55 dBA (Seife, 1999). The constant noise made it difficult for the astronauts to get a good night's sleep; it also disrupted work and made voice communication difficult.

A possible barrier against ambient noise is to wear earplugs (a physical barrier system). This would protect the astronauts when they worked in the noisiest parts of the space station. Unfortunately this solution means that it is difficult to hear the acoustic warning signals (alarms). The barrier thus has the intended positive effect of preventing the effects of noise as well as the unintended negative effect of possibly hindering the detection of acoustic warnings. It is not unusual that barriers have side effects, although they are not always as obvious as in this case. The proper solution would, of course, be to reduce the ambient noise but this seems to be so costly that it is out of the question. Another solution would be to switch alarms to another mode or medium, or to increase their volume (intensity) so that the level would overcome the attenuation provided by the ear plugs.

Since few of us are astronauts, a less exotic example is found in the problem of ticking alarm clocks. Many people find it difficult to fall asleep – or indeed to go on sleeping – if there is a ticking alarm clock nearby. (This problem may be less serious today, since most clocks now are electrically driven. Yet there are other noises during the night that may make it hard to sleep.) One solution would be to move the alarm clock further away, so the sound is softer. Another solution is to use earplugs, which will also guard against other types of noises. This solution unfortunately has the unwanted side effect that it becomes more difficult, if not impossible, to hear the alarm clock when it goes off. The situation is illustrated in Figure 4.13.

As this example illustrates, there is no simple solution to the problem, except to change the modality of the wanted input so that it is different from the modality of the noise. Only by doing that will it be possible to provide a barrier against the noise.

Bi-Directional Barriers

A door has several times been used as an example of a functional barrier system which serves to prevent the entrance in to or out of a room. In most cases there is no conflict between getting into or out of a room, since the status of the functional barrier system can be changed at will. Or, in other words, the door can be locked or unlocked on demand. There are, however, situations in which this is not the case, and these illustrate the complex nature of even seemingly simple barrier functions.

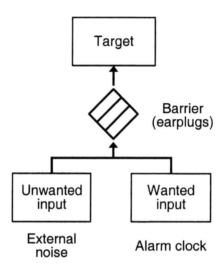

Figure 4.13: Barriers with intended and unintended effects

On July 31, 2003, a fire broke out in the psychiatric clinic at Saint Sigfrid's hospital in the town of Växjö, Sweden. The fire apparently started because one of the inmates had smuggled in some matches or a lighter to her cell and, for unknown reasons, set fire to her bed sheets. The fire fighters arrived four minutes after the alarm had sounded, but found the ward completely filled with smoke and with very low visibility.

The ward in question contained female prisoners sentenced to institutional care. For that reason the doors to the individual rooms, or rather cells, were securely locked and in most of them the windows were made of armoured glass. The intention was, of course, to make it impossible for anyone inside the rooms to get out unless they were let out. The problem in this case was that it was equally difficult for the fire fighters to get in to the rooms, either through the doors or by breaking the windows. As it happened, in the room where the fire started the door had been opened and the windows broken, which was why the fire had spread so rapidly. The tragic outcome of this event was that two of the inmates, 17 and 18 years of age, died while three had to be taken to nearby hospitals for treatment.

In terms of barrier functions, the door functions as a barrier in two directions, both for getting out of the cell and for getting into it, cf. Figure 4.14. Under normal conditions, the staff in the ward have keys so that they can open the doors. The fire happened during the night, the alarm was received at 03:55 in the morning, and the staff were therefore not immediately available. Since the fire fighters did not have access to the keys when they arrived, they instead had to try to break through doors and windows. The situation was made worse by the fact that the staff were uncertain about which rooms the inmates were in.

(In this case the facility also lacked several other barriers, namely a sprinkler system, proper training of the night-time staffs, and procedures for emergency access to rooms at night. The accident was therefore the result of a combination of factors, rather than a single cause.)

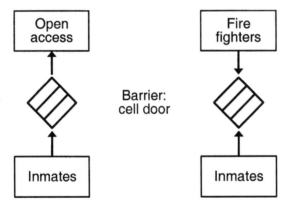

Figure 4.14: Unintended effects of bi-directional barriers

Barriers and Accident Prevention

The main motivation trying to understand accidents is to prevent them from happening again. A cynic might point out that very rare accidents will not happen again, at least not in the same form or with the same manifestation. According to this view it would be rational to do nothing about them, once their uniqueness had been determined. As an example, the explosion of the space shuttle Challenger on January 28,

1986, could be seen as an extremely rare event that would never happen again. (The same could obviously not be said after the loss of the space shuttle Columbia on February 1, 2003.) Yet there are several good reasons why such an attitude is unacceptable. Firstly, we cannot live with the uncertainty, but our whole moral or ethical code requires that a cause must be found and responsibility assigned. Secondly, and more importantly, the analysis may reveal weaknesses in the system, which may lead to other similar accidents, even if the very same accident will never occur again. Thirdly, it always turns out that the very rare accidents are not due to unique causes, but rather are due to an unexpected – and therefore in this sense unique – combination of common factors. This means that other combinations should be expected, hence that it makes sense to do something to prevent these. Note, however, that any response should address the commonness of the factors rather than the uniqueness of the combination.

If we look at how people and organisations respond to accidents, it is possible to distinguish a relatively limited set of typical responses. The concepts of barrier systems and barrier functions discussed in Chapter 3 account for a part of those, but there are other ways to respond than by introducing new barrier functions.

Responding to Accidents

When considering which response to choose, it is first of all necessary to make clear whether the accident really was an unusual – or freak – event or whether it was something that can be expected to happen again. In the case that it is considered a freak or rare event, the decision may be to do nothing. This can either be because it is considered so rare that it is practically 'an act of god' (which means that no reasonable explanation can be constructed using the current scientific vocabulary and beliefs) or because it is objectively known to be so rare that it is not worthwhile to do anything about it. If this way of reasoning seems strange, one need only go to the field of probabilistic risk assessment to realise that it is a fully accepted logic. The main purpose of PSA/PRA is to establish the probabilities of future, risky events and through system design ensure that the probabilities are so low that all worries can be put aside.

In most cases, however, it is necessary to do something, and looking at how people and systems normally respond it is possible to distinguish a characteristic set of ways of responding. Assuming that an acceptable cause has been found, and keeping in mind the cynical definition of causes from Chapter 1, i.e., that a cause is a social construction after the fact (with hindsight) rather than an objective 'truth', there are several characteristic modes of response, listed as the first column in Table 4.1. These are:

Table 4.1: Possible strategies for accident prevention

Main strategy	Type	Example
Replacement	Identical unit or component	
(complete or partial)	Improved unit or component	
	Functional barrier system	Alarms
		Interlocks
		Interface
Prevention	Physical barrier system	Buildings, fences.
	Symbolic barrier system	Rules, tasks
		Procedures
	Incorporeal barrier system	Safety culture
	Task redesign	
Facilitation	Training	
(simplification /	Interface design	Regularisation
clarification)		Grouping
	Support	Attention, memory
	Physical barrier system	Wall
	Functional barrier system	Airbag
	Recovery	System design
Protection		Operational support
		Fault tolerance
	Mitigation	Feedback
		Detection
		Undoing
Elimination	System redesign	
	Recall (withdrawing)	

- *Replacement*, which means that the offending component, i.e., the part of the system that was found to have failed or malfunctioned, is replaced. The replacement can either be by an identical module or component, or by an improved module or component. Replacement is used both for hardware, software, and humans (sometimes called humanware). In the case of software there is, of course, not much gained by replacing with an identical module, since software is not susceptible to tear and wear in the same way as hardware. In the case of humans, the identical module can be another person with the same nominal qualifications, for instance because the 'old' person has become more unreliable or begun to lose his/her capabilities or faculties. The replacement can of course also be used for functions of organisations or, indeed, in rare cases whole organisational units. A common form of replacement is when a product is recalled for improvements, e.g., automobiles. In the case of software, customers have been persuaded to pay for the replacements themselves, incredible as it may seem.

- *Prevention.* As discussed in Chapter 3, prevention is always accomplished by using the four barrier systems, either individually or in combination. Chapter 3 has also given a number of examples of either use. The choice of which barrier system to use often represents a trade-off between time and effort, since complex and resource demanding barriers take time to put into place. Yet while it may be both fast and inexpensive to issue a new guideline or set up a number of warning signs, the effect may soon wear off and thereby make the barrier system ineffective in the long run.

- *Facilitation.* By this is meant that the system is changed or redesigned so that it is easier to use correctly, hence that by default it is more difficult to use incorrectly or to do something wrong. Facilitation is thus in a sense a barrier, but since the barrier function is indirect, it will here be considered as facilitation *per se*. Facilitation can focus on the tasks, by making them less complex, hence easier to do, or on users, in the form of training and re-education. Task redesign can be for the system as a whole, for operational support, or for task design and task/function allocation (roles). Facilitation can occur through interface design, which is a major topic in the fields of human-computer interaction or human-machine systems design; and finally by providing various types of operational support for users, such as procedures, attention monitoring, etc.

- *Protection.* This is the other main group of barrier functions and the other side of the prevention-protection coin. Protection can involve the use of physical or functional barrier systems (whereas symbolic and non-material barrier systems offer little protection).

Protection can also be achieved in different ways, one being to provide means of mitigation, the other being to provide means of recovery. The difference between the two is that mitigation can be used while the system is still functioning or the process is still running, while recovery is something that takes place to restore system functioning after it has gone down or made the transition from an operational to a non-operational state (e.g., hot standby). There are in practice many ways in which mitigation and recovery can be accomplished, but it will be impossible to go into these here. Interested readers may find Kanse (2003) a useful starting point.

- *Elimination.* At the other end of the scale we have elimination, which is the complete removal of the offending system or component. This is a relatively rare occurrence, one of the few examples being the Ford Pinto, which was recalled by Ford Motor Company on June 9, 1978.

The range of options listed in Table 4.1 can be seen as a kind of complement to Figure 1.7, which presented the developments in the typical causes used by accident analysis. Table 4.1 makes clear that barriers are not the only solution to accident prevention, and that the use of barriers for prevention and protection must be seen as relative to other solutions (replacement, facilitation, and elimination). As argued in Chapter 2, the choice of solution will very much depend on the accident model that is being used.

A graphical representation of the potential accident is almost indispensable to choose the proper means of accident prevention. It can help both in suggesting where (and how) barrier functions should be deployed, and also which type of barrier functions (and consequently also barrier systems) should be used. The first step is in many ways easier than the second, since a properly conducted risk analysis will make it evident where barrier functions must be located to bring about the necessary improvements in safety. The second step will inevitably bring issues of cost and efficiency into the choice, and considerations of risk and safety must confront the reality of priorities and resources. While the final decision often is out of the hands of the experts on accident and risk – or even safety – it may still be useful to apply the evaluation criteria and checklists presented in Chapter 3. At the very least it will make it clearer what the pros and cons are of each alternative.

Chapter 5

A Systemic Accident Model

'... I am always unjust, always partial, always exclusive. My excuse is necessity – the necessity which my finite and practical nature lays upon me. My thinking is first and last and always for the sake of my doing, and I can only do one thing at a time.'
(William James, *The Principles of Psychology*, (1890), pp. 959-60)

Introduction

The socio-technical systems on which modern society is based tend to increase in complexity, partly because the technology in itself becomes more powerful and partly because we come to depend more and more on the systems we have created, hence keep tinkering with them to improve their performance. The increasing complexity is not confined to each system by itself but also has the unavoidable consequence that the systems become more closely coupled, i.e., that the interaction and dependency between individual systems increase. It seems as if we are caught in a vicious circle that goes as follows: (1) technological innovations open up new possibilities and enable the construction of new or improved systems; (2) we use the improved systems to make our lives 'easier' – faster planes and trains that travel with shorter intervals, more powerful power plants with narrower operating limits, longer tunnels in difficult environments, communication (sight, sound, data) everywhere and anytime, and so on – and thereby quickly come to depend upon them; (3) in order to meet the demands for safe and reliable operation we require further technological innovation, which – unintentionally – may create new possibilities, etc.

This development led Charles Perrow to put forward the argument that accidents should be considered natural occurrences rather than abnormal and unusual phenomena (Perrow, 1984). The argument was based on the finding that systems had become so complex that humans were unable to control them, neither directly at the sharp end nor indirectly through design and automation. Perrow specifically pointed to the growing complexity of systems, the tighter couplings and the concomitant human inability to understand and control them, as summarised by the following four points.

- Complex systems consist of multiple parts that depend on each other, and there is only a limited possibility of delaying processes or in carrying out actions.
- Actions must generally follow in invariant sequence and there is often only one method to achieve a goal.
- There is limited possibility of slack or of substituting supplies, resources or personnel.
- Buffers and redundancies exist only as they have been designed into the system, and cannot be adjusted to fit unforeseen demands.

The tighter couplings mean that the systems become more difficult to use, not only in terms of actual operation, monitoring and control, but also in terms of maintenance, management, etc. This in turn has consequences for how control stations and interaction facilities are designed, even if we only consider the aspects of operation.

The position taken here is superficially the same as Perrow's, namely that accidents are normal occurrences. But the reasons for taking this position are somewhat different. The argument is that human performance must be variable and approximate because of the complexity of the socio-technical environment, and that it is the variability of performance rather than the complexity of systems as such that is the main reason for accidents. The variability is furthermore not the same as 'human error', and should not be considered as erroneous or unconstructive as such. On the contrary, the variability is a necessary condition for the proper functioning of systems of even moderate complexity and without that they would not work.

The performance variability is not due to human variability as such, if it is understood as coming from the perceptual-motor and cognitive limitations of the human as a controller – although such limitations do exist and are well documented. The variability rather comes from the need to be adaptive in a constructive manner, to be able to make ends meet. It is a deliberate and purposeful variability rather than the residual variability due to a fallible human 'machine' with limited capabilities.

The variability is thus induced by the complexity and demands from the system, which must therefore be considered the source. Since it is impossible significantly to reduce this complexity – as Perrow so forcefully argued, and as his arguments have been borne out by general experience – the alternative is to try to manage the variability. Managing something requires being able to observe or detect it, being able to determine when it is getting out of hand, and being able effectively to introduce countermeasures or mitigating actions. This is in a nutshell what accident prevention is about.

Time and Variability

A system, and the performance or output of a system, is said to be variable if it changes over time – or more precisely if the differences between two measurement values that indicate the status of the system exceed a given threshold. This means that the rate of change of the system is important. Since every system by definition comprises a set of subsystems, it also means that variability can take place on several time scales simultaneously. There is the typical variability of moment-to-moment performance, i.e., performance variability proper, in response to short-term fluctuations in, e.g., resources, demands and working conditions. This takes place on a second or minute level, depending on the nature of the process and the performance. Then there is the variability in the demands from the working environment, which usually are a little slower, although even these can be quite marked and rapid. Examples are the military, electronic commerce, and open-heart surgery. And finally there is the variability of the organisation itself, the slow drifting to new norms and emerging tacit standards for performance. NASA is a good – or perhaps bad – example of that as argued by the report from the Columbia Accident Investigation Board (CAIB, 2003).

For the humans in the system, the different types or ranges of variability correspond to the moment-to-moment adjustments during work, the changes in patterns or modes of work over days or weeks, and the long term changes where experience is consolidated and through which interpersonal and intraorganisational relations – social as well as emotional – fall into place. In this context we are interested mainly in the variability that is related to sources within the work environment itself, since these can be addressed by system design, hence are amenable to efforts of accident prevention.

The variability of performance at various levels can be seen as the way in which people try to remain in control of a situation. It can be argued that human performance requires simultaneous control at several layers, which correspond to different characteristic time-spans or time dynamics of the work environment. A specific suggestion is to describe control on four different layers, called tracking, regulating, monitoring and targeting (Hollnagel et al., 2003). This can be seen as a parallel to the engineering description of multiple embedded control loops, for instance the four loops of flight control, guidance, navigation and tactical flight management in the case of modern aircraft (e.g., Tarnowski, 2003).

If performance variability is the main reason for accidents, one may rightly ask why there were fewer accidents in the past, i.e., before the 20th Century. The reason for that is simply that the systems were less complex, which means that there was less variability in working conditions and demands, hence less need to adjust. In the terminology developed by Perrow (1984), the systems were more loosely coupled and there was therefore sufficient slack in them to absorb the variability of inputs and demands. This is typically also the case when people interact with each other, or when the pace of the process is set by people rather than by technology. Consider, for instance, if two people have to work together to accomplish a task (cutting trees, repairing a machine, etc.). Even though people vary individually, they do on the whole work in the same way and with roughly the same 'natural' speed (John Henry and other supermen excluded). For instance, if each task in an assembly process is done by hand by groups of people, work will flow at a naturally pace – neither too fast nor too slow. If, however, machines or technology does part of the work, the pace will be determined by the optimal speed of the machine, rather than the optimal speed of the human. One need only refer to the – comical – situations depicted by Charlie Chaplin in the film 'Modern Times' to realise that. To make matters worse, machines themselves work at a stable speed or pace and have little if any capability to respond to the variability of their environment, e.g., if the following step in a process is not yet ready. Humans under normal circumstances are quick to detect changes in the conditions of their fellow workers and will respond in a generally constructive and predictable manner. Machines can only detect what they have been told to recognise and are limited to a small set of stereotypical responses. Since the reasons for these responses may not always be clear to the humans in the system, hence creating various situational or even fundamental surprises, the result may be a deteriorating situation once things start to go wrong.

The Principle of Efficiency-Thoroughness Trade-Off

There are very few things that we can do without first ensuring that some conditions are fulfilled or making sure that the necessary resources or materials are available. That goes from cooking *spaghetti carbonara*, to driving to work, to giving medicine to a patient or handing it out to a customer, to starting a nuclear power plant (or any other industrial installation) after a shut-down period, to taking an airplane into the air, etc. In the first case, we must ensure that we have both the necessary ingredients and the necessary equipment (pots and pans) ready. In the second case we must ensure that the car has enough fuel, that we know where to go and how to get there, that there is sufficient time for the travel. When giving medicine to a patient, we must ensure that it is the right medicine in the right dose, and that it is given to the right patient. When starting a nuclear power plant after a shutdown period, all systems must be operationally ready – not least the safety related systems, e.g., Gauthereau & Hollnagel, 2001. And finally, before beginning take-off, even before leaving the gate, a number of checks must be made to ensure that the aircraft is in a ready status.

Similar requirements exist while actions are carried out. In addition to preconditions there are numerous executing conditions that must be monitored and maintained. This is particularly the case for systems that exist in a dynamic equilibrium, such as an aircraft during flight with little or no possibility of reverting to a safe state. In some cases the monitoring of execution conditions is strictly regulated and assisted – or even taken over – by technology, for instance in the form of critical functions (Corcoran et al., 1981). In the majority of cases the monitoring is left to the discretion of people, which means that it is an additional task, although clearly a necessary one. In most work domains, work is further regulated either explicitly by procedures and instructions or implicitly by rules and standards of good practice. These may be present as symbols, instructions, or 'cultures'.

Nominal and Actual Conditions of Work

When a work situation is planned or designed, a number of assumptions are usually made. First, that the inputs to the work process are regular and predictable. (They are obviously predictable if they are regular, but they may be predictable for other reasons as well.) This specifically goes for the input from other people who are part of the work process. And as we have discussed above, this can normally be taken for granted in systems with a low level of technology, where the pace is set by people. Second, that demands and resources are within limits, i.e., that people are not asked to do anything beyond their capacity (in the short or the long run), and that they are not asked to do something without being given the means to do it. (Again, time is among the most important resources.) Here it is important to note that capacity is never fixed, but can vary in complex ways. Third, that working conditions in general fall within normal limits, which means that the system – and especially people – are able to provide the desired output in quality and quantity. Fourth, and finally, that the output, i.e., whatever is produced by the system, complies with the expectations or norms. The ideal situation may look as shown in Figure 5.1.

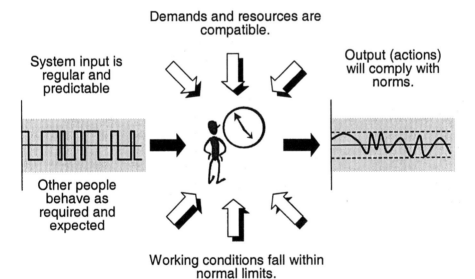

Figure 5.1: Work according to design assumptions

If the design assumptions are correct, that is if the conditions of work match the expectations most of the time, then there is little need for the people involved to deviate from rules and procedures and to make adjustments to the way they work. Another way of stating that is to say that the procedures actually match the conditions. The term *procedures* is used in a wide sense, covering not only what is written, but also the unwritten and unspoken assumptions about details of work. However, it is the case more often than not that the design assumptions are oversimplified, hence in that respect wrong.

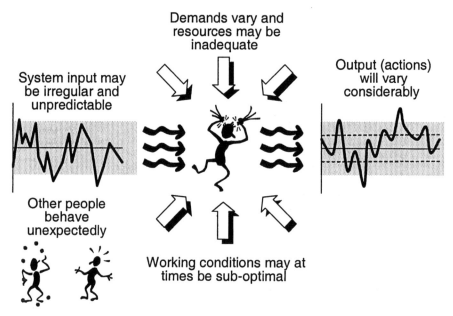

Figure 5.2: Work as it is in reality

In practice it is often found that the inputs to the work process are irregular and unpredictable. This specifically goes for the inputs from other people who are part of the work process, one reason being the couplings in the system (see below). Second, that demands and resources are inadequate and/or incompatible. People are therefore constantly asked to do something beyond their capacity (in the short or the long run), and they are asked to do something without being given the proper means – or time – to do it. Third, that working conditions may fall outside of normal limits, which means that the system – and especially people – are unable to provide the desired output in sufficient quantity and with sufficient quality. Fourth, and finally, that the output, i.e., what is produced by the system, fails to comply with the expectations or norms. Since this output often is part of the input to other people in the system, and definitely to the next step in the process, it provides the link referred to above, hence begins to create a *circulus vitiosus*. The realistic situation may look as shown in Figure 5.2.

The characterisation of the conditions of work has a strong resemblance to some of the details of the hexagonal function representation described in Chapter 4. The similarity is, of course, not fortuitous. The hexagonal representation proposed a formalised way of representing the main factors that have an effect on how a function is carried out. The six connectors corresponded to preconditions, resources, time, and controls – as well as the inputs and outputs. The same factors are found in the descriptions of Figure 5.1 and Figure 5.2, although some of them have been combined.

The Paradox of Optimal Performance

Human actions always have to meet multiple, changing, and often conflicting criteria to performance. Humans are usually able to cope with this imposed complexity because they can adjust what they do and how they do it to match the current conditions. This ability has been described in several ways by terms such as adaptation, optimisation (and sub-optimisation), satisficing, *suffisance*, minimising cognitive effort, minimising workload, balancing arousal, etc. It is probably impossible to account for this behaviour using a single criterion or concept, and the issue here is not to attempt a comprehensive description of how this adjustment, adaptation or optimisation takes place, nor to spell out the possible psychological 'mechanisms' behind, but rather to consider the consequences it has.

As a starting point, we take for granted that people constantly try to optimise their performance. This can be seen as trying to achieve an acceptable balance or trade-off between thoroughness and efficiency – between resources and demands, where both may vary over time. On the one hand people genuinely try to meet their (internalised) goals, i.e., they try to do what they are supposed to do – or at least what they believe it is reasonable to do – and to be as thorough as they find it necessary. On the other hand they try to do this as efficiently as possible, which means without spending any unnecessary effort or time to do it.

The reason for this is not that people are lazy or 'cognitive misers'. The reason is rather that it improves the chances of survival. If all capacity is used for a single purpose, if something is done with the use of complete attention, then there is no capacity left to keep an eye on other things nor any possibility of thinking ahead to prepare for what may be coming. In evolutionary terms this will reduce the chances for survival, since 'enemies' can come too close for comfort. From a strict engineering point of view it also makes sense to retain some spare capacity for general monitoring and planning of what may come next (feedforward), since a system that relies completely on feedback easily will lose control.

In trying to achieve this trade-off, people are greatly helped by the regularity of their work environment and, indeed, the regularity of the world at large. If the work environment were continually changing it would be unpredictable. This lack of predictability would effectively make it impossible to take any shortcuts or indeed to learn how things could be done in a more efficient manner. It is precisely because the work environment has some measure of regularity or stability that it becomes predictable, and therefore allows performance to be optimised by making various shortcuts, which in turn frees capacity and increases the chances of survival.

The benefits of making shortcuts are obvious: they save time and effort. If a person 'always' can assume that condition A is true in situation B, then there is no real need to check for the condition. Instead of checking every possible condition or prerequisite of an action, efforts can be reserved to check conditions that are known to vary across situations, or conditions that are seen as being more salient and important. In the case of RO-RO ferries, if the bow port always is closed when the ferry leaves harbour, then there is no need explicitly to verify this condition. And the bow port is always closed, because regulations say that it should be. Or, to take another example, if a hospital laboratory has routines to ensure that the right type of blood is issued, then it is only necessary to check that the identification of the patient is correct. The nurse has to bring the blood to the right patient, but need not check whether the blood is of the right type.

The Need for Local Optimisation

The net result is that human performance is efficient because people quickly learn to disregard those aspects or conditions that normally are insignificant. This adjustment is furthermore not only a convenient ploy for the individual, but also a necessary condition for the joint system (i.e., people plus other people plus technology) as a whole. Just as individuals adjust their performance to avoid wasting effort, so does the joint system. This creates a functional entanglement, which is essential for understanding why failures occur. The performance adjustment on the joint system level cannot be effective unless the aggregated effects of what individuals do are relatively stable, since this constitutes an important part of the joint system's environment. On the other hand, the efficient performance of the joint system contributes in a significant manner to the regularity of the work environment for the individuals, which is a pre-condition for the performance adjustments they make.

The reasoning behind this is simple. System A constitutes part of the environment for system B, and vice versa. System A can perform in an orderly manner if its environment is predictable. That in itself makes system A's performance orderly and predictable. This in turn enables system B to perform in an orderly manner, hence improving the conditions for system A. Conversely, if the output from system A for some reason breaks down or becomes irregular, system B will be affected because its environment becomes more unpredictable. This will in turn affect system A, and so on. The two systems are effectively coupled to each other and depend on each other in the sense that each contributes to the environment of the other (Figure 5.3). In cybernetics this is known as mutual deviation-amplifying loops (Maruyama, 1963), and in systems theory as dissipative structures (e.g., Capra, 1997).

As far as the level of individual human performance is concerned, the local optimisation – through shortcuts, heuristics, and expectation-driven actions – is the norm rather than the exception. Indeed, normal performance is not that which is prescribed by rules and regulation but rather that which takes place as a result of the adjustments, i.e., the equilibrium that reflects the regularity of the work environment. This means that we should not look for the cause of failures in the actions that constitute normal performance since they, by definition, are not wrong. This is consistent with the view of complexity theory according to which some properties of the system cannot be attributed to individual components but rather emerge from the whole system.

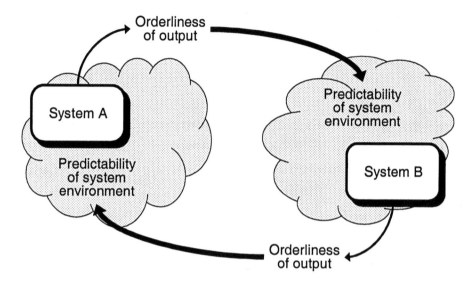

Figure 5.3: Mutually coupled systems

The conclusion is that both normal performance and failures are emergent phenomena, hence that neither need be attributed to or explained by specific components or parts. Instead we should look for how mutual dependencies can arise within the system. For the humans in the system this means in particular that the reason why they sometimes fail, in the sense that the outcome of their actions differs from what was intended or required, should be seen as due to the variability of the context and conditions, rather than to the variability of their actions.

The adaptability and flexibility of human work is the reason for its efficiency. At the same time it is also the reason for the failures that occur, although it is never the cause of the failures. The implications of that will be explored further in the following sections.

Why Things (Sometimes) go Wrong

It is important to understand how normal performance can be the source of both successes and failures. The systemic view emphasises the importance of understanding the dynamics of performance and that people and social systems – but not technological artefacts – are involved in a continuous process of local optimisation. This does not mean, however, that everything that goes wrong should be explained by the same simple principle. There are, indeed, many reasons why people experience a demand-related incapacity where it is difficult to understand what is happening and where they therefore may have problems either in finding the right response or in predicting correctly the consequences of what they are doing. Without claiming to be complete, the following list at least contains the main known sources of problems:

- Lack of training and/or experience for the task at hand or for the situation.
- Inappropriate work schedules and working hours; diurnal (circadian) disruptions.
- Deficient working conditions in general (temperature, noise, humidity, dust, vibration, etc.)
- Misleading design of equipment and interfaces; inadequate or inconsistent operational support.
- Underspecified tasks and ambiguous performance criteria.
- Conflicting, changing or unreasonable demands.
- Incomplete or incorrect procedures and plans.
- Inefficient teamwork and/or collaboration.
- Inefficient communication either in the social level or due to technological problems.
- Detrimental, non-supportive organisational climate.

In addition there may be some situations where the inherent variability of perceptual-motor performance plays a role, such as inadequate control of muscles leading to pressing the wrong button or sudden bursts of colour blindness or retinal insensitivity meaning that a signal is missed. Such situations are, however, very rare and normally not among the main sources of performance variability.

Most of the problems listed above force people to adjust what they do to get the best out of the current conditions. In many cases this means that the tasks have to be modified in some way, because the equipment does not fit, because the resources are inadequate, because the situation is different from what was expected (or taught), or because there are competing demands. Many of these adjustments can be described by a single principle, namely as a case of trading off thoroughness for efficiency.

ETTO Rules

When Dan Goldin, previously an engineer and manager with the US aerospace company TRW, took over as head of NASA in 1992 he inherited an organisation that had its share of trouble. In Goldin's view the problem was that NASA spent too much on single missions and took too long to build them; even worse, the missions were not always successful. Rather than focus on large and expensive missions that could incur costly losses, NASA should build large numbers of smaller, cheaper spacecraft, so that losing one would be bearable. This was dubbed the 'faster, better, cheaper' (FBC) philosophy.

In 1999, after the highly publicised losses of two missions to Mars within a couple of weeks, NASA came under heavy criticism from both external and internal sources (Oberg, 2000). One outcome was the realisation that the FBC philosophy clashed with an old engineering proverb: 'Faster, better, cheaper – choose two of the above.' In other words, it was impossible to meet all three criteria at the same time, and something therefore had to give.

In the experimental study of human performance it is generally found that people tend to make more errors when they respond more rapidly, and conversely that they tend to be more accurate when they take longer. The experiments use situations where people, for instance, have to respond by pressing one of several buttons depending on which signal they are given. This effect is known as the speed-accuracy trade-off, and it is assumed that people make a choice of some kind of whether they want to be fast or to be accurate. The speed-accuracy trade-off is by no means restricted to experiments with choice reaction-time, but can also be found in everyday activities. It has in common with the FBC philosophy that it is impossible to fulfil both criteria at the same time, i.e., people cannot be both fast and accurate – at least not in the long run.

It has already been mentioned that people, in trying to optimise their performance, seem to be trying to achieve an acceptable balance or trade-off between thoroughness and efficiency. Thoroughness means that they try as best they can to do the right thing and do it in the right way, i.e., to choose the correct action and to carry it out as well as possible. Efficiency means that they try to do this without spending too much effort in order to meet the demands of the situation, regardless of whether these demands are imposed by an external source or of their own making.

This efficiency-thoroughness trade-off (ETTO) is common feature of human performance that seems to play a role on the level of individuals and on the level of organisations alike. On the individual level the ETTO principle can be found both in the characteristics of cognitive functioning as well as in how people go about their work.

ETTO on the Level of Cognitive Functioning. In the early 1970s two psychologists, Amos Tversky and Daniel Kahneman, published the results from a number of studies of the mental operations people use in judgment under uncertainty (e.g., Tversky & Kahneman, 1974). The research addressed problems that are fundamental to understand how humans make decisions, and how they determine the likelihood of the events that the decisions are about. It had generally been assumed that people tried to assess probabilities according to the normative models, although with obvious difficulties. What Tversky and Kahneman demonstrated was that people do nothing of the sort, but rather rely on a small number of heuristics, i.e., mental shortcuts that reduce the complex tasks of assessing probabilities to simpler judgmental operations. Prime among these were *representativeness*, meaning that people rely on the degree of similarity between a sample and a reference set; *availability*, meaning that people assess the probability of an event based on the ease with which instances or occurrences can be brought to mind; and *anchoring*, meaning that people make estimates by starting from an initial value but fail to adjust it sufficiently in the light of evidence.

Some years later, Reason (1990a) described a number of error forms, defined as 'pervasive varieties of fallibility that are evident at all performance levels ... (and) ... rooted in universal processes that influence the entire spectrum of cognitive activities' (p. 97). The two main ones were similarity matching and frequency gambling. *Similarity matching* was proposed as being the primary basis of memory search, where the result of a search, e.g., in answer to a question, would be items with attributes that matched wholly or partially the 'calling conditions' of the question. In cases where an immediate answer could not be given, *frequency gambling* was proposed as a way by which a selection was made from partially matched 'answer candidates' so that the more frequently-encountered items prevailed.

ETTO on the Level of Individual Work. Both of the above examples refer to trade-offs made on the level of cognitive functioning, i.e., as a trait of human cognition rather than as a deliberate choice. The latter can be found on the level of how people go about their work. Here it is possible to describe a large number of ETTO rules, of which the following are the typical.

- *Looks OK.* 'It looks fine to me, no real need to go into details. I take responsibility, of course.' A quick judgment replaces a more through check of the status and conditions of the system.
- *Not really important.* 'It looks fishy, but I don't think the consequences really are that serious.' The threshold for taking action in response to a symptom is temporarily raised.
- *Normally OK, no need to check it now.* 'Let's get down to work, this is usually OK.' A check is skipped in order to meet production goals.
- *It will be checked by someone else later.* 'We can skip this step now. Someone else will take care of it later.' A check is skipped, often because of time pressure, on the assumption that it will be done later.
- *It has been checked by someone else earlier.* 'We can skip this step now, it has already been done by someone.' A check is skipped, often because of time pressure, on the assumption that it has already been done.
- *Cannot remember how to do it.* 'There is no one to ask, and it takes too long to find out by oneself.' A step is skipped because the person does not know how to do it, and cannot be bothered to find out. This often indicates substandard training and work organisation.
- *Insufficient time or resources, will do it later.* 'Let's get on with the work, we can deal with this later.' 'Let's finish what we are doing now.' 'We don't have time to do that now.' A task or activity is postponed, because it is not seen as essential for the current assignment.

- *It worked the last time around.* 'There is no need to test this now, the previous batch / time around was fine.' 'Last time I used it, it worked fine.' A check is replaced by reference to anecdotal evidence, often based on wishful thinking.
- *Don't worry, it is perfectly safe and nothing will happen.* Trying to instil a false sense of security in someone else, by referring to authority or experience rather than facts.

Most people will easily recognise one or more of the ETTO rules, and perhaps even have recent experience with them. The reason why people behave in this way is given by the name of the principle: they try to be sufficiently efficient, and they do this by only being as thorough as they believe is necessary. The criterion for making the trade-off is, however, not a fixed one, but depends on the context. For instance, if the external or internal pressure to complete a task or meet a deadline is very high, people will lower their demands to thoroughness, i.e., they are willing to take greater risks. The converse is, of course, also the case, but generally attracts less interest because it rarely leads to unwanted outcomes. It is important to emphasise, though, that people on the whole do not like to take unnecessary risks, but that the conditions sometimes make the risks seem necessary.

The efficiency-thoroughness trade-off can be found on the level of individuals and groups, as well as in the interaction between groups. For example, in chemotherapy it is vital that drugs intended for intrathecal (IT) administration are kept separate from drugs intended for intravenous (IV) administration. It is therefore a requirement within pharmacies that IT and IV drugs should be labelled, packaged, and delivered separately. At a particular hospital it had become practice for ward staff to request the pharmacy to send the two types of drugs together, and the pharmacists complied since they did not want to compromise patient care. The pharmacists presumably thought that they could safely relax their procedure because the drugs would be checked before being administered at the ward. Similarly, the procedure at the ward gradually became relaxed, partly because the staff assumed that the pharmacy had delivered the correct drugs. One day, when many other things were a little out of the normal, the inevitable happened and the wrong drug was administered, with the tragic consequence that a patient died.

ETTO on the Organisation Level. Organisations are at least as prone as individuals to make trade-offs. A pessimistic view would be that they are even more prone, partly due to the separation between the sharp end and the blunt end (more about this in Chapter 6). The main components of organisations are people, and it would be most surprising if their behaviour changed just because they were described as a group and not as individuals.

A quick look at behaviour in organisations suggests the following examples of ETTO rules.

- *Negative reporting.* This is the rule that only deviations from the normal state are to be reported. This means that a lack of information is interpreted as confirmation that everything is safe.
- *Reduction of redundancy.* Efforts are saved by eliminating double checks and independent verifications.
- *Management double standards.* This is a situation where people are pushed to make efficiency-thoroughness trade-offs because of an official management policy that clashes with the official one. Typically, the official policy puts safety first, but in practice people know that efficiency is the more important.

The following section will give a few examples of the ETTO principle as it can be found in practice.

ETTO in Practice

Examples of the ETTO principle can be found daily, both in what we do ourselves and in what others do. Such examples generally illustrate the benign or advantageous aspects of the principle, the ways in which we carry out our work or get through the day without spending unreasonable amounts of effort. Studies of social cognition, from the pioneering work of William James (1842-1910) to the present day, have made clear that people are 'good-enough' perceivers, i.e., they only put as much effort into what they do as is sufficient for them to achieve their goals. 'The pragmatic perceiver does not necessarily maximize accuracy, efficiency, or adaptability; good-enough understanding, given his or her own goals, is the rule' (Fiske, 1992, p. 879). This underscores the argument that ETTO generally is a source of success rather than a source of failure. Unfortunately, we often focus on the more dramatic examples of the negative aspects of ETTO that can be found in practically every incident and accident report.

One area where people often have to make efficiency-thoroughness trade-offs is in the use of procedures. In a questionnaire study with 286 aircraft maintenance engineers, McDonald (2003) found that a full 34% reported not following the official procedure for a task they had just completed. Of these 45% stated that there was an easier way than the official method while 43% said that there was a quicker way.

Trading off thoroughness for efficiency can involve violating a procedure or a safety rule. Polet et al., (2002), reported a study of operators of an industrial rotary press. Since there are a number of serious hazards associated with a rotary press – including burns, falls, and electrocution – operators must respect the prescribed safety procedures. On the other hand, operators are also acutely aware of the compromise between repair quality and lost production time, and therefore tend to take shortcuts wherever feasible. From observations of the operations used to clean the rolls of the rotary press, Polet et al. found two characteristic deviations in the procedure. One was that operators chose not to use rubber gloves, and the other that they worked on the machine while it was still running. When the two deviations were combined, the time taken to complete the procedure was reduced by 57% or 90 seconds. This was clearly a gain in efficiency paid by a loss in thoroughness. The fact that operators were willing to take significant risks to save 90 seconds of time suggests a considerable pressure towards production, hence a double management standard.

The capsizing of the ferry *Herald of Free Enterprise* outside the port of Zeebrügge on March 6, 1987 provides a most dramatic and tragic, example of the compound effects of the ETTO principle under adverse conditions. The *Herald of Free Enterprise* was a modern Ro-Ro passenger and vehicle ferry with two main vehicle decks. At Dover and Calais double-deck ramps were connected to the ferry. At Zeebrügge there was only a single-level access ramp, which could not quite reach the upper vehicle deck. It was therefore necessary to pump water into the bow tanks to facilitate loading.

When the ferry left Zeebrügge not all water had been pumped out of the ballast tanks, causing her to be some 3 feet down at the bow. The *Herald* backed out of the berth stern first. As the ship rapidly accelerated to 22 knots' service speed, a bow wave began to build up under her prow. At 15 knots, with the bow down 3 feet lower than normal, water began to break over the main car deck through the open doors at the rate of 200 tons per minute.

The *Herald* had clamshell doors, which opened and closed horizontally. This made it impossible for the ship's master to see from the bridge if the doors were closed. The captain apparently assumed that doors were safely closed unless he was told otherwise. The assistant bosun, who was directly responsible for closing the doors, was asleep in his cabin, having just been relieved from maintenance and cleaning duties by the bosun. It was later made clear that the bosun did not see door closing as part of his duties. The chief officer, responsible for ensuring door closure, testified he thought he saw the assistant bosun going to close the door.

The *Herald* accident can be viewed in many ways, demonstrating that there is no single truth about any accident. While it is often used as an example of an organisational accident (e.g., Reason, 1990a), it also shows how a combination of efficiency-thoroughness trade-offs can lead to an accident. In the case of the *Herald*, the following were the most important.

- Not all water had been pumped out of the tanks at the time of departure from Zeebrügge. The reason was that this would have delayed the departure. (ETTO rule: Insufficient time.)
- The captain assumed that the doors were closed unless told otherwise. (This is the organisational ETTO rule of negative reporting.)
- The bosun, who had released the assistant bosun from work, did not consider that it was part of his duties to close the bow doors or even to make sure that someone else did it. (ETTO rule: It will be checked by someone else – or perhaps even an additional rule saying it is not my responsibility.)
- The chief officer, responsible for ensuring door closure, testified he thought he saw the assistant bosun going to close the doors. (ETTO rule: Normally OK, looks OK.)

When looked at from this point of view the accident can be seen as an aggregation of trade-offs that creates the conditions for the unwanted outcomes. In the systemic accident model this can be described as the confluence of a set of functions where the normal connections are violated in the sense that preconditions for actions are ignored. Similar to the case of the wrong medicine handed out, this creates connections that were not anticipated when the rules for ferry operation were written. These connections taken together produce the unexpected outcomes.

The Sources of Success

In human performance, local optimisation – through shortcuts, heuristics, and expectation-driven actions – is the norm rather than the exception on both the individual and organisational levels. Normal actions are successful because people find ways of adjusting to the local conditions and learn correctly to anticipate the developments. Failures occur when this adjustment goes awry, but neither the actions nor the principles of adjustment are wrong as such. It is therefore a mistake to look for the cause of failures in normal actions.

The real reason why the outcome of actions sometimes differs from what was required or intended must be found in the variability of the context and conditions rather than in the failures of actions. The adaptability and flexibility of human work is, at the same time, the source of success and the source of failures, but it should never be seen as the cause of failures. Herein lies the paradox of optimal performance at the individual level. *If anything is unreasonable, it is the requirement to be efficient and thorough at the same time – or rather to be thorough when with hindsight it was wrong to be efficient.*

Stochastic Resonance as a Model for Accidents

Chapter 2 presented three different ways of thinking about accidents, corresponding to a sequential, an epidemiological, and a systemic accident model respectively. It was argued that only the latter represented a true non-sequential understanding of accidents, and that it was the preferred alternative for that reason alone. Chaos theory was mentioned as an example of a systemic model, but chaos theory is of limited practical value as an accident model.

Systemic models are, by their nature complex and are therefore also harder to find than the other types. A good candidate for a systemic accident model is found in the principle of stochastic resonance, which describes how noise can induce order in a complex system (Benzi et al., 1981). To understand that, it is necessary briefly to recapitulate what resonance is.

Resonance is a fundamental physical phenomenon, which is well understood and which is the basis for many technical inventions, such as radio and television, to name but two. A simple example of resonance is provided by a playground swing, which in physical terms is a pendulum. Every pendulum has a natural frequency that depends on its length, which means that the swing has a natural frequency that depends on the length of the ropes. As every child soon learns, if you push someone sitting on the swing at the right moment, the amplitude of the swing will increase. In this way even a small child can make a large adult swing by synchronising the pushing with the swing's back and forth cycle. In terms of physics, the push is a forcing function, which makes the swing resonate when it is applied at the natural frequency. The person in the swing can also provide the forcing function, by changing the position of the legs or torso and thereby shift the centre of mass very slightly. This produces a small pushing force which makes the swing go higher and higher. But as everyone also knows, it has to be timed perfectly. Indeed, if the force is applied out of phase with the natural frequency of the swing, it will cancel the movement and gradually bring the swing to a halt.

More formally, resonance is defined in physics as a relatively large selective response of an object or a system that vibrates in step or phase with an externally applied oscillatory or pushing force. Resonance is the increase in amplitude of oscillation of an electric or mechanical system exposed to a periodic force whose frequency is equal or very close to the natural undamped frequency of the system. As illustrated by the example of the swing, resonance requires three basic conditions (cf. Figure 5.4):

- An object or a system that pulsates with a natural frequency. This can be either a mechanical or physical device (think of a guitar or a violin) or an electronic circuit.
- A forcing function that is applied in phase and at the same frequency as the natural frequency of the object and which thereby creates a resonance or makes the object resonate.

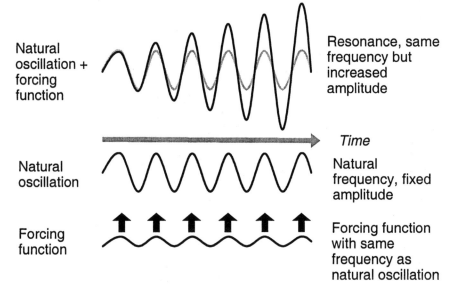

Natural oscillation + forcing function — Resonance, same frequency but increased amplitude

Time

Natural oscillation — Natural frequency, fixed amplitude

Forcing function — Forcing function with same frequency as natural oscillation

Figure 5.4: Classical resonance

- A lack of damping or energy loss. The latter is necessary for the resonance to occur. If the energy loss – due to, e.g., internal damping or friction – is greater than the energy of the forcing function, then there can clearly not be any resonance effect. In order for an object to resonate, mechanical or electrical energy has to build up in the object and anything that removes these forms of energy tends to interfere with resonance. Thus if the person on a swing counteracts the push, the swing will not go higher.

Resonance has been known and used in practice long before it was explained as a physical phenomenon, for instance in musical instruments such as flutes or string instruments. The oscillation can be a mechanical vibration, as is the case when the string is strummed, or when you blow across the top of an empty bottle. An example of acoustical resonance is the vibration induced in a violin or piano string of a given pitch when a musical note of the same pitch is sung or played nearby. Resonance is an efficient way of getting a large output – or forceful result – by amplifying an oscillation. There is, however, a downside to resonance in cases where the amplification is unwanted and where the effect is a loss of control of the system. Resonance is therefore not only an advantage but can also constitute a risk and therefore be the cause of accidents. In modern times the best known example of that is the collapse of the Tacoma Narrows Bridge on November 7, 1940.

Tacoma Narrows Bridge

The bridge was built across the Tacoma Narrows, WA, which is the single point where the Washington mainland and the Olympic Peninsula are close. The bridge was constructed as a 5,000 foot, two-lane suspension bridge, which at the time was the third longest bridge of this type in the world. Work on the $6.4 million bridge began in early 1939 and on July 1, 1940 it was ready to be opened. The Tacoma Narrows Bridge was revolutionary in its design but also known for being peculiarly sensitive to high winds. The shape of the bridge was much like that of an aircraft wing and under windy conditions it would generate sufficient lift and become unstable, swaying and vibrating. It quickly became known as 'galloping Gertie', and people travelled from afar to experience the movements of the bridge.

On Thursday November 7, 1940, the centre span had been rising and falling three to five feet in winds of 35 to 46 miles per hour. Shortly after 10:00 A.M. the motion changed from a rhythmic rising and falling to a two-wave twisting motion, which caused the roadbed to tilt 45 degrees from horizontal one way and then 45 degrees from horizontal the other way. The combined force of the winds and internal stress finally became too great for the bridge and after several hours it broke apart. (This is one of the best-known and most closely studied engineering failures, due in large part to the film and photographs that recorded the collapse. A good analysis of the collapse can be found in Petroski (1994) who also points out that there were a number of precedents. As early as 1949, a report by Professor Burt Farquharson listed ten cases between 1818 and 1889 where suspension bridges had been severely damaged or destroyed by wind.)

To bring the story to an end, designs for a new bridge were completed in 1947 and checked aerodynamically with the use of models. The Tacoma Narrows Bridge opened to traffic on October 14, 1950, and all components of the structure were finally in place by November, 1951. The bridge still stands.

London Millennium Bridge

A – fortunately – less dramatic illustration of resonance occurred 60 years later in London, England. On Saturday June 10, 2000, the London Millennium Bridge was opened for the public. The 320 m long Thames crossing, built at a cost of £18.2 million, linked St Paul's Cathedral in the City with the Tate Modern gallery in Southwark. It was also the first new river crossing in central London since Tower Bridge opened in 1894. The bridge was to be a symbol of the new millennium, a structure so sleek and elegant that its designers called it a 'blade of light'. It was an immediate success, and more than 160,000 people visited it during the weekend. At 22:00 on Monday June 12 the bridge was, however, closed. The reason was that the bridge swayed alarmingly, terrifying those who walked across. After extensive modifications it was opened again for the public on February 22, 2002.

The London Millennium Bridge, or the Bridge of Sways as it became known, was a flat suspension bridge that rested on two concrete piers in mid-river; with four cables running along each side to take some of the load and stiffen the structure. The bridge had been designed using computer simulations to model its behaviour, yet the designers failed to recognise two rather simple facts.

Normal walking pace is about two strides a second, which according to conventional wisdom produces a vertical force at around 2 Hertz. What the engineering intelligence had overlooked was that as a person walks one foot first pushes left, then the other pushes right, which leads to a 1 Hertz horizontal force. This unfortunately corresponded to the natural oscillation frequency of the bridge. It is nevertheless reasonable to assume that if a large number of people walk on a bridge they will be walking out of step, i.e., at different paces, so that the input will be random noise rather than a synchronous force. Indeed, when a company of soldiers are to cross a bridge, they are usually ordered to break step to avoid setting up vibrations.

This assumption is unfortunately only correct if the ground does not move. The second fact that was missed by the engineers is that when people walk on an oscillating or swaying surface, they tend to move in synchrony with the surface. Think, for instance, of people walking on the deck of a boat, where it is natural to match the steps to the movements of the deck. Exactly the same thing happened on the Millennium Bridge. The bridge probably started to sway a little due to the high winds on the day. People on the bridge naturally tried to adjust their balance as the bridge moved slightly, and this created an unintentional synchrony of walking. The synchronised walking made the bridge wobble even more, thereby amplifying the effect to the point where people started to feel unsafe, and the bridge had to be closed.

Unlike the Tacoma Narrows Bridge this did not result in the destruction of the bridge – although it certainly destroyed the confidence of the engineers who had designed it. In time the problem was identified and remedied. In the case of the London Millennium Bridge it turned out – as so often seen – that a number of similar cases had happened before, but that the lessons for one reason or another had not been disseminated through the bridge-building community. One case was the Toda Park footbridge, which spans a river in Tokyo's suburbs. In connection with a boat race on the river, more than 30,000 people crossed the bridge before and after the races. Slight vibrations of the bridge had made the pedestrians walk in step, as reported by Fujino et al. (1993). Several years later the Pont Solferino, a new footbridge over the Seine in Paris, opened on December 14 but closed within a few weeks because of the vibrations pedestrians could feel when walking on it. It was reopened in September 2000 after suitable modifications.

Stochastic Resonance

In all of the above cases the cause of the problems was resonance, and therefore something that in principle should have been foreseen. Since the phenomenon of resonance is well known, the solution was in each case easy once the problem had been recognised. At Tacoma, the bridge had been destroyed and it was therefore necessary to build a new and more stable bridge. In London, the Millennium Bridge was still intact, and the solution was to develop a set of devices that effectively dampened the oscillations. In both cases the resonance was of the classical type and the accidents could be described in terms of a sequential model. The cause was the forces applied to the bridge(s), which created the resonance, rather than the resonance as such. The solution was therefore to block the effect of the forces by introducing dampening, i.e., prevention by a functional barrier system.

In stochastic resonance the relations among forces are a little trickier although the basic principles are the same, namely that an external force amplifies a naturally occurring oscillation. But in order to understand why stochastic resonance is relevant as an accident model, it is necessary first to take a look at noise.

In physical, as well as in practical terms, noise is something that distorts or disturbs. From a technical perspective, noise is something that may degrade a signal. In the introduction to the *Mathematical Theory of Communication*, commonly referred to as information theory, Shannon & Weaver (1969; org. 1949) wrote that:

> In the process of being transmitted, it is unfortunately characteristic that certain things are added to the signal which were not intended by the information source. These unwanted additions may be distortions of sound (in telephony, for example) or static (in radio), or distortions in shape or shading of a picture (television), or errors of transmission (telegraphy or facsimile), etc. All of these changes in the transmitted signal are called *noise*. (Op. cit. p. 78)

Noise is here defined as an error, which is superimposed on top of a true signal, and this is the common view of information theory. For most purposes noise is something to be avoided, and considerable ingenuity has over the years been dedicated to finding ways of avoiding the effects of noise both in technological systems, at work, and in daily life.

In the world of classical resonance, noise degrades either the natural oscillation or the forcing function and therefore produces a more irregular and less distinct outcome. Stochastic resonance in some sense turns the situation on its head since in this case noise can be used to enhance a signal, at least for some non-linear systems. The clue to this lies in the phenomenon of resonance. Noise, and more specifically white noise, can be understood as a signal that includes all frequencies within a given range at equal amplitude. If noise therefore is added to another signal – the message – some components of the noise will obviously amplify the signal, i.e., they will 'push' the signal at the right moment. Unfortunately, other components of the noise will dampen or attenuate the signal, and the net effect is usually that the signal as a whole becomes distorted and harder to distinguish. In everyday language, the signal becomes 'drowned by noise'.

If, however, the signal is weak and hard to recognise in the first place, the addition of random noise may make the signal partly recognisable. In other words, the amplification may at times bring the signal strength over the detection threshold, whereas the attenuation does not make any discernible difference, since the signal is too weak to be recognised in the first place. Without going into the mathematics, the phenomenon of stochastic resonance can be represented as shown in Figure 5.5.

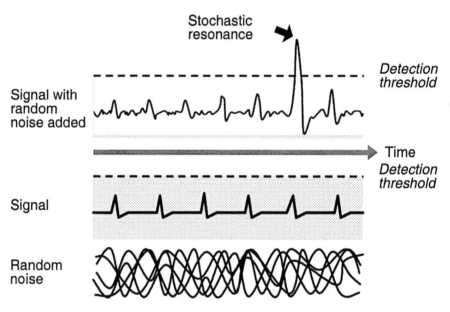

Figure 5.5: Stochastic resonance

More formally, stochastic resonance is a phenomenon in which a non-linear input is superimposed on a periodic modulated signal so weak as to be normally undetectable, but which becomes detectable due to a resonance between the weak deterministic signal and the stochastic noise. Stochastic resonance is generally used to illustrate the noise-controlled onset of order in a complex system. Since stochastic resonance was first described, it has been observed in a variety of physical systems and used, for instance, to account for climate changes. More recently it has also been observed in biological sensory neurons. It has been suggested that it is useful as a way for the brain to extract small amounts of information from quite noisy stimuli. (A further example on a different scale may be in the explanation of the dreaded freak waves.)

A simple – although not everyday – example of stochastic resonance is the following. If you sail along a coastline it may happen that you run aground. If the bottom is sandy, the boat may just get stuck (if it is rocky, the outcome can be more serious). The solution is to push or pull the boat to get it lose. This is done by applying a force to the boat, usually by jumping into the water and pulling a rope while careening the boat to reduce the draft. In many cases the force of the pull is insufficient to get the boat lose. But it may happen that a wave comes along and lifts the boat, so that this in combination with the pull is sufficient to get the boat off the ground. (Technically, the lift reduces the drag.) This is a case of stochastic resonance, in the sense that the wave adds to the force from the person pulling the rope. The wave is in this case the stochastic (or random) input. (A more common example may be, e.g., to pull a boat onto the shore while using the waves to provide additional lift.)

Resonance in Complex Systems

Stochastic resonance can be used to describe how order can arise in a seemingly unordered or noisy system. Accidents are, however, the opposite of order and rather represent conditions where order and regularity breaks down. It may therefore seem strange to propose stochastic resonance as an analogy for accidents. The paradox is nevertheless easily resolved by using the concept of performance variability, which we have already encountered in the description of the efficiency-thoroughness trade-off principle.

Performance is necessarily variable in any complex system, including all joint human-machine systems as symbolised by Figure 5.6. This is due both to the performance variability of subsystems and components, and to the complexity of their interactions (cf. Perrow, 1984). In the case of technological components the performance variability is due partly to imperfections of manufacturing and operation, and partly to the limitations of design in the sense that there are working conditions and combinations of input that have not been and perhaps could not be foreseen. In such cases the performance of a subsystem or component becomes variable. In the case of humans and social systems, performance is variable for many different reasons, prime among which is the human tendency to adjust performance to current conditions, as described above in terms of the efficiency-thoroughness trade-off (ETTO), lack of constancy of perceptual and cognitive functions (such as attention), etc.

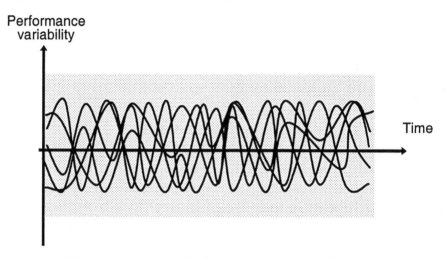

Figure 5.6: Performance variability – multiple weak signals

A complex system will typically comprise a large number of subsystems and components, and the performance variability of each of these can be seen as a periodic weak signal. It is weak in the sense that it is too small to constitute a hazard or to have noticeable effects, mainly because the rest of the system normally catches these before they have time to develop into something bigger. Most complex systems are in practice self-correcting either by design or by nature. The very same perspective can, however, be applied to any subsystem or component and relative to that the performance variability of the rest of the system can be seen as stochastic noise. This means that the definition of what is the 'signal' and what is the 'noise' is relative to the focus. The principle of stochastic resonance makes it clear that every now and then a weak signal, which normally is too weak to represent any problems or be a cause of concern, will be amplified by the background noise so that it rises over the detection threshold (cf. Figure 5.7). The weak signal can be the variability of any part or component of the system and the noise is the aggregated variability of the rest of the system. This corresponds to the view of systemic accident models, according to which accidents generally are due to coincidences or an alignment of conditions and occurrences each of which is necessary but none alone sufficient to lead to the accident.

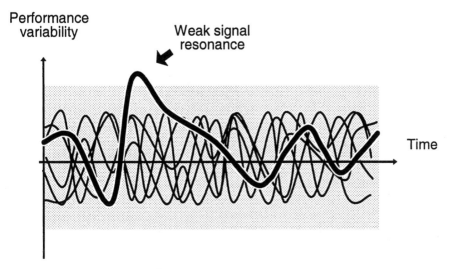

Figure 5.7: Weak signal resonance

As an example, consider a power generating plant that is temporarily shut down for maintenance. This is something that happens regularly in every country, and carrying out the maintenance is indeed (and in this context, paradoxically) often seen as a preventive barrier function on a macroscopic level. The scheduled shutdown does not normally cause any problems since it is carefully planned and co-ordinated. However, it may happen that the shutdown coincides with severe weather, either very hot or very cold, which creates a surge in the demand for power. This may lead to insufficient capacity and cause a brown-out or black-out in a region or a country. In this example the normal weak signal is the maintenance (or rather, the reduced generating capacity that results from that), and the random noise is the variability in temperature or environmental conditions. If the two happen to coincide, the reduced generating capacity may become too small, hence leading to an unwanted outcome. (Conversely, the signal corresponding to the capacity deficit becomes too large.) The problems are exacerbated because power plants are coupled to each other via a grid, so that any disturbance quickly propagates through the system. Since power plants furthermore are designed to protect themselves against overload, either by shutting down or by disconnecting from the grid, a single disturbance can quickly be amplified and lead to a major blackout. In 2003 a number of such events happened in quick succession, one in the US and Canada on August 14, one in London on August 28, one in Sweden and Denmark on September 23, and one in Italy on September 28.

From Stochastic to Functional Resonance

In stochastic resonance the noise is a truly random input that is superimposed on the signal. In that sense the signal is a property of the system while the noise is a property of the environment. In the systemic accident model the delineation between system (weak signal) and environment (noise) is relative, as described above. In principle, any part of the system variability can be the signal with the rest being the noise. The noise is furthermore not truly stochastic but is, to a large extent, determined by the variability of the functions of the system. Since the resulting resonance does not depend on an unknown source but is a consequence of the functional couplings in the system, it is more correct to call it functional resonance than stochastic resonance. Even though functional resonance does not provide the final explanation of why accidents happen, it can serve as a useful analogy to think about accidents and understand how large effects can accrue, with none of the shortcomings of linear and epidemiological models.

Based on the concepts presented and discussed above, it is possible to make a concrete proposal for a systemic accident model. As shown by Figure 5.8 it has the following main components:

- Human performance variability. This comprises both individual performance variability and the variability of social systems (organisations). As described above, two main sources of the performance variability are the ETTO principle and temporary (demand-related) incapacity.
- Technological glitches (shortcomings) or outright failures, either as abrupt malfunctioning or as gradual performance degradation due to tear and wear. Examples of major sources of this are inadequate maintenance and design flaws and oversights.
- Latent conditions in general, which may arise from a number of conditions, such as deficient or slack safety culture, or unclear indications when something has gone wrong.

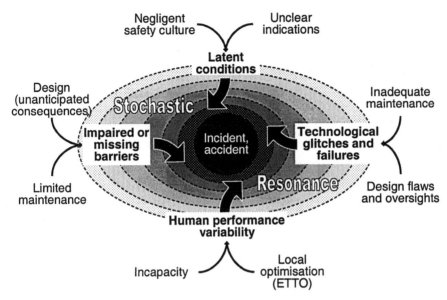

Figure 5.8: Functional resonance as a systemic accident model

- Finally, impaired or missing barriers. This may be due to limited or inadequate maintenance or inadequate design (unanticipated consequences).

Figure 5.8 tries to illustrate that these four main 'forces' do not simply combine linearly thereby leading to an incident or accident. The model rather suggests that their influence is mediated or carried by functional resonance. When looked at separately each source of variability (humans, technology, latent conditions, barriers) is a weak signal and the other sources are random noise. The principle of functional resonance tells us that every now and then they will combine in such a way that the weak signal (human variability, technical failure, latent conditions, or barrier impairment) will rise and lead to a detectable and unwanted outcome. (The model is, of course, not limited to four 'forces' but can be extended whenever needed. The four functions referred to here are, however, sufficient to illustrate the principles.) This model has several consequences for how one should deal with accidents.

- It will normally be of limited value to try to identify the *specific* causes of an accident. For any accident that has occurred there will always be a specific constellation of factors and conditions that led to the accident and thus, in a sense, was the cause. But this constellation is the result of non-linear processes and trying to base prevention on that is therefore unlikely to succeed. Instead one should look at the constellation and try to understand what brought it about. In the case of serious accidents, it is practically guaranteed that the same constellation will not occur again, hence that the same accident will not occur again. This does not rule out that another event may lead to the same consequences, which means that in that sense it *is* the same accident. Indeed, if we consider accidents and classify them in terms of their consequences, many of them are alike, even the serious ones such as controlled flight into terrain, chemical spills, oil spills, explosion, and train crashes. But if we look closer to the aetiology of the accident, no two of them are identical. One should therefore strive to find what is typical for an accident, rather than what is unique.

- We cannot predict exactly when accidents will occur or which types of accidents they will be. (There seems to be the same problem in predicting earthquakes, although probably for a different reason, as argued by Buchanan, 2000.) The timing of accidents is unpredictable because they are the result of non-linear processes. We can, however, forecast where accidents are likely to occur by characterising the variability of the system, specifically the variability of components and subsystems and how this may combine in unwanted ways. This can be done by looking at how functions and subsystems depend on each other. (It is of course also possible to consider how they may combine in desirable ways, such as in supporting creativity and innovation.)

- On the assumption that accidents are due to the unforeseen aggregation of variability, their prevention can be of two kinds: barriers and performance variability management. As noted in Chapter 3, barriers are valuable because they are effective against a specific type of disturbance even if the cause or origin of that disturbance is unknown. Unfortunately, barriers are themselves susceptible to functional resonance, hence may fail at unpredictable times. A second form of prevention is therefore to manage the performance variability. Even though we cannot always isolate the critical variability from an analytical basis, experience tells us that some forms of variability are more troublesome than others. The functional resonance model can be used to define effective ways to monitor and manage performance variability so that harmful developments can be detected and mitigated at an early stage.

Functional Resonance Accident Model (FRAM)

Chapter 4 put forward the proposal for a systemic accident model with individual functions as the elements. Each function was characterised in terms of how it was coupled to other functions using six different connectors (inputs, outputs, preconditions, resources, time and control). This turns out, not coincidentally, to be useful to describe also how functional resonance can occur by considering how the variability of each function may be affected by the variability of other functions. To illustrate how this can be done the previous example of handing out the wrong drug will be used.

The drug dispensing procedure comprises five steps or segments that are significant for the outcome and which can meaningfully be described on their own (cf. Figure 4.4). As in all cases of task decomposition, there are no absolute criteria for what constitutes a meaningful elementary function or activity. It depends on the nature of the domain and the purpose of description. In this example each of the five functions occurs once. But it is entirely possible that a function may occur more than one time, or that the same function may be part of several situations.

The five functions are: 'register prescription', 'fetch drug from supply', 'check barcode or drug identification number', 'check preparation and dose details', and 'customer dialogue'. The five functions are described below using the same template as in Chapter 4, but with some details added.

Function	Fetch drug from supply (cabinet of drawers)
Input	New prescription
Output	Drug has been taken from supply
Preconditions	Prescription has been registered (by drug name)
Resources	Drug is available in supply
Time	Not applicable
Control	Correct drug is taken from supply (name, dose, etc.)

Function	Customer dialogue
Input	Prescribed drug has been verified
Output	Customer has received prescribed drug
Preconditions	All customer items have been handled
Resources	Not applicable
Time	Sufficient time for dialogue, no pressure from queues
Control	Customer understands what pharmacist says

Function	Check preparation and dosage details
Input	Drug taken from supply
Output	Drug preparation details have been verified
Preconditions	Drug name / identity has been verified
Resources	Access to computer
Time	Sufficient time for data entry, no pressure from colleagues
Control	Computer dialogue (software)

Function	Check barcode or item identification number
Input	Drug taken from supply
Output	Drug name / identity has been verified
Preconditions	Drug name has been recorded
Resources	Access to computer
Time	Sufficient time for data entry, no pressure from colleagues
Control	Computer dialogue (software)

Function	Register prescription
Input	Prescription received from customer
Output	Prescription has been registered (by drug name)
Preconditions	N/A (possibly: preceding task completed)
Resources	Access to computer
Time	Do as soon as possible
Control	Data entry validation (software)

The five functions are not listed in any specific order, partly to emphasise that the purpose is to describe the functions rather than the sequence in which they should be carried out, or alternatively the sequence in which they were carried out. (In the concrete case, the two differed.)

The dependencies among the functions are emphasised by using the same descriptions when feasible. For instance, the output (outcome) from 'register prescription' is 'prescription has been registered (by drug name)'. The very same phrase is used to describe the precondition for 'fetch drug from supply'. The reason is that this makes it easier to identify dependencies among functions at a later stage.

The accident model is based on this representation of individual functions, and since the governing principle is that of functional resonance, the model is called the Functional Resonance Accident Model (FRAM). The characteristics of each function provide the basis for describing its potential variability, and the connections are used to find which other functions may be affected. The purpose of characterising the variability is to determine how likely it is that the output will be different from what was stipulated – or in plain language, that it will be wrong. In principle, a wrong output should be caught by the preconditions of the functions that use it, but the variability of performance may mean that the preconditions fail to serve their purpose. In fact, most of the ETTO rules described above refer to various ways in which a check or precondition test can be curtailed or bypassed, and Chapter 4 provided a concrete example of how this could happen.

To make this characterisation of the functions requires detailed knowledge about the domain and the type of work, as well as a good understanding of how performance conditions may affect how a function is carried out. In the first instance it is relevant to consider the proximal factors, such as resources, control, and time. If either of these varies or is deficient, it is likely that the output also will be deficient. Further details of the way in which this can be done will be provided in Chapter 6.

About FRAM

The name of the model has been chosen first and foremost because it provides a meaningful and pronounceable acronym. People with some knowledge of the Scandinavian languages will also recognise that the word *fram* in Swedish and Norwegian means 'forward'. (In Danish the word is spelled *frem*.) Etymologically it is derived from the Greek word *promos*. It is therefore quite appropriate as the name of a model to support accident prediction.

More interestingly, FRAM is also the name of a Norwegian vessel that served in a number of polar expeditions, including Fridtjof Nansen's expedition across the Polar Sea, 1893-1896, with his attempt to ski to The North Pole; Otto Sverdrup's expedition to the areas Northwest of Greenland, 1898-1902; and Roald Amundsen's conquest of The South Pole, 1910-1912. FRAM is reputed to be the strongest vessel in the world, and has advanced further north and further south than any other surface vessel.

Chapter 6

Accident Prevention

'We're prepared for anything, but we like to have luck on our side.'
Rud Moe, Hubble Mission Manager at NASA Goddard Space Flight Center.

Introduction

This last chapter of the book deals with accident prevention, including – as we know by now – the protection against unwanted consequences. Although it is impossible to prevent accidents from happening in an absolute sense, it is, of course, still highly desirable to prevent as many as possible from taking place, especially the serious ones. Similarly, when accidents happen it is useful to learn as much as possible about why they happen.

Chapter 2 discussed how we can understand accidents and presented three model types, called the sequential, the epidemiological and the systemic accident models. The chapter ended by summarising the consequences of each model for accident analysis and accident prevention.

- If accidents are described using a sequential type of model, then the analysis becomes a search for well-defined causes and distinct cause-effect links. The underlying assumption is that once such causes and links have been found they can either be eliminated or rendered ineffective by encapsulation.

- If accidents are described using an epidemiological type of model, then the analysis becomes a search for known carriers and latent conditions. The underlying assumption is that defences and barriers can be strengthened to prevent future accidents from taking place, even though the detailed pathways may be uncertain. Since it may be inefficient to look for a large number of specific carriers and latent conditions, an alternative approach is to rely on reliable indications of general system safety 'health'.

• Finally, if a systemic accident model is used, then the analysis becomes a search for the combinations of performance variability and dependencies that create functional resonance. This reflects the assumption that the variability in a system can be monitored and controlled.

The differences among the models do not mean that only a systemic accident model should be used and that the sequential and epidemiological models should be sent on early retirement. In accident analysis, as in many other aspects of work, it is prudent to be pragmatic and not make things more complex than necessary. Although a systemic model is more powerful and complex than an epidemiological model, which in turn is more powerful and complex than a sequential model, there may certainly be cases where the latter will suffice and where it would be unreasonable not to use it. Indeed, if a single and simple cause can be found one should take advantage of that since it may be easier to do something about it. Experience shows, however, that it is worthwhile to look also at the more complex models and to describe the accident in more detail even if a distinct cause has been found. A single cause in most cases only describes the proximal causes or antecedents (the ones that are nearest in time to the accident), and may miss both latent conditions and causes that are removed in space and time. Since the systemic model in practice comprises the perspectives of both the sequential and epidemiological accident models, hence also the possibilities of both eliminating causes and strengthening barriers, there is good reason to use it as long as it is done in a flexible and considered manner.

The Reality of Risks

A fundamental requirement for any kind of accident prevention is the ability to understand that a risk may exist and to understand it concretely. This may seem trivial and hardly worth mentioning for people who deal with risks in their professional capacity. Yet the ability to appreciate the reality of risk cannot be taken for granted since even hardened professionals at times may become blinded by hope, fear, or hindsight. It is therefore pertinent to take a short look at the issue of how risks can be appreciated. The challenges to understanding and preventing system failures are:

- Whether it is possible to understand what the problem is.
- Whether it is possible to envisage the consequences and to differentiate between large and small risks.
- Whether there are any known means by which the risks can be reduced or eliminated.

A good, although now somewhat remote, example of these problems is the concerns about the transition into the new Millennium – at least according to the Western way of counting years – and the problems this might cause in the use of computers. In the West, considerable commotion surrounded the so-called Y2K problem, since the transition was seen as a potential risk due to some peculiarities of the computing systems in use. This risk was furthermore not confined to the West, since the same information technology had been successfully exported to most of the world.

In the end, nothing untoward happened on a cataclysmic scale. Aeroplanes did not fall from the sky, patients did not die as sophisticated hospital machinery failed, nuclear power plants did not experience scrams, telecommunication systems did not grind to a halt, etc. There were, of course, lots of minor disturbances, but for better or worse life went on as usual. In the aftermath people started asking questions of whether the risks were grossly overestimated and if all the work therefore had been in vain, or whether the risk assessment had been correct and the counteractions effective.

In this case the problem was easy to understand. Everyone, from the man or woman in the street to managing directors and politicians, could see that it was impossible to write a four-digit number with two digits only. It was also easy to understand that a failure to distinguish between, e.g., 1901 and 2001 could have some consequences, although the detailed mechanisms by which it could happen were somewhat obscure. However, everybody knew that computers were all over the place, and everybody had at some point in time had the experience of a computer system failure – either in the bank, at the ticket counter, at work, or at home. It was therefore easy to imagine that seriously bad things might happen if computers began to crash on a large scale.

Finally, there seemed to be an obvious solution, namely to go through the software and change all the places where a year was represented by two digits only. Overall the Y2K problem thus benefited from having a clearly described and easily understood cause, concrete and probable consequences, and finally a clearly defined solution – at least in principle.

The situation is, however, radically different for most of the problems that occur in day-to-day practice. First, it is often not easy to understand what the problem is, or to see that there is a problem at all – at least not until an accident has happened. This is in no small measure due to the success of eliminating the simpler problems, i.e., those due to really bad interface design, to improper working procedures, to poor workmanship, to incompatible working conditions, etc. As a result of that, practically all of the obvious problems have been taken care of, which means that only the complex ones remain. System failures are therefore mostly due to unusual combinations of conditions, which involve the poorly described characteristics of socio-technical systems and organisations. While specialists in human factors, cognitive engineering, or risk analysis may still be able to understand what the problems are, this understanding often eludes other people at both the blunt and the sharp ends.

Second, because the problems are difficult to understand, it also becomes difficult to envisage the consequences and to pinpoint significant risks. The events that one would want to avoid may only occur very infrequently or even possibly be so-called rare events – meaning that they are almost never repeated. Since their aetiology is unclear, it may be very difficult both to determine what consequences may obtain and to assess their likelihood. Finally, even if the risks can be assessed, the complexity of causes makes it hard to identify simple and robust countermeasures. Without a clear focus, it is very difficult to know how to respond, particularly when the response must be cost-efficient.

There is no shortage of examples that can illustrate the above analysis. Indeed, the fact that the first comment to many accidents often is 'we did not think that this could happen here!' is ample proof of that. Any of the major industrial or technological accidents that have been so diligently documented in the past could serve as evidence. If further evidence is needed, just think of the series of blackouts that hit the USA and Europe in August-September, 2003.

In relation to the fields of human-machine interaction and cognitive systems engineering, the lesson to be learned one more time is that *accidents are due to usual actions under unusual circumstances, rather than unusual actions under usual circumstances.* In other words, the exceptions are not nicely tucked away in one spot of the joint system, such as the operator or the interface, but are rather due to the dynamics and the complexity of the functional couplings. People always try to optimise their work, at the sharp end as well as the blunt end and through all stages of the system's life cycle. Sometimes this leads them to lose control of what they do. The challenge is to understand when and why it happens.

Requisite Imagination

One of the important ingredients in understanding that a risk exists, and also in being able to understand the details, is to have imagination. This does not just mean wild speculations but rather the ability systematically to explore the set of possible events.

A common reaction to serious accidents is that they were thought to be impossible. This means that the accidents were imaginable, but that their likelihood of occurrence was assumed to be so low as to be practically non-existing. An even more extreme reaction to some events is to declare them unimaginable. A case in point is the attack on the World Trade Centre in New York on September 11, 2001. Such an attack was to most people beyond the limits of imagination although it need not have been. This leads to some thoughts on the concept of requisite imagination.

Requisite variety is an important concept in cybernetics and control theory. These disciplines are concerned with how a system or a process can be controlled, so that in the end the system behaves as required. Without going into technical details, the principle of requisite variety says that the variety of a controller should match the variety of the system to be controlled. The variety of the system to be controlled comes from the functional characteristics of the system as well as the disturbances that may affect the system. We can think of the variety as all the different conditions that can possibly exist, or all the possible situations that may occur. It stands to reason that in order to control a system, in order to be able to produce the effective corrective or compensating actions (known as the control input), the controller must have at least the same variety as the system to be controlled, i.e., there must be a possible response for every possible condition. The Law of Requisite Variety, formulated in cybernetics in the 1940s and 1950s (Ashby, 1956), states that the variety of the outcomes (of a system) can only be decreased by increasing the variety in the controller of that system. In a striking formulation that achieved a certain degree of fame, the authors expressed the principle by saying, 'every good regulator of a system must be a model of that system' (Conant & Ashby, 1970).

In dealing with accidents in complex systems, Westrum (1993) noted that:

> ... imagination is frequently required to identify possible modes of failure and also possible modes of testing the system. The use of such 'requisite imagination' not only characterizes the top performers, but its absence often figures in the major system failures. (Westrum, 1993, p. 402)

Requisite imagination thus means the ability to speculate constructively about the possible ways in which something can go wrong. Since we know that everything can go wrong, the requisite imagination should in principle be infinite. Gall (1975, p. 92) noted that 'a complex system can fail in an infinite number of ways', that 'the mode of failure of a complex system cannot ordinarily be predicted from its structure', and finally that 'the crucial variables are discovered by accident'. Most accident prediction methods fail to recognise this and continue to work blissfully on the basis of a simple accident model. While the imagination can never be infinite, hence never fully match the possibilities that sooner or later will be realised in practice, much can be done to foster a greater imagination. Indeed, even a small improvement is worthwhile, since many accidents illustrate an extraordinary lack of imagination.

A classical example of this is the aborted launch of the Redstone rocket described in Chapter 1. Seen in retrospect it seems strange that no one realised that the consequence of reducing the length of the tail plug would be that it one day would be shorter than the control cables, hence be pulled out first. Another example is the effect of installing reflector posts along roads. The assumption was that this would give motorists a clearer idea of where the edge of the road was and that they therefore would drive more safely. But the reality turned out to be different. An experiment in Finland in 1990 compared 20 pairs of similar roads. One road of each pair, chosen at random, was equipped with reflectors posts and the other was used as a control. On roads where the speed limit was 80 km/h, drivers drove between 5 and 10 km/h faster and about 60 centimetres closer to the edge, if reflector posts were present. On average the number of accidents increased by 20 per cent, the number of accidents where someone was injured increased by 43 per cent, and the number of night-time accidents soared by 160 per cent! Yet these results should not have been completely unexpected, not least because they were consistent with the theory of risk homeostasis (Wilde, 1982). For most drivers the effect of being able better to see where the road goes is to adjust the driving (position and speed) to take advantage of that. In relation to barriers this means that actual effect possibly may be the opposite of the intended one. This is obviously something one should consider in connection with the design of barriers, as in the following piece of advice:

> Requisite imagination is the ability to imagine key aspects of the future we are planning ... Most importantly, it involves anticipating what might go wrong, and how to test for problems when the design is developed. Requisite imagination often indicates the direction from which trouble is likely to arrive ... It provides a means for the designer to explore those factors that can affect design outcomes in future contexts. (Adamski & Westrum, 2003)

Harnessing Imagination

In both of the above cases (the Redstone rocket, the reflective posts) the undesirable consequence could have been foreseen either by the help of imagination or by using a systematic method. The latter is obviously the more important, because it provides a way of methodically producing the set of possible outcomes and identifying those that are undesirable.

The technique for doing this is generally known as Hazard and Operability Analysis (HAZOP) which was developed by Imperial Chemical Industries in England in the early 1960s (CISCH, 1977). The purpose of HAZOP is to identify all possible deviations from a design's expected operation and all hazards associated with these. The most important part is to analyse each step in a process or procedure using a set of HAZOP guidewords, which represent the following conditions: negation, quantitative increase and decrease, qualitative increase and decrease, logical opposite, and substitution. A typical list of HAZOP guidewords is, for instance, 'no; not; none; more; less; as well as; part of; reverse; other than' (Harms-Ringdahl, 2001). The essence of the method is simply to combine each step with the list of guidewords and consider whether something could happen other than what was intended. If, for instance, a step reads 'pressurise system to 5 kg/cm²', the HAZOP guidewords will force the analyst to consider whether any of the following possibilities may occur: tank is not pressurised, pressure is too low, pressure is too high, two connected tanks are pressurised, tank is depressurised, and another (wrong) tank is pressurised.

The principle of combining guidewords with the description of an activity in order to explore all possible combinations is not unique to risk analysis but has been part and parcel of problem solving techniques at least since the 1940s (Duncker, 1945). The HAZOP guidewords were developed for risk assessment of technical systems, and while they may be used for socio-technical systems as well, it is reasonable to revise the set of guidewords to be able to address also the variety of human failure modes. A good candidate for a revised list is the systematic set of failure modes presented in Table 3.6. If we apply this list to the Redstone accident, we find that the situation can be described either by 'duration, too short' or 'distance / length, too short'. In the case of driving on roads with reflective posts, a systematic examination of failure modes similarly shows that 'distance, too small' – meaning the distance to the road edge – or 'speed, too fast' could describe the unintended outcome.

The use of a systematic list of failure modes is, of course, no panacea. It is a way of ensuring that every possible combination is considered, but cannot guarantee that every combination is considered with equal seriousness or that every possible failure is found. The guidewords are helpful as a principled approach, but cannot and should not be seen as a substitute for human reasoning and imagination. It is clearly necessary to find ways of improving requisite imagination and it is fortunately also possible to do so, as suggested above.

Accident Prediction

In order to prevent incidents and accidents it is necessary to predict them. As we move from the sequential accident model to the systemic, predictions become more difficult because the models become more complex. On the other hand, the predictions also become more realistic, for exactly the same reason. Even a sequential model can be used to predict accidents – but only those that are in accordance with the model! A sequential accident model is, however, a gross simplification of reality and the while the predictions may have a high degree of precision they have a low degree of possibility or likelihood of being correct. The precision is furthermore in terms of the model's phenomena and not in terms of the real world phenomena.

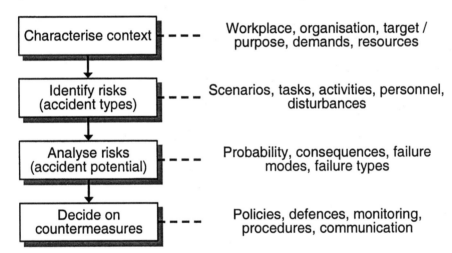

Figure 6.1: A generic approach to risk assessment for socio-technical systems

In a systemic accident model, such as the Functional Resonance Accident Model, it may be impossible to predict accidents exactly. The best that we can do is to make a qualitative prediction of types of incidents / accidents and try to determine the probability that an accident may occur (i.e., calculate the likelihood of functional resonance). This may nevertheless be adequate for most purposes, since it usually is sufficient to know *what* may happen and *how* it will manifest itself, even if it is uncertain *when* it will happen.

Accident prediction is in many ways very similar to risk assessment, since that by definition aims to identify the possibilities for unwanted consequences and events in a system. Risk assessment – or risk analysis – has been used for technical systems for many years and a considerable number of methods and approaches abound, many of proven value (e.g., Aven, 2003; Park 1987; Harms-Ringdahl, 2001). In recent years there has been a growing interest in risk assessment for socio-technical systems as well, and the approach has quite sensibly been to modify technical risk assessment methods to take into account the additional features of socio-technical systems, first and foremost the distinctiveness of human and organisational behaviour. Risk assessment for socio-technical systems – rather than for purely technological systems – often follows the generic approach shown in Figure 6.1.

The generic approach does not specify which type of accident model is used. This may lead to various interpretations of the approach, in particular to differences in emphasis on the various steps or stages. A sequential accident model will put little weight on the first step and rather go directly to the second. An epidemiological accident model might in contrast put more weight on the first step and less on the others.

A systemic accident model makes certain assumptions about how a system should be described and understood and this has consequences for the approach to accident prediction or risk assessment. Whereas a risk analysis normally looks for how individual functions or actions may fail, a systemic accident models focuses on how conditions leading to accidents may emerge. In practical terms accident prediction therefore requires an approach with these steps:

- Identify and characterise essential system functions; the characterisation can be based on the six connectors of the hexagonal representation.
- Characterise the (context dependent) potential for variability using a checklist.
- Define functional resonance based on identified dependencies among functions.
- Identify barriers for variability (damping factors) and specify required performance monitoring.

The following sections will describe each of the four steps in detail, to give a concrete idea of what they entail in practice. The description will refer to the drug dispensing procedure used earlier in the book.

Step One: Identify Essential System Functions

In Chapter 1 a system was defined as the ordered arrangement of a collection of components and functions. The arrangement is ordered because the system is built to achieve a specific purpose (or set of purposes). The determination of what constitutes a system and what constitutes the components is therefore relative to the purpose and the chosen level of description.

It follows from this definition that the identification of the functions of a system cannot be absolute. This is, however, not a problem since functions easily can be defined in terms of their purpose or the goals they can bring about. Functions can be identified in a number of ways, such as a top-down analysis of goals and means, a hierarchical task analysis (Annett, 2003), etc. For example, if the goal or purpose is to deliver the drug specified on a prescription, the necessary functions are to fetch the drug, to check that it is the correct drug as specified, and hand it over. (Other issues that are not described here are to charge the right amount for the drug, to receive payment, to update the inventory list, etc.) The acts of fetching the drug and of establishing that it is correct, in turn become goals or objectives that can be achieved by other functions, cf. Figure 6.2. This recursive identification of goals and functions will after a while identify all functions that are needed to achieve a specific purpose, hence all functions that must be considered for accident prediction.

Most descriptions lead to an arrangement of the functions, such as the one shown in Figure 6.2. This typically depicts the normal or stipulated order akin to a procedure or a task specification. It is, however, important for the purpose of accident prediction not to be bound by such an arrangement, since that invariably constrains the possibilities for finding out how an accident can emerge. This is why the strict format of the event tree makes it unsuitable for accident prediction (but not necessarily for probability calculation for a specific event). This is also a limitation of the fault tree, although that format is far more open to considering alternatives than is the event tree.

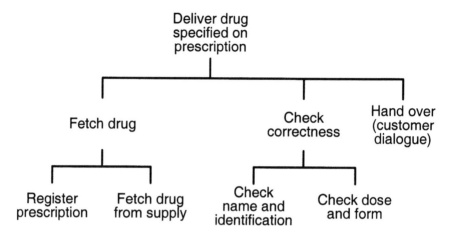

Figure 6.2: Functional decomposition of drug dispensing procedure

The simple solution to overcome this limitation is to do away with the links in the graphical representation. As discussed in Chapter 4, the two main limitations of graphical representations are that they are visually misleading and that they make it difficult to show connections between components that are not neighbours. On the other hand graphical representations are very useful to provide an overview of a system or an event. The main problem seems to be that a graphical representation often comes before the analysis, and therefore may constrain it. If instead the graphical representation is produced after the analysis, the negative side effects will be reduced.

Chapter 5 ended by showing how the five main functions of the drug dispensing procedure could be described in a common object-oriented form without linking the functions explicitly to each other. This description can, of course, easily be reproduced as five independent hexagonal functions or 'snowflakes', following the principles of the FRAM as shown in Figure 6.3. The stipulated normal connections among inputs and outputs have deliberately been left out, but as an exercise the reader is encouraged to indicate them and also to add descriptions of the connectors. When the functions become connected the resulting structure is a FRAM network.

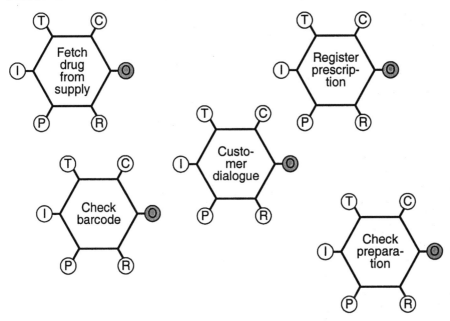

Figure 6.3: FRAM representation of drug dispensing procedure

Step Two: Determine the Potential for Variability

The fundamental feature of functional resonance is that the variability of any function is affected by the variability of the rest of the system. It is therefore an important part of the FRAM method to characterise the potential for variability of each function as well as of the system as a whole.

The potential for variability depends on the nature of the function in question and on its context. The context is normally taken to be the circumstances in which an event occurs or the environment of a system, i.e., that which is outside the boundary. Since the system boundary is relative to the chosen point of view, the distinction between system and environment is also relative rather than absolute. In relation to the FRAM, the context of a function, however, also includes the complement of functions within the system. This complement of functions may in model terms be considered as a first-order context, while the system's environment is a second-order context.

In any practical case there may be a fairly large number of functions to describe and it cannot be known in advance which they will be. It is nevertheless possible to classify any function as belonging to one of three main categories, which usually are called human (M), technological (T), and organisational (O). (The use of M for human comes from the practice in the Scandinavian countries, which have a long tradition of what is called MTO analysis. In the Scandinavian languages the word for human is *menneske* or *människa*, hence the initial M.) The criterion for an M-type function is that it primarily involves the activity of an individual – typically something that takes place at the sharp end. The criterion for a T-type function is that it primarily involves the functioning of a technological system. And the criterion for an O-type function is that it primarily involves an organisational function – typically something that takes place at the blunt end.

The three main categories of M, T, and O functions differ with respect to how volatile the functions are, how much they depend on the context, and their overall speed or rate of change – all relative to the duration of the events under consideration, of course. Human functions – i.e., what humans do – depend very much on the context and are rather volatile, but their rate of change is low. People learn slowly, for instance, or are slow to change tactics. Technological functions (T), are less volatile and depend less on the context. Indeed, technology is usually designed to provide stable performance over a given range of conditions. The rate of change is high since a technological system can change state or mode of functioning abruptly, often without any recognisable indications thereof. O-functions, finally, are sluggish rather than volatile. In most cases they also *are* the context rather than depend on it. The rate of change is very slow, and if they change it is likely to be between situations or events rather than within. They may therefore in practice be considered as constant during a given event.

As an illustration of this, single technological processes typically have a low intrinsic variability, are relatively independent of the context or operating environment, and take place at a high speed. In contrast to that, social and psychological processes have a very high intrinsic variability, depend on the working conditions to a considerable degree, and take place at a slower speed.

Common Performance Conditions. In order to assess the potential for variability it is, however, necessary to increase the level of resolution beyond talking about M, T, and O-functions. Since specific functions cannot be known in advance of any analysis, the alternative is to describe the context or performance conditions in more detail. It has long been generally acknowledged that the performance of humans, as individuals or in a group, to a significant extent is determined by the context. The same actually goes for technological functions although these are somewhat less susceptible. Descriptions of context have traditionally referred to a limited, but not necessarily small, set of factors, which from the start were called performance shaping factors (Swain & Guttman, 1983). Originally suggested as a part of human reliability models to calculate 'human error' probabilities, performance shaping factors slowly changed their role from merely shaping performance to actually determining it. In *A Technique For Human Error Analysis* (ATHEANA) the context was referred to directly as error forcing conditions (Cooper et al., 1996), which perhaps is the strongest possible way of expressing how the context affects functioning. A related suggestion is the notion of General Failure Types (Reason, 1997) defined as the workplace and organizational factors most likely to contribute to unsafe acts.

The FRAM does not endorse the strong assumption that performance conditions directly cause failures or lead to unsafe acts. Instead it simply proposes that the context affects the variability of functions, recognizing that the variability can have positive as well as negative consequences. *The FRAM terminology does not include the concept of unsafe acts, but instead refers to variations of normal actions that for one reason or another may lead to unwanted consequences.* The interest is therefore on how to describe the conditions that may affect performance variability. One proposal for this is the set of common performance conditions that was developed for use in the Cognitive Reliability and Error Analysis Method (CREAM; Hollnagel, 1998). The set originally comprised nine different common performance conditions, but has grown as a result of practical experience so that there now are eleven. Each of the common performance conditions is defined below, including an indication of whether it primarily applies to M, T or O functions.

- *Availability of resources (M, T).* Adequate resources are necessary for stable performance, and a lack of resources increases variability. The resources primarily comprise personnel and material.
- *Training and experience (M).* The level and quality of training, together with the operational experience, determines how well prepared

people are for various situations, hence how variable their performance will be.

- *Quality of communication (M, T).* Another important condition is the efficiency of communication, both in terms of timeliness and adequacy. This refers both to the technological aspects (equipment, bandwidth) and the human or social aspects.

- *HMI and operational support (T).* This refers to the human-machine interaction in general, including interface design and various forms of operational support. The HMI is known to have a significant influence on performance variability.

- *Access to procedures and methods (M).* The availability of procedures and plans (operating and emergency procedures), routine patterns of response, etc., also affect the variability of performance. This can create a synergistic effect with training and experience.

- *Conditions of work (T, O).* The nature of the physical working conditions such as ambient lighting, glare on screens, noise, temperature, interruptions from the task, etc. Working conditions may range from the advantageous to the detrimental.

- *Number of goals and conflict resolution (M, O).* The number of tasks a person must normally attend to and the rules or principles (criteria) for conflict resolution. Clear rules for conflict resolution may significantly reduce performance variability.

- *Available time (time pressure) (M).* The time available to carry out a task; this may depend on the synchronisation between task execution and process dynamics. Lack of time, even subjective, is likely to increase performance variability. Lack of time may be due to too many goals, but can also occur for other reasons.

- *Circadian rhythm (M).* Whether or not a person is adjusted to the current time (circadian rhythm). Lack of sleep or asynchronism can seriously disrupt performance.

- *Crew collaboration quality (M).* The quality of the collaboration among crew members, including the overlap between the official and unofficial structure, level of trust, and general social climate. This comprises the effects of crew resource management, as well as people's enthusiasm for work.

- *Quality and support of organisation (O).* The quality of the roles and responsibilities of team members, safety culture, safety management systems, instructions and guidelines for externally oriented activities, role of external agencies, etc.

For the purpose of determining the possibility of functional resonance, each of the common performance conditions can be rated as above with regard to how volatile they are, how much they depend on the context, and their rate of change. An even more specific description can be used to rate the quality of each common performance condition for a given scenario. In the FRAM the following categories are proposed: (1) stable or variable but adequate; (2) stable or variable but inadequate; and (3) unpredictable. In general, if a common performance condition is stable or variable but adequate, then the associated performance variability will be low. Conversely, if a condition is stable or variable but inadequate, then the associated performance variability will be high. Finally, if a condition is unpredictable, then the variability will be very high. It is easily possible to use a more detailed rating, for instance by making a distinction between the 'stable and adequate' and 'variable but adequate' conditions, but for the initial assessment of performance variability this is not required.

As an illustration, consider the function 'register prescription'. This function involves both M and T aspects, since it is carried out by people but makes use of technology. The variability of this function can therefore be affected by ten of the eleven common performance conditions. Considering that this function is carried out by a single person rather than a team, and that the place of work furthermore is a pharmacy with regular working hours, the set of relevant common performance functions can be further narrowed to the following five: availability of resources, HMI and operational support, conditions of work, number of goals, and available time. What remains is, for the given scenario, to assess the quality of each common performance condition.

Step Three: Define Functional Resonance Based on Dependencies among Functions

After identifying and characterising the essential functions in Step 1 of the FRAM procedure, and determining their potential variability in Step 2, the next step is to describe the dependencies among functions. Since the dependencies must account for both correct and incorrect connections between functions, it is not sufficient to rely on the normal procedure or task. Indeed, the main purpose of this step is to look for connections that could occur under certain conditions even though they should not.

It is possible to find the dependencies in a system by noting whether the variability of one function A can affect another function B. This requires that function B is connected to function A, in the sense that the outputs from function A provide one or more of the inputs to function B (input, preconditions, resources, control, time). Any single function may obviously depend on two or more other functions, just as any single function may constitute the pre-condition for two or more other functions (i.e., a many-to-many mapping). By using this simple principle to describe the dependencies between pairs of functions and then combining these, it is possible to produce an overall description of the dependencies that exist for the aggregated larger system.

Finding the Expected Connections. The expected connections can be found simply by looking for matching descriptions of input and output. (This is one reason why it is useful to be concise in the descriptions, and to use similar terms wherever possible.) The outputs may well go outside the system, i.e., cross the boundary. In that case they need not be considered further, except if there are external demands to the quality and quantity of outputs. In the drug dispensing procedure, the expected connections are easily found, and look as shown in Figure 6.4. Each connection also names the 'common element'.

In some cases the same output goes to more than one other function. This is the case for 'fetch drug from supply' where the output 'drug taken from supply' feeds into three other functions. (It is also the case for 'Prescription received from customer', although this is the output from an external function.) In other cases there are several inputs to a function. Consider, for instance, 'check preparation' where one input is material, the 'drug taken from supply' from the function 'fetch drug from supply', and the other is information, the 'drug identity verified' from the function 'check barcode'. The latter is the input to the precondition, which means that the drug preparation only should be checked if the drug name has been verified previously, i.e., it serves as a functional barrier system. It is finally also possible that there may be several qualitatively different outputs from a function, although this is not the case in the present example.

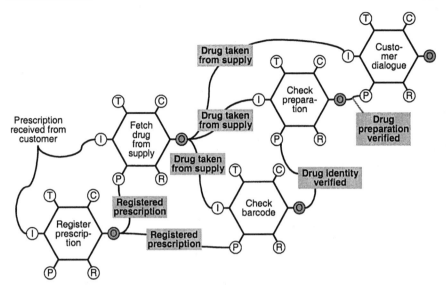

Figure 6.4: FRAM network for expected function connections

The connections shown in Figure 6.4 represent the normal and expected steps through the drug dispensing procedure. This FRAM network is incomplete because it only shows the details of the input, output, and precondition connectors. The three other connectors (time, resources, and control) should also be filled out to provide the full basis for appreciating how events may develop. The time input will, for instance, affect the variability of the function as discussed above. In Figure 6.4, four of the functions will only be carried out if the preconditions are fulfilled. This provides a protection against unwanted outcomes, i.e., against incidents and accidents. It is easily seen that this presentation is different from both an event tree and a fault tree, primarily because it represents a flow of material (the drug) as well as a flow of information (the outcome of the checks). In general, a FRAM network should represent all the connections or flows of importance and define them clearly. It is also evident that the network structurally is more similar to a fault tree than an event tree. Whereas a fault tree shows the logical conditions required for something to fail, i.e., the top event, the FRAM network shows the logical conditions for something to go right. It thereby provides the basis for finding out what can go wrong, hence what may be done to prevent an accident.

Finding the Unexpected Connections. For the purpose of accident prevention it is necessary to consider how something can go wrong and why. The FRAM network provides an easy way of doing that simply by considering how specific connections may be invalidated or fail. This can be shown as in Figure 6.5, where all the preconditions are marked as failed. (This can obviously be done also for any other connectors that are in use.)

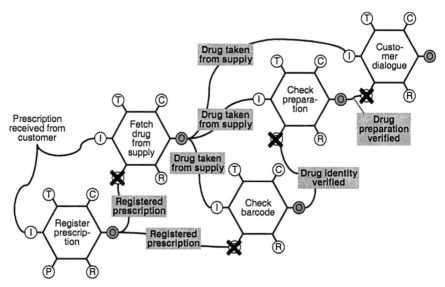

Figure 6.5: FRAM network for unexpected function connections

Consider, for instance, the function 'Customer dialogue'. This should not normally take place unless the drug preparation has been verified, which in turn requires that the drug identify has been verified. But if the precondition test for 'Customer dialogue' is relaxed or even fails, then it is possible for the customer to get the 'Drug taken from supply' without it having been verified. If that drug in turn is a wrong one, then the final outcome will be unwanted. 'Customer dialogue' is an M-function and the important common performance condition for the precondition is available time; should time be too short, the precondition may be curtailed by an efficiency-thoroughness trade-off. Since time is a common mode (cf. below), this may lead to a functional resonance condition where consequently the whole procedure fails and the customer is given a wrong drug.

The same considerations should clearly be made for each of the other functions, as well as for all the functions together, i.e., for the task as a whole. An equivalent, but possibly simpler, way of determining whether functional resonance is likely is by relaxing the matching requirements. For the FRAM network shown in Figure 6.4, the requirement is a complete match, e.g., that the output from 'fetch drug from supply' (= drug taken from supply) matches the input to 'check barcode or item identification number'. If, however, the condition is relaxed to read just, e.g., 'some drug' corresponding to a condition of reduced attention or limited time available, then additional matches become possible, cf. Figure 6.6. This is obviously equivalent to the failure of a precondition test, but simpler to implement because it can be done directly from the template description of functions, thereby avoiding rendering unnecessary the graphical representation.

Figure 6.6 does not show the whole task, but only the first-order connections that involve 'some drug' as an output-input. Once these have been found, the same procedure can be repeated for the outputs of the functions involved to see which further connections may become possible if the matching requirements are reduced. (In the present example, the number of functions is regrettably too small to illustrate this. For a larger set of functions this exercise should be done directly from the template descriptions, since a graphical representation quickly becomes unwieldy.) In this way all possible connections can gradually be found, expected as well as unexpected ones. Figure 6.6 shows that one of the first-order connections goes directly to the final step of the drug dispensing procedure. This means that a wrong outcome may result if this condition obtains, independent of whether any of the other functions fail.

A major reason for functional resonance is that people (and artefacts) exist within a common context, which may affect the variability of several functions in the same way. If, for instance, the pressure to perform at the sharp end is high due to production or efficiency demands, then that will likely affect all tests and checks that are part of the procedure. For any given function the context, defined as the complement of functions within the system boundary, therefore becomes more variable and the variations may unexpectedly reinforce each other leading to a state of functional resonance.

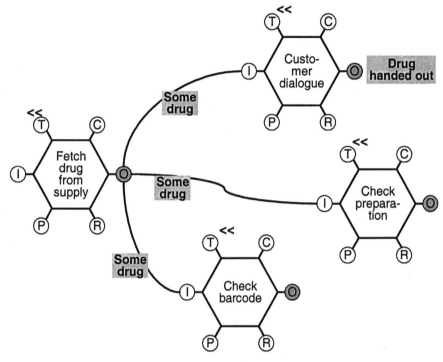

Figure 6.6: First-order links in a FRAM network

For technological systems this condition has been recognised as the common cause failure or common mode error, the main effect of which is that components do not fail independently. What is true for technological systems is obviously also true for humans, and the effect is probably much stronger here. This can be shown as in Figure 6.6, where the '<<' marks at the time connectors indicate that time is limited throughout. If people have common assumptions or work under common conditions (such as limited time or inadequate resources), they are likely to make the same kinds of efficiency-thoroughness trade-off. The effect of the performance conditions is thereby amplified, allowing a small deviation to produce a disproportionately large result. One consequence of that is that the only reasonable way to guard against functional resonance is to have qualitatively different barrier functions rather than the same function repeated for redundancy.

Step Four: Deciding on Countermeasures

Both accident analysis and risk analysis may identify a need of prevention or protection. When this happens, the first question is clearly *where* in the system barrier functions should be introduced or, in other words, where the barriers should be placed. A barrier serves to stop or block the flow of something, regardless of whether it is mass, energy or information and regardless of whether the flow is going in or out. Although a barrier function in the analysis is a virtual function, it must be realised or implemented in a concrete manner. That usually involves determining where in the system it is going to be located, since all systems have a physical basis. Some suggestions for how this can be done were described in Chapter 4. A FRAM network can certainly also be used for this purpose.

Although it may be tempting to use a description of past accidents as the basis for decisions about changes or improvements to barrier functions, it is not advisable to do so. The reason is that the same development is unlikely to occur again, even if the system is only moderately complex. This is not the same as adopting the cynical view described in Chapter 4, according to which it is unnecessary to guard against the repetition of a complex accident sequence since in practice it never will happen. It is rather an acknowledgement of the fact that it is impossible to have sufficiently detailed knowledge about the actual conditions that existed for an accident situation, and likewise to be equally precise in predicting future accidents. Even a systemic model such as the FRAM is a simplification of reality, although it avoids the fallacy of assuming complete determinism and the linear propagation of effects.

The second question is *which* type of barrier functions – and obviously also barrier system – to use. The natural approach here is to start from barrier functions since they often can be realised in several different ways. Choosing a barrier function and an associated barrier system is not just a question of considering the primary purpose, i.e., the immediate and specific effectiveness of the barrier function, but must also include other aspects such as costs, delays in implementation, requirements to maintenance and support, etc. The choice must therefore be based on a detailed assessment of the various aspects of barrier systems that were presented in Chapter 3. In doing this it must also be kept in mind that the design and use of barriers itself is vulnerable to the biases of human reasoning that have been found in judgement and decision making, as described, e.g., by Tversky & Kahneman (1974), and to efficiency-thoroughness trade-offs. It may even be more affected by other factors, such as economic considerations, political convenience, or public opinion. (For an alternative analysis of this see Merton's (1979) discussion of the Law of Unintended Consequences that was mentioned in Chapter 1.)

Performance Variability Management

The main message of this book is that the way we think about systems has consequences for how we respond to them, both in direct interaction and in developing more considerate responses. Each of the three accident models described in Chapter 2 has consequences for how unwanted performance outcomes are dealt with, and specifically for the measures that are taken to improve system safety during design and operation. The corresponding three approaches to accident prevention can be called 'error' management, performance deviation management, and performance variability management, respectively.

- *'Error' management* is based on the assumption that the development of an accident is deterministic, as implied by the sequential accident model. Consistent with that assumption, it should be possible to identify a clear 'root cause' – or set of 'root causes' – and therefore to prevent future accidents by eliminating or encapsulating the identified causes. 'Error' management represents a 'seek and destroy' approach according to which 'errors' should be either eliminated or encapsulated so that they can do no harm. It thus corresponds to the policies of elimination or replacement, as described in Table 4.1.

- *Performance deviation management* recognises that accidents may have both manifest and latent causes corresponding to the epidemiological accident model. Instead of looking for the 'root cause', which may be difficult or impossible to find, the search looks for traces or signatures of deviations or unsafe acts on the assumption that suppressing or eliminating these will prevent accidents. Although performance deviation management is a step forward from 'error' management, it still entails the view that 'errors' or deviations are negative and therefore undesirable. As argued by Amalberti (1996), among others, 'errors' or deviations have a useful function as well, since they make it possible to learn from incidents and accidents. Indeed, deviations from the norm can have a distinct positive value and be a source not only of learning but also of innovation. In order for this to work the system must have sufficient resilience to withstand the consequences of the uncommon action and it must be possible for users to see what has happened and how it happened.

- *Performance variability management* is a way of recognising the dual nature of performance. This approach recognises that unwanted outcomes are the result of the functional resonance that emerges from the variability in coupled systems. This variability can be seen at every level of system description and for every kind of system – from mechanical components to organisations. This approach shares the assumption with performance deviation management that there are specific profiles or signatures of variability that can be monitored. The difference is that the monitoring can be the basis for suppressing the variability that may lead to unwanted outcomes as well as for enhancing or amplifying the variability that may lead to positive outcomes.

Performance variability management comprises the belief that accidents generally represent the outcome of complex interactions and coincidences rather than specific failures, and that accidents cannot be explained by simplistic cause-effect relations. Such coincidences are due more often to the normal performance variability in the system, rather than to actual failures of components or functions. (One may, of course, consider failure as an extreme form of performance variability, i.e., the tail end of a distribution.) To prevent accidents it is therefore necessary to describe the characteristic performance variability of a system, to explain how such coincidences may build up, and to propose how they can be detected.

Detection and Control of Performance Variability

Accidents usually build up over time, although there may also be cases where they happen abruptly and without warning – although it is often found with hindsight that warnings were present but that they were not noticed. It should therefore be possible to find indicators of the accident before the actual onset and use these as a basis for preventive actions. This is, as we have seen, a central feature of the epidemiological accident model. While monitoring the performance variability is an important part of accident prevention, the variability that precedes the accident is not the only thing to be controlled. The aftermath of an accident is also important, particularly since it can be of a considerable duration. A very general characterisation of accident development recognises four distinct phases, which are: (1) normal operation, (2) pre-accident build-up, (3) the actual accident with the immediate consequences, and (4) the post-accident period with the long-term consequences. For each of these phases performance variability management takes a separate form as monitoring, detection, dispersion, or correction (Figure 6.7). Monitoring and detection correspond to what in Chapter 3 was called prevention; similarly dispersion and correction correspond to what was called protection. The four functions can by themselves be considered as four high-level barrier functions.

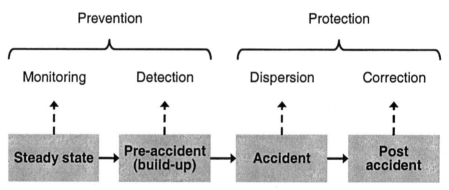

Figure 6.7: Performance variability management functions

- *Monitoring of steady-state performance.* Here the main concern is to keep an eye on how the system performs, including individual (critical) functions. While monitoring is not a barrier function as such, effective monitoring can prevent accidents. Monitoring may involve functions such as observation, confirmation, managing, and recording, and the observation of system states and trends.

- *Detection during pre-accident build-up.* During this stage the main objective is to detect large or unusual variations in the performance of functions and systems. Detection is a genuine part of accident prevention, and many specific solutions have been developed. Examples of technological solutions are alarm systems; examples of organisational solutions are incident reporting and quality control. Detection involves functions such as identification, verification, and questioning or probing, and typically relies heavily on functional barrier systems.

- *Dispersion during the accident itself.* When the accident happens, the first stage of protection is to reduce or disperse the immediate consequences. Some characteristic functions here are attenuating, partitioning, and reducing the direct effects, as well as strengthening defences and resources. Dispersion generally works by separating objects in time and space or reducing contact area or duration of exposure.

- *Correction during the post-accident phase.* The post-accident or recovery period constitutes the second stage of protection. This covers a longer time period and can be seen as a way of correcting what went wrong, involving replacement, modification and improvement of both barrier systems and barrier functions. This may lead to the replacement of functions and resources as well as modifications of rules, criteria and procedures, or even a complete redesign of the system in part or in whole. The correction is usually a long-term affair that goes on for weeks or months, sometimes taking even years in the case of exceptionally large accidents.

The high-level barrier functions of monitoring, detection, dispersion, and correction correspond to characteristic stages in the development of an accident, as mentioned above. Each of the high-level barrier functions can be implemented by one or more barrier systems, where the choice depends on the stakeholder's requirements and constraints as well as the prerequisites for the individual functions. For example, a correction implemented by an incorporeal barrier system, such as a new rule, can be taken into use very quickly and inexpensively. On the other hand, incorporeal barrier systems are rarely effective in the long run, since they require a high degree of compliance by those involved.

The relation between the four high-level functions and the four types of barrier systems is developed in more detail below.

- *Monitoring* involves an act of reasoning or interpretation of data and can therefore be provided by a functional barrier system (e.g., an early warning system, a long-term detection system), as well as by a symbolic barrier system – provided there is someone to interpret the symbols. For the very same reasons it is not possible to implement monitoring by a physical barrier system or an incorporeal barrier system. Monitoring can be considered as a management function in two different ways. First, because it is important for actually managing the process in the long term. Second, because it often is done by the higher echelons of the organisation, i.e., the management level.
- For *detection*, a similar line of argument can be used. Detection is usually functional and can be implemented by technology (as a functional barrier system) with or without human collaboration. Detection by humans (either unaided or aided by machines) can also rely on symptoms, which in that respect serve as complex symbols for the process state. Detection cannot be provided by a material barrier system, nor by an incorporeal one, since it involves an act of reasoning or an act of identification / interpretation.
- *Dispersion* is usually provided by a material barrier system, such as a wall, a fire corridor, etc. It can also be provided by a functional barrier system, such as interlocks, airbags or sprinklers. Dispersion cannot be provided by a symbolic barrier system, since it requires concrete changes to the direction of matter and energy. The same argument goes for incorporeal barrier systems.
- *Correction* can take place for a material barrier system, such as restoring it. Correction can also be applied to a functional barrier system, e.g., by developing new interlock. It can be provided for a symbolic barrier system such as developing new signs and symbols, and finally also for an incorporeal barrier system such as instituting new laws. In each case, however, the correction is not brought about by the barrier system itself, but requires the actions of an external agent such as a team of specialists or an organisation.

In terms of barrier functions, performance variability management comprises both prevention and protection. It is usually thought of in relation to the processes and events at the sharp end, since this is where accidents show themselves. On that level of performance the people at the sharp end, i.e., the operators, implement variability management. Their performance may in turn be subject to performance variability management, which in this case is carried out as a managerial function within the organisation. In the true spirit of the systemic accident model, the managerial functions should also be subject to performance variability management, since they in their own way may be fully as variable as the processes and events at the sharp end. This must be done recursively since there is a limit to how many times yet another layer can be added to the organisation.

The Receding Sharp End

The concepts of sharp end and blunt end were introduced because accident analyses often found that satisfactory explanations could not be found at the sharp end and that the conditions of the accident were determined by factors that were removed in time or in space. In one of the early descriptions of the sharp end, blunt end concept, Reason (1993) associated the sharp end with active failures and the blunt end with latent failures. Active failures were defined as 'unsafe acts committed by those at the "sharp end" of the system' and latent failures as 'fallible decisions, taken at the higher echelons of the organisation' (Reason, 1993, p. 224). The main thrust of the sharp end, blunt end description of accidents is thus a distinction between how proximal factors (working here and now) and distal factors (working there and then) in combination may lead to the accident. By nominating an event as the focus for the analysis, it becomes by default the sharp end while all other events, which naturally must precede it, become the blunt end. (To avoid too much confusion, we shall use the terms virtual sharp end and virtual blunt end, respectively, to indicate the relative view in an analysis rather than the concrete view of an accident.)

However, from another point of view the failures were all active when they were made, regardless of who made them or where and when it happened. This is a consequence of the relativity of the sharp end, blunt end distinction as argued in Chapter 2. An accident analysis must obviously start from something that happened, i.e., from the sharp end where the operators are, in the cockpit, in the operating room, etc. However, as soon as the analysis begins, it works its way slowly backwards through the possible antecedents to the observed manifestation – from the phenotype to the genotype (Hollnagel, 1993). This is done iteratively, which means that at any point in time the current antecedent being investigated is a virtual sharp end. In other words, blunt end events or factors become virtual sharp end events or factors as soon as they are being scrutinised. This has elegantly been expressed by saying that 'everybody's blunt end is someone else's sharp end.'

It follows from this that when actions at the blunt end took place they were actions at a virtual sharp end. There is, however, an important difference between the actions 'here and now' and actions 'there and then', which has to do with the possibilities for acting correctly, specifically the possible of finding out if a failure has been made. Failures at the sharp end can in the majority of cases be seen straight away. The opposite is the case for the blunt end where the effects of actions and decisions usually cannot be seen until long after and possibly in a different part of the system. Actions taken at the actual sharp end usually affect the people themselves here and now. Actions at the actual blunt end usually affect other people in a different part of the organisation some time into the future. This is why the effects remain latent, and also why they cannot easily be seen by those who made the actions.

It is ironical that whereas people at the actual sharp end experience the accidents, it is mostly people at the actual blunt end who are responsible for preventing them. People at the sharp end can certainly take local precautions against acute hazards, but for many reasons they are not usually allowed to make permanent changes to their work environment. It is therefore important to realise how the working conditions are for people at the blunt end rather than blame them wholesale. While everyone basically is subjected to the same influencing factors, the conditions at the blunt end are in many ways worse than at the sharp end as shown by Table 6.1.

People at the sharp end usually work with well-defined tasks in carefully designed environments. In order to do their work they are provided with proper tools, they often receive extensive training and are normally provided with sufficient resources. Since their tasks are well defined, the scope of decisions is usually prescribed and often limited with reasonable opportunities for detecting when something goes wrong. Technological artefacts may support this detection in various ways and provide reasonable opportunities for recovery as long as incorrect actions are within the design-base. The time horizon is normally short and efforts are made to ensure good predictability. In other words, considerable efforts have been made to provide the best possible conditions for work.

Table 6.1: Working conditions at the sharp end and the blunt end

	Blunt end	Sharp end
Constraints	Unclear, often economical and time	Part of work, but not always sufficiently clear
Resources, tools	Few, general	Many, specific, part of design
Scope of decisions	Wide, vague	Limited (by design)
Detection, correction	Few opportunities, long delays	Good opportunities, often supported by technology
Predictability	Low due to complexity of system	Reasonable in normal cases (by design)
Time horizon	Decisions: short, consequences: delayed	Decisions: short, consequences: immediate

The conditions are less optimal for people at the blunt end. They are often confronted with tasks that are incompletely specified and mostly have access to generic tools such as computerised office systems. The scope of their decisions is wide, often stretching far into the future and usually affecting a work environment and working conditions (the actual sharp end) of which they have limited knowledge and experience. Predictability is also low, both because the time horizon can be very long, and because the 'processes' that the decisions concern are rarely well defined. In consequence, possibilities for detection and correction of actions that fail to achieve their objectives are few and far between. Time pressure, on the other hand, can be rather high because of the momentum of the surrounding bureaucratic machinery. Feedback about the outcomes is sporadic and delayed, and is often only provided if something serious occurs, such as an accident. Whenever this happens the process of recovery can be slow, partly because of the several layers between the blunt end and the sharp end, and partly because it may involve major changes to systems and procedures.

Altogether, people at the blunt end are rarely in an enviable position, cf. Reason (1997, Chapter 8).

Since decisions about accident prevention often are made by people who do not actually work at the sharp end, it makes it all the more important that such decisions are based on an adequate model or understanding of the accident. The Law of Requisite Variety also applies here in the sense that we can only do something effectively to prevent accidents if our understanding of them is at least as complex as the accidents themselves. A first step towards that is to be aware of which accident model we use, both for analysis and prevention, and to refrain from reasoning in simple causal terms. We should also face up to the fact that the outcome of an accident analysis, as an explanation or an identified set of causes, itself is subject to a trade-off between efficiency and thoroughness, usually with time and resources being the determining factors. So, indeed, are the decisions about accident prevention, if they are not outright prone to wishful thinking. The understanding of accidents should always remain open to reinterpretation, either if new facts come to light or if our ability to understand the world around us improves.

In accident prevention we should be prepared for everything, and we preferably should not have to rely on luck. This little book can hopefully be a help to achieve that.

Bibliography

Adamski, A. J. & Westrum, R. (2003). Requisite imagination. The fine art of anticipating what might go wrong. In E. Hollnagel (Ed.), *Handbook of cognitive task design*. New Jersey: Lawrence Erlbaum.

Allen, J. (1983). Maintaining knowledge about temporal intervals. *Communication of the ACM, 26*, 832-843.

Amalberti, R. (1996). *La conduite des systèmes à risques*. Paris: PUF.

Annett, J. (2003). Hierarchical task analysis. In E. Hollnagel (Ed.), *Handbook of cognitive task design*. Mahwah, NJ: Lawrence Erlbaum Associates. (pp. 17-36).

Ashby, W. R. (1956). *An introduction to cybernetics*. London: Methuen & Co.

Aven, T. (2003). *Foundations of risk analysis. A knowledge and decision-oriented approach*. Chichester: John Wiley & Sons, Ltd.

Beer, S. (1964). *Cybernetics and management*. New York: Science Editions.

Benzi, R., Sutera, A. & Vulpiani, A. (1981). The mechanism of stochastic resonance. *J. Phys. A: Math. Gen.* 14L 453.

Bignell, V. & Fortune, J. (1984). *Understanding systems failures*. Manchester, UK: Manchester University Press.

Bird, F. (1974). *Management guide to loss control*. Atlanta: Institute Press.

Bogner, M. S. (1994). *Human error in medicine*. Hillsdale, NJ. Lawrence Erlbaum Associates.

Boone, J. & van Ours, J. (2002). *Cyclical fluctuations in workplace accidents*. CEPR Discussion Paper no. 3655. London, Centre for Economic Policy Research.

Boorstin, D. J. (1993). *The creators: A history of heroes of the imagination*. New York: Vintage Books.

Buchanan, M. (2001). *Ubiquity*. London. Phoenix.

CAIB (2003). *Columbia accident investigation board: Report Volume 1*. Washinton, D.C.: Government Printing Office.

Capra, F. (1997). *The web of life*. London: Flamingo.

CISHC (Chemical Industry and Safety Council), (1977). *A guide to hazard and operability studies.* London: Chemical Industries Association.

Cojazzi, G. & Pinola, L. (1994). *Root cause analysis methodologies: Trends and needs.* In G. E. Apostolakis & J. S. Wu (Eds.), Proceedings of PSAM-II, San Diego, CA, March 20-25.

Conant, R. C. & Ashby, W. R. (1970). Every good regulator of a system must be a model of that system. *International Journal of Systems Science, 1*(2), 89-97.

Cooper, S. E., Ramey-Smith, A. M., Wreathall, J., Parry, G. W., Bley, D. C., Luckas, W. J., Taylor, J. H. & Barriere, M. T. (1996). *A technique for human error analysis (ATHEANA)* (NUREG/CR-6350). Washington, DC: US Nuclear Regulatory Commission.

Corcoran, W. R., Finnicum, D. J., Hubbard III, F. R., Musick, C. R. & Walzer, P. F. (1981). Nuclear Power Plant Safety Functions. In *Nuclear Safety,* Vol 22, No 2, March-April 1981.

Dingus, T. A. & Hulse, M. C. (1993). Some human factors design issues and recommendations for automobile navigation information systems. *Transportation Research Part C: Emerging Technologies, 1*(2), 119-131.

Dörner, D. (1980). On the difficulties people have when dealing with complexity, *Simulation and Games,* 11, 87-106.

Duncker, K. (1945). On problem solving. *Psychological Monographs, 58*(5), (Whole No. 270).

Fiske, S. T. (1992). Thinking is for doing: Portraits of social cognition from Daguerreotype to Laserphoto. *Journal of Personality and Social Psychology, 63*(6), 877-889.

Fragola, J. R. (1995). Space shuttle probabilistic risk assessment. *Reliability Society Newsletter, October 1995,* 6-8.

Fujino, Y., Pacheco, B. M., Nakamura, S. & Warnitchai, P. (1993). Synchronization of human walking observed during lateral vibration of a congested pedestrian bridge. *Earthquake Engineering and Structural Dynamics, 22,* 741-758.

Gall, J. (1975). *Systemantics: How systems work and especially how they fail.* Quadrangle Books.

Gauthereau, V. & Hollnagel, E. (2001). *Operational readiness verification (ORV): A study of safety during outage and restart of nuclear power plants.* Proceedings of 8th Conference on Cognitive Science Approaches to Process Control. 24-26 September, Munich, Germany.

Green, A. E. (1988). Human factors in industrial risk assessment – some early work. In L. P. Goodstein, H. B. Andersen & S. E. Olsen (Eds.), *Task, errors and mental models*. London: Taylor & Francis.

Grimes, K. (2003). To trust is human. *New Scientist, 178*(2394), 32-37.

Haddon, W. (1966). The prevention of accidents. In *Preventive medicine* (pp. 591-621). Boston, MA: Little, Brown & Co.

Hale, A., Guldenmund, F., Goosens, L. & Bellamy, L. (2000). Focussed auditing of major hazard management systems. In I. Svedung & G. M. Cojazzi (Eds.), *Risk management and human reliability in social context* (EUR 20141 EN). Ispra, Italy: EC Joint Research Centre.

Hale, A., Goosens, L., Ale, B., Bellamy, L., Post, J., Oh, J. & Papazoglou, I. A. (2004). *Managing safety barriers and controls at the workplace*. Seventh International Conference on Probabilistic Safety Assessment and Management, June 14-18, Berlin, Germany.

Harms-Ringdahl, L. (2001). *Safety analysis. Principles and practice in occupational safety* (2nd Ed.). London: Taylor & Francis.

Heinrich, H. W. (1931). *Industrial accident prevention*. McGraw-Hill: New York.

Heinrich, H. W., Petersen, D. & Roos, N. (1980). *Industrial accident prevention* (5th Ed). McGraw-Hill: New York.

Hollnagel, E. (1993). *Human reliability analysis: Context and control*. London: Academic Press.

Hollnagel, E. (1995). The art of efficient man-machine interaction: Improving the coupling between man and machine. In: J.-M. Hoc, P. C. Cacciabue & E. Hollnagel (Eds.), *Expertise and technology: Cognition & human-computer co-operation*. Lawrence Erlbaum.

Hollnagel, E. (1998). *Cognitive reliability and error analysis method*. Oxford, UK: Elsevier Science.

Hollnagel, E. (2002). Understanding accidents: From root causes to performance variability. In J. J. Persensky, B. Hallbert & H. Blackman (Eds.), *New Century, New Trends*. Proceedings of the 2002 IEEE 7th Conference on Human Factors and Power Plants, September 15-19, Scottsdale, AZ, USA. New York: IEEE.

Hollnagel, E., Nåbo, A. & Lau, I. (2003). *A systemic model for Driver-in-Control*. 2nd International Driving Symposium on Human Factors in Driver Assessment, Training, and Vehicle Design, Park City, UT.

INSAG (1995). *Defence in depth in nuclear safety*. Vienna: International Atomic Energy Agency.

Itoh, K., Seki, M. & Andersen, H. B. (2003). Approaches to transportation safety: Methods and case studies applying to track maintenance train operations. In E. Hollnagel (Ed.), *Handbook of cognitive task design* (pp. 603-632). Mahwah, NJ: Lawrence Erlbaum Associates.

Kanse, L. (2004). *Recovery uncovered: How people in the chemical process industry recover from failures*. Eindhoven University Press.

Kecklund, L. J., Edland, A., Wedin, P. & Svenson, O. (1996). Safety barrier function analysis in a process industry: A nuclear power application. *Industrial Ergonomics, 17*, 275-284.

Kjellen, U. (2000). *Prevention of accidents through experience feedback*. London, UK: Taylor & Francis.

Knox, N. W. & Eicher, R. W. (1983). *MORT user's manual* (DOE 76/45-4). Idaho Falls, Idaho: EG&G Idaho, Inc.

Leplat, J. & Rasmussen, J. (1987). Analysis of human errors in industrial incidents and accidents for improvement of work safety. In J. Rasmussen, K. Duncan & J. Leplat (Eds.), *New technology and human error*. John Wiley & Sons, Ltd. (pp. 157-168).

Leveson, N. G. (1994). High pressure steam engines and computer software. *IEEE Computer*, October.

Leveson, N. G. (1995). *Safeware – system safety and computers*. Reading, MA: Addison-Wesley.

Lind, M. (2003). Making sense of the abstraction hierarchy in the power plant domain. *Cognition, Technology & Work, 5*(2), 67-81.

Lorenz, E. (2003). *The essence of chaos*. London: Routledge.

Maruyama, M. (1963). The second cybernetics: Deviation-amplifying mutual processes. *American Scientist, 55*, 164-179.

May, J. & Horberry, T. (1994). *SPaD human factor study: Directory of relevant literature*. Derby: University of Derby.

McDonald, N. (2003). Culture, systems and change in aircraft maintenance organisation. In G. Edkins & P. Pfister (Eds.), *Innovation and consolidation in aviation*. Ashgate. (pp. 39-57).

Meric, M., Monteau, M. & Szekely, J. (1976). *Techniques de gestion de la securitè*. Rapport No. 234/RE, INRS, 54500 Vandouevre, France.

Merton, R. K. (1979). *Sociological ambivalence and other essays*. New York: The Free Press, pp. 145-155.

Nietzsche, F. (1990). *Twilight of the idols*. Harmondsworth: Penguin Books.

NTSB (1997). *Grounding of the Panamanian passenger ship Royal Majesty on the Rose and Crown shoal near Nantucket, Massachusetts, June 10, 1995.* Washington DC: National Transportation Safety Board.

NTSB (2000). *In-flight Breakup Over the Atlantic Ocean Trans World Airlines Flight 800 Boeing 747-131, N93119, Near East Moriches, New York, July 17, 1996.* Washington DC: NTSB.

NTSB (2002). *EgyptAir Flight 990 Boeing 767-366ER, SU-GAP 60 Miles South of Nantucket, Massachusetts, October 31, 1999.* Washington DC: NTSB.

Oberg, J. (2000). Houston, we have a problem. *New Scientist*, 166(2234), 26.

Parasuraman, R. (1998). *Neuroergonomics:The Study of Brain and Behavior at Work.* http://www.cua.edu/students/org/csl/neuroerg.htm

Park, K. S. (1987). *Human reliability. Analysis, prediction, and prevention of human errors.* Amsterdam: Elsevier.

Perrow, C. (1984). *Normal accidents: Living with high risk technologies.* New York: Basic Books, Inc.

Petroski, H. (1994). *Design paradigms: Case histories of error and judgment in engineering.* Cambridge, UK: University of Cambridge Press.

Poincaré, H. (1912). *Calcul des probabilities.* Paris.

Polet, P., Vanderhagen, F. & Wieringa, P. A. (2002). Theory of safety-related violations of system barriers. *Cognition, Technology & Work*, 4(3), 171-179.

Rasmussen, B. & Petersen, K. E. (1999). Plant functional modelling as a basis for assessing the impact of management on plant safety. *Reliability Engineering and System Safety, 64*, 201-207.

Rasmussen, J., Duncan, K. & Leplat, J. (Eds.) (1987). *New technology and human error.* London: John Wiley & Sons.

Reason, J. T. (1987a). An interactionist view of system pathology. In J. Wise and A. Debons (Eds) *Information systems: Failure analysis.* Berlin: Springer-Verlag.

Reason, J. T. (1987b). The Chernobyl errors. *Bulletin of the British Psychological Society, 40* (April), 201-206.

Reason, J. T. (1990a). *Human error.* Cambridge, U.K.: Cambridge University Press.

Reason, J. T. (1990b). The contribution of latent human failures to the break down of complex systems. *Philosophical Transactions of the Royal Society (London)*, Series B. 327: 475-484.

Reason, J. T. (1991). Too little and too late: A commentary on accident and incident reporting systems. In T. W. van der Schaaf, D. A. Lucas & A. R. Hale (Eds.), *Near miss reporting as a safety tool.* Oxford: Butterworth-Heinemann. (pp. 9-26).

Reason, J. T. (1993). The identification of latent organizational failures in complex systems. In Wise, J. A., Hopkin, D. V. & Stager, P. (Eds.), *Verification and validation of complex systems: Human factors issues.* Berlin: Springer Verlag.

Reason, J. T. (1997). *Managing the risks of organizational accidents.* Aldershot: Ashgate Publishing Limited.

Ross, D. T. (1977). Structured analysis (SA): A language for communicating ideas. *IEEE Transactions on Software Engineering, SE-3*(1), 16-34.

Scriven, M. (1964). Views of human nature. In T. W. Wann, Ed. *Behaviorism and phenomenology.* Chicago: The University of Chicago Press.

Seife, C. (1999). Dangerous din. *New Scientist,* 17 April, 1999, p. 4.

Senders, J. W. & Moray, N. P. (1991). *Human error. Cause, prediction, and reduction.* Hillsdale, NJ: Lawrence Erlbaum.

Shannon, C. E. & Weaver, W. (1969). *The mathematical theory of communication.* Chicago: University of Illinois Press.

Sheridan, T. B. (1992). Telerobotics, automation, and human supervisory control. Cambridge, MA: MIT Press.

Sjöfartsverket (2000). *Rapport. Passagerarfartyget Stockholm – SGLD – grundstötning 2000-07-20.* Norrköping, Sweden. (URL: http://www.sjofartsverket.se/tabla-d/pdf/d14/rapporter/stockholm.pdf; accessed 2004-01-25.)

Snook, S. A. (2000). *Friendly fire: The accidental shootdown of U.S. Black Hawks over Northern Iraq.* Princeton, NJ: Princeton University.

Suchman, E. (1961). A conceptual analysis of the accident phenomenon. *Behavioral approaches to accident research.* New York: Association for the Aid of Crippled Children.

Svenson, O. (1991). The accident evolution and barrier function (AEB) model applied to incident analysis in the processing industries. *Risk Analysis, 11*(3), 499-507.

Svenson, O. (2001). Accident and incident analysis based on the accident evolution and barrier function (AEB) model. *Cognition, Technology & Work,* 3(1), 42-52.

Swain, A. D. & Guttman, H. E. (1983). *Handbook of human reliability analysis with emphasis on nuclear power plant applications* (NUREG CR-1278). Washington, DC: NRC.

Tarnowski, E. (2003). *Automation in the air transport system, today, tomorrow, the future.* Sixth International Australian Aviation Psychology Symposium, December 1-5, Sydney, Australia.

Taylor, J. R. (1988). *Analysemetoder til vurdering af våbensikkerhed.* Glumsø, DK: Institute for Technical Systems Analysis.

Taylor, J. R. (1993). *Risk analysis for process plant, pipelines and transport.* London, UK: Taylor & Francis.

Tenner, E. (1997). *Why things bite back.* New York: Vintage Books.

Trost, W. A. & Nertney, R. J. (1985). *Barrier analysis* (DOE 76-45/29). Idaho Falls, Idaho: EG&G Idaho, Inc.

Turner, B. (1987). *Man-made disasters.* London: Wikeham Press.

Tversky, A. & Kahneman, D. (1974). Judgment under uncertainty: Heuristics and biases. *Science, 185*, 1124-1131.

Vaughan, D. (1996). *The Challenger launch decision.* Chicago, IL: The University of Chicago Press.

Wason, P. C. & Johnson-Laird, P. N. (1972). *Psychology of reasoning: Structure and content.* London: B. T. Batsford Ltd.

Weick, K. E. & Sutcliffe, K. M. (2001). *Managing the unexpected: Assuring high performance in an age of complexity.* San Francisco, CA: Jossey-Bass.

Westrum, R. (1993). Cultures with requisite imagination. In J. A. Wise, V. D. Hopkin & P. Stager (Eds.), *Verification ad validation of complex systems: Human factors issues.* Berlin: Springer Verlag. (pp. 401-416).

Wilde, G. J. S. (1982). Risk homeostasis. *Risk Analysis, 2*(4), 209-225.

Wilpert, B. & Qvale, T. (Eds.), (1993). *Reliability and safety in hazardous work systems: Approaches to analysis and design.* London: Taylor & Francis.

Wogalter, M. S., DeJoy, D. M. & Laughery, K. R. (Eds.) (1999). *Warnings and risk communication.* London: Taylor & Francis.

Woods, D. D., Johannesen, L. J., Cook, R. I. & Sarter, N. B. (1994). *Behind human error: Cognitive systems, computers and hindsight.* Columbus, Ohio: CSERIAC.

Author Index

Subject Index

For Product Safety Concerns and Information please contact our EU
representative GPSR@taylorandfrancis.com
Taylor & Francis Verlag GmbH, Kaufingerstraße 24, 80331 München, Germany

www.ingramcontent.com/pod-product-compliance
Ingram Content Group UK Ltd.
Pitfield, Milton Keynes, MK11 3LW, UK
UKHW021830240425
457818UK00006B/140